PRAISE FOR *EQUAL IS UNFAIR*

"This book is like an oasis in the desert. At LAST *the voice of reason breaks through the prejudices and presumptions and outright misrepresentations that are at the heart of the hysterical cries of the inequality fighters."*

–Mark Pellegrino, *star of* Lost, Dexter, Supernatural *and* Quantico

"More bad ideas are promoted under the beguiling banner of 'equality' than anything else these days. If you've been seduced into thinking that it's the key to personal or material progress, this book is your antidote. Read it cover to cover and you'll never see humanity, the economy or public policy the same again."

–Lawrence W. Reed, *President of the Foundation for Economic Education*

"Equal Is Unfair demolishes the Left's myths and demonstrates that the campaign against income inequality is actually an attack on the concept of the 'land of opportunity'—America's unique sense of life. As Watkins and Brook show, reason and freedom, not handouts and high taxes, are the foundations of human progress. And production, not redistribution, is the source of human flourishing."

–John A. Allison, *retired President and CEO of the Cato Institute, and retired Chairman and CEO of BB&T*

"There are basically two ways of thinking about policy responses to inequality—raising or leveling. Leveling tends to promote the idea that there is a fixed pie of wealth in society and distribution is a function of luck, while raising tends to promote the idea that wealth must be created by individuals who realize the gains from trade and the gains from innovation, and as such, distribution is a function of rewards for superior talent and insight into how to satisfy the demands of others in the market. Human excellence must be acknowledged before it can be rewarded, and talents are to be celebrated rather than explained away as a consequence of luck. In Equal Is Unfair, Watkins and Brook provide a persuasive defense of human excellence, and of true capitalism which brings out the best in humanity and unleashes the creative genius in man in the arts, science and commerce. Highly recommended."

–Peter Boettke, *University Professor of Economics and Philosophy, George Mason University*

"Arguing the unarguable, Watkins and Brook blow the top off established wisdom on the evil of income inequality and the culpability of the 1%. Today's one-sided debate on income inequality amounts to envy politics, not logic or fact, as these authors demonstrate in their explosive and entertaining book, Equal Is Unfair: America's Misguided Fight Against Income Inequality. This book shows why the profit motive is noble and shows that government intervention in all areas of our lives—not income inequality—is what's really threatening the American Dream. A must read for those who desire prosperity for more of the world's people."

—Mallory Factor, New York Times *bestselling author of* Shadowbosses *and* Big Tent, *FoxNews contributor and professor at The Citadel, Oxford University and Buckingham University*

EQUAL
IS
UNFAIR

EQUAL
IS
UNFAIR

AMERICA'S MISGUIDED
FIGHT AGAINST
INCOME INEQUALITY

DON WATKINS AND YARON BROOK

St. Martin's Press

New York

www.stmartins.com

Library of Congress Cataloging-in-Publication Data

Watkins, Don, 1982– author.
  Equal is unfair : America's misguided fight against income inequality / Don Watkins and Yaron Brook.
    pages   cm
  Includes index.
  ISBN 978-1-250-08444-6 (hardcover)
  ISBN 978-1-250-08445-3 (e-book)
  1. Income distribution—United States. 2. Equality—United States. 3. Capitalism—United States. 4. Wealth—United States. 5. Entrepreneurship—United States. 6. Social mobility—United States. 7. United States—Economic conditions. I. Brook, Yaron, author. II. Title.
  HC110.I5W34   2016
  339.2'20973—dc23

2015030166

Our books may be purchased in bulk for promotional, educational, or business use. Please contact your local bookseller or the Macmillan Corporate and Premium Sales Department at 1-800-221-7945, extension 5442, or by e-mail at MacmillanSpecialMarkets@macmillan.com.

First Edition: March 2016

10 9 8 7 6 5 4 3

CONTENTS

PART ONE
MAKING SENSE OF THE INEQUALITY DEBATE

CHAPTER ONE

WHO CARES ABOUT INEQUALITY?

THE DEFINING CHALLENGE OF OUR TIME?

A few years ago, one of the authors of this book, Yaron Brook, was invited to give the keynote address at the Virginia Republican Party State Convention. Here's how he started.

> I was not lucky enough to be born an American citizen. I became an American citizen by choice. I immigrated to this country. I was born and raised in Israel. I served in the Israeli military where I met my wife of twenty-seven years. And when we got married, after we had fought for our country, we sat down and said, you know, you only live once and we want to make the most of our lives, we want to be someplace where we can enjoy freedom, where we can make the most of the life that we have, where we can pursue our happiness, where we can raise our children to the best of our ability. And we looked around the world. We weren't committed to any particular place, so we looked around the world and we said, "Where are we going to go?" We chose this country because America is the greatest nation on earth, and really is the greatest nation in human history.[1]

Of all the questions Yaron considered before he made his decision, one that never came up was how much *economic inequality* there was in

America. Like millions before him, Yaron came to America seeking to make a better life for himself and his family: he wanted to experience the American Dream, in which he would be free to set his own course and rise as far as his ability and ambition would take him. Would that put him in the top 1 percent or the bottom 10 percent of income earners in America? It would never have occurred to him to ask, and if someone *had* asked him, his answer would have been: "Who cares?"

Yaron is not unique in this regard. Polls consistently show that inequality is very low on Americans' list of concerns.[2] Even people who live in rural Michigan and struggle to make their mortgage payments apparently don't care that, hundreds of miles away in New York, a handful of hedge fund managers fly on private jets and dine at Nobu. What we do care deeply about is the opportunity to make a better life for ourselves—and we are more likely to celebrate the fact that this allows some people to succeed beyond their wildest dreams than lose sleep over it.

But hardly a day goes by in which we aren't told that our attitude toward economic inequality is wrong—that even if we don't care about inequality in and of itself, we *should* care, because it threatens the American Dream. In one of his most celebrated speeches, President Obama declared that "the defining challenge of our time" is "a dangerous and growing inequality and lack of upward mobility that has jeopardized middle-class America's bargain—that if you work hard, you have a chance to get ahead."[3]

Obama is hardly a lone voice on this issue. Nobel Prize–winning economist Joseph Stiglitz writes of "the large and growing inequality that has left the American social fabric, and the country's economic sustainability, fraying at the edges: the rich [are] getting richer, while the rest [are] facing hardships that [seem] inconsonant with the American Dream."[4] Journalist Timothy Noah warns that "income distribution in the United States is now more unequal than in Uruguay, Nicaragua, Guyana, and Venezuela, and roughly on par with Argentina. . . . Economically speaking, the richest nation on Earth is starting to resemble a banana republic."[5] French economist Thomas Piketty, in his celebrated work, *Capital in the Twenty-First Century,* warns that "capitalism automatically generates arbitrary and unsustainable inequalities that radically undermine the meritocratic values on which democratic societies are based," and so "the risk of a drift toward oligarchy is real and gives little reason for optimism about where the United States is headed."[6] The bottom line, according to Obama, is that the "combined trends of increased inequality and decreasing mobility pose a fundamental threat to the American Dream, our way of life, and what we stand for around the globe."[7]

In his 1931 book *The Epic of America*, James Truslow Adams introduced the phrase "the American Dream" into the lexicon, referring to "that dream of a land in which life should be better and richer and fuller for everyone, with opportunity for each according to ability or achievement."[8] The American Dream is about *opportunity*—the opportunity to pursue a better life, where one's success depends on nothing more (and nothing less) than one's own ability and effort, and where, as a result, innovators can come from nowhere to spearhead limitless human progress.

On the face of it, that dream would seem to entail enormous inequality: in a land where there are no limits on what you can achieve, some will earn huge fortunes, many will earn a decent living, and others will fail for one reason or another. Yet critics insist that economic inequality is at odds with the American Dream. Their specific arguments vary, but they all boil down to three general claims: in one way or another, inequality conflicts with economic mobility, economic progress, and fairness.

1. Inequality vs. Mobility. The best proxy for opportunity, according to the critics, is economic mobility. There are different ways of assessing mobility, but however you measure it, they say, the fact is that if you're born poor in America, chances are you'll stay poor, and if you're born rich, you'll probably stay rich. Some critics argue that rising inequality is a result of the same forces that are limiting mobility, such as the decline of unions or the minimum wage. Others paint inequality as a cause of declining mobility—citing, for instance, the ability of affluent Americans to send their children to exclusive schools that poorer parents cannot afford. In many cases, the connection between rising inequality and declining mobility is never fully spelled out: we are simply told that, for instance, the highly unequal United States has less economic mobility than our counterparts in Europe, and that we can increase mobility by molding ourselves in the image of European social welfare states.

2. Inequality vs. Progress. According to the critics, economic inequality is at odds with economic progress. The dominant view is that the last

forty years have been marked by a startling rise in income and wealth inequality, as the rich got richer and the poor and middle class stagnated.
Some argue that this rising inequality is a telling *symptom* of underlying
economic problems, such as tax and regulatory policies that favor "the
rich." Others claim inequality *causes* economic progress to slow, citing statistical correlations between high inequality and lower growth. Explanations for *how* inequality slows growth are all over the map, ranging from
the claim that it reduces consumer spending, supposedly the driving force
of economic growth, to the claim that inequality makes workers less happy
and therefore less productive.

3. Inequality vs. Fairness. One of the reasons we value opportunity is
that it reflects our commitment to fairness. We believe that a person's level
of success should be tied to merit, and that if you lie, cheat, or steal—or
simply make dumb decisions—your "privileged position" shouldn't protect you from failing. But rising inequality, the critics claim, is at odds with
fairness.

Sometimes the claim is that inequality undermines fairness by giving
"the rich" the power to rig the political system in their favor. "Ordinary
folks can't write massive campaign checks or hire high-priced lobbyists
and lawyers to secure policies that tilt the playing field in their favor at
everyone else's expense," President Obama tells us.[9] In other cases, the
claim is that rising inequality is the result of injustice. According to Stiglitz, "Too much of the wealth at the top of the ladder arises from exploitation. . . . Too much of the poverty at the bottom of the income spectrum
is due to economic discrimination and the failure to provide adequate
education and health care to the nearly one out of five children growing
up poor."[10]

Often, however, the underlying message is that economic inequality, at
least beyond a certain point, is inherently unjust. In Obama's words, "The
top 10 percent no longer takes in one-third of our income [as they did prior
to the 1970s]—it now takes half. Whereas in the past, the average CEO
made about 20 to 30 times the income of the average worker, today's CEO
now makes 273 times more. And meanwhile, a family in the top 1 percent
has a net worth 288 times higher than the typical family, which is a record
for this country."[11] These ratios, the president assumes, are self-evidently
unjustifiable.

Whatever account any given critic endorses, the conclusion is always the same: if we care about the American Dream, we have to reduce inequality by propping up those at the bottom and by *bringing down those at the top.* And so along with proposals to increase the minimum wage and bolster unions, the inequality critics also advocate top marginal income tax rates well above 50 percent, huge taxes on inheritances, vast amounts of regulation designed to restrain big business, salary caps on CEO pay, and campaign finance laws to constrain political speech by the wealthy, to name only a few of their schemes. In Piketty's runaway bestseller, *Capital in the Twenty-First Century,* the chief proposals for fighting inequality are an annual global wealth tax of up to 10 percent a year, and a self-described "confiscatory" top marginal income tax rate as high as 80 percent.[12]

For some, even this doesn't go far enough. There are critics of economic inequality who are largely indifferent to its impact on opportunity and want to level down society even if it means crippling economic progress. In their popular critique of economic inequality, *The Spirit Level,* Richard Wilkinson and Kate Pickett tell us that "we need to limit economic growth severely in rich countries," because "[o]nce we have enough of the necessities of life, it is the relativities which matter."[13] Similarly, best-selling author Naomi Klein argues that to truly deal with the problem of inequality, we must reject capitalism altogether, give up on the idea of economic progress, and embrace a decentralized agrarian form of socialism.[14] Left-wing radio host Thom Hartmann will settle merely for banning billionaires: "I say it's time we outlaw billionaires by placing a 100% tax on any wealth over $999,999,999. Trust me, we'll all be much better off in a nation free of billionaires."[15]

SHOULD WE BE SUSPICIOUS OF INEQUALITY?

The inequality critics paint a bleak picture of modern America—one so bleak that many of us do not recognize it in our daily experience—and offer up solutions that many of us find deeply troubling. But at the same time, these critics are addressing issues of profound concern, and their claims come backed by seemingly persuasive evidence: statistics, studies, and books by some of today's leading intellectuals and journalists. We want

America to be a land of limitless opportunity, and so their claims warrant serious consideration.

But right at the outset there's a huge obstacle to assessing their claims objectively: namely, the inequality critics have smuggled into the discussion a perspective on wealth that tacitly *assumes* that economic inequality is unjust.

The "fixed pie" assumption. The inequality critics often speak of economic success as if it was a fixed-sum game. There is only so much wealth to go around, and so inequality amounts to proof that someone has gained at someone else's expense. Arguing that "the riches accruing to the top have come at the *expense* of those down below," Stiglitz writes:

> One can think of what's been happening in terms of slices of a pie. If the pie were equally divided, everyone would get a slice of the same size, so the top 1 percent would get 1 percent of the pie. In fact, they get a very big slice, about a fifth of the entire pie. But that means everyone gets a smaller slice.[16]

What this ignores is the fact of *production*. If the pie is constantly expanding, because people are constantly creating more wealth, then one person's gain doesn't have to come at anyone else's expense. That doesn't mean you *can't* get richer at other people's expense, say by stealing someone else's pie, but a rise in inequality per se doesn't give us any reason to suspect that someone has been robbed or exploited or is even worse off.

Inequality, we have to keep in mind, is not the same thing as poverty. When people like Timothy Noah complain that "income distribution in the United States is now more unequal than in Uruguay, Nicaragua, Guyana, and Venezuela," they act as if it's irrelevant that almost all Americans are rich compared to the citizens of those countries. Economic inequality is perfectly compatible with widespread affluence, and *rising* inequality is perfectly compatible with a society in which the vast majority of citizens are getting richer. If the incomes of the poorest Americans doubled while the incomes of the richest Americans tripled, that would dramatically increase inequality even though every single person would be better off. Inequality refers not to deprivation but *difference*, and there is nothing suspicious or objectionable about differences per se.

The "group pie" assumption. In his speech on inequality, President Obama said, "The top 10 percent no longer takes in one-third of *our* income—it now takes half."[17] (Emphasis added.) This sort of phraseology, which is endemic in discussions of inequality, assumes that wealth is, in effect, a social pie that is created by "society as a whole," which then has to be divided up fairly. What's fair? In their book *The Winner Take All Society*, economists Robert Frank and Philip Cook begin their discussion of inequality with a simple thought experiment. "Imagine that you and two friends have been told that an anonymous benefactor has donated three hundred thousand dollars to divide among you. How would you split it? If you are like most people, you would immediately propose an equal division—one hundred thousand dollars per person."[18] In their view, if the pie belongs to "all of us," then absent other considerations, fairness demands we divide it up equally—not allow a small group to arbitrarily take a larger share of "our" income.

But although we can speak loosely about how much wealth a society has, wealth is not actually a pie belonging to the nation as a whole. It consists of particular values created by particular individuals (often working together in groups) and belonging to those particular individuals. Wealth is not distributed by society: it is produced and traded by the people who create it. To distribute it, society would first have to *seize* it from the people who created it.

This changes the equation dramatically. When individuals *create* something, there is no presumption that they should end up with equal shares. If Robinson Crusoe and Friday are on an island, and Crusoe grows seven pumpkins and Friday grows three pumpkins, Crusoe hasn't grabbed a bigger piece of (pumpkin?) pie. He has simply created more wealth than Friday, leaving Friday no worse off. It is dishonest to say Crusoe has taken 70 percent of the island's wealth.

It's obvious why the fixed pie and group pie assumptions about wealth would lead us to view economic inequality with a skeptical eye. If wealth is a fixed pie or a pie cooked up by society as a whole, then it follows that economic equality is the ideal, and departures from this ideal are *prima facie* unjust and need to be defended. As Piketty puts it, "Inequality is not necessarily bad in itself," but "the key question is to decide whether it is justified, whether there are reasons for it."[19]

But if wealth is something that individuals *create*, then there's no reason to expect that we should be anything close to equal economically. If we look at the actual individuals who make up society, it is self-evident that human beings are unequal in almost every respect: in size, strength, intelligence, beauty, frugality, ambition, work ethic, moral character. These differences will necessarily entail huge differences in economic condition—and there is no reason why these differences should be viewed with skepticism, let alone alarm.

If we keep in mind that wealth is something individuals *produce*, then there is no reason to think that economic equality is an ideal and that economic inequality is something that requires a special justification. That doesn't mean the claims about mobility, progress, and fairness are necessarily false. That remains to be seen. But it does mean that we have no reason to suspect at the outset that economic inequality is at odds with the American Dream. On the contrary, if we look at what made America the land of opportunity, there is every reason to think that opportunity goes hand in hand with economic inequality.

THE IDEAL OF OPPORTUNITY

If you want to understand what made America the land of opportunity— and what threatens opportunity today—the thing to know is that this was the first country that celebrated and protected the individual's pursuit of success.

Historically, particularly in Europe, the earthly ideal most societies aspired to was a life of leisure—not relaxation after a hard day's work, which America would provide in abundance, but a life free from work. The epitome of this ideal was the gentleman aristocrat, who didn't sully his hands with business.[20] The American attitude was different. Even before the American Revolution, visitors to the New World were stunned by the numbers of Americans "whose 'whole thoughts' were 'turned upon profit and gain.'"[21] In *Letters from an American Farmer,* written during the American Revolution, French-American J. Hector St. John de Crèvecœur stated "we are all animated with the spirit of an industry which is unfettered and unrestrained, because each person works for himself. . . . Here the rewards of his industry follow with equal steps the progress of his labour; his labour is founded on the basis of nature, SELF-INTEREST: can it want a stronger allurement?"[22]

By mid-nineteenth century, this focus on productive achievement had been ingrained in the nation's soul. As one commentator notes:

> Almost without exception, visitors to the Northern states commented on the drawn faces and frantic busyness of Jacksonian Americans and complained of bolted meals, meager opportunities for amusement, and the universal preoccupation with what Charles Dickens damned as the "almighty dollar."[23]

It's hard for us to grasp today just how central productive work was to American life during this country's first century and a half. People of that era showed up to cheer the launch of new bridges and trains the way Americans today greet the Super Bowl. Popular music celebrated technological achievements such as the telephone and the automobile. Daniel Yergin notes in his history of oil that during the late nineteenth century, "Americans danced to the 'American Petroleum Polka' and the 'Oil Fever Gallop,' and they sang such songs as 'Famous Oil Firms' and 'Oil on the Brain.'"[24]

Summarizing America's obsession with productive achievement, Viennese immigrant Francis Grund observed in the early nineteenth century:

> There is probably no people on earth with whom business constitutes pleasure, and industry amusement, in an equal degree with the inhabitants of the United States of America. Active occupation is not only the principal source of their happiness, and the foundation of their national greatness, but they are absolutely wretched without it, and . . . know but the horrors of idleness. Business is the very soul of an American: he pursues it, not as a means of procuring for himself and his family the necessary comforts of life, but as the fountain of all human felicity; . . . [I]t is as if all America were but one gigantic workshop, over the entrance of which there is the blazing inscription "*No admission here except on business.*"[25]

This distinctively American spirit was bolstered by the distinctively American system of government. Before the creation of the United States, every system of government took it for granted that some people were entitled to rule others, to take away their freedom and property whenever some allegedly "greater good" demanded it—that, after all, is what enabled the European nobility to live those lives of leisure. Such systems were rigged against any outsider or innovator who wanted to challenge convention, create something new, and rise by his own effort and ability rather than through political privilege. But building on the achievements of thinkers like John Locke, the Founding Fathers established a nation based on the principle, not of economic equality, but *political equality.*

Political equality refers to equality of *rights.* Each individual, the Founders held, is to be regarded by the government as having the same rights to life, liberty, and the pursuit of happiness. When the Founders declared that "all men are created equal," they knew full well that individuals are unequal in virtually every respect, from intelligence to physical prowess to moral character to wealth. But in one respect we *are* equal: we are all human beings, and, despite our differences, we all share the same mode of survival. Unlike animals that have to fight over a fixed amount of resources in order to survive, our survival is achieved by using our minds to *create* what we need to live. We have to think and produce if we want to live and achieve happiness, and as a result we must have the *right* to think and produce (and to keep what we produce) if we are to create a society in which individuals can flourish.

What can violate those rights? What can stop us from supporting our lives through thought and production? Basically, just one thing: physical force. The only way human beings can coexist peacefully is if they "leave their guns outside" and agree to live by means of production and voluntary trade rather than brute violence. As Locke explained, this was the purpose of government: to protect the rights of the "industrious and rational" from violation by "the quarrelsome and contentious."[26]

By making the government the guardian of our equal rights rather than a tool through which the politically privileged controlled and exploited the rest of society, the Founders transformed the state from an instrument of oppression into an instrument of liberation: it liberated the individual so that he was free to make the most of his life. (That the Founders failed to fully implement the principle of equality of rights, above all by allowing the continued existence of slavery, is an important but separate issue.)

This was the foundation of the American Dream. The reason America became a land in which there was "opportunity for each according to ability or achievement" was because political equality ended the exploitation of the individual by the politically powerful. If you wanted to make something of your life, nothing would be given to you—but no one could stop you. In place of the guild systems, government-granted monopolies, and other strictures that had stifled opportunity in the Old World, the New World provided an open road for the visionaries, inventors, and industrialists who would transform a virgin continent into a land of plenty.

Is it any wonder, then, that the nation was obsessed with commerce? In America, if you decided to devote yourself to productive work, it was within your power to rise from rags to riches—or, at the very least, to rise further than was possible anywhere else on the globe. If you could offer a better product or a better service or a lower price or better skills, no one could prevent you from improving your station in life. Freedom made success primarily a matter of choice rather than chance, of merit rather than privilege. That is what drew millions of immigrants to our shores. This 1850 poster calling for Irish immigrants was typical of this view:

> In the United States, labour is there the *first* condition of life, and industry is the lot of all men. . . . In the remote parts of America, *an industrious youth* may follow any occupation without being looked down upon or sustain loss of character, and he may rationally expect to *raise himself* in the world by his labour.
>
> In America, *a man's success* must altogether rest with himself—it will depend on his *industry, sobriety, diligence* and *virtue;* and if he do not succeed, in nine cases out of ten, the cause of the failure is to be found in the *deficiencies* of his own character.[27]

To be sure, political equality and the opportunity it unleashed went hand in hand with enormous economic inequality. There was no contradiction in that fact. Political equality has to do with how individuals are treated by the government. It says that the government should treat all individuals the same—black or white, man or woman, rich or poor. But political equality says nothing about the differences that arise through the voluntary decisions of private individuals. Protecting people's equal rights inevitably leads to enormous differences in economic condition, as some people use their freedom to create modest amounts of wealth while others reach the highest levels of success. The reason Americans have never cared about economic inequality is precisely because they recognized that it was the inevitable by-product of an opportunity-rich society.

But Americans *are* concerned about the state of opportunity today—and rightfully so. When the inequality critics say that the American Dream is on life support, their arguments often resonate because, in many instances, the problems they are pointing to are real (if sometimes exaggerated). In some ways, the road to success is *not* as open as it once was. Progress *is* slower than it should be. There *are* people getting their hands on money that they do not deserve. But these things are not happening in the ways, or for the reasons, that the inequality critics say.

THE REAL THREAT TO
THE AMERICAN DREAM

If we agree with the opponents of economic inequality about anything, it's that today's status quo is unacceptable. There are genuine barriers to opportunity, and the deck *is* becoming stacked against us—but not because "the rich" are too rich and the government is doing too little to fight economic inequality. The real threat to opportunity in America is increasing *political* inequality.

In a land of opportunity, an individual should succeed or fail on the basis of merit, not political privilege. You deserve what you earn—no more, no less. Today, however, some people are being stopped from rising on the basis of merit, and others are achieving unearned success through political privilege. As we'll catalog in the pages ahead, the source of this problem is that we have granted the government an incredible amount of arbitrary power: to intervene in our affairs, to pick winners and losers, to put roadblocks in the way of success, to hand out wealth and other special favors to whatever pressure group can present itself as the face of "the public good." Some of these injustices *do* increase economic inequality, but it isn't the inequality that should bother us—it's the injustice.

When a bank or auto company that made irrational decisions gets bailed out at public expense, that *is* an outrage. But the root of the problem isn't their executives' ability to influence Washington—it's Washington's power to dispense bailouts. When an inner-city child is stuck in a school that doesn't educate him, that *is* a tragedy. But the problem isn't that other children get a better education—it's that the government has created an educational system that often doesn't educate, and that makes it virtually impossible for anyone but the affluent to seek out alternatives.

Of course people will try to influence a government that has so much arbitrary power over their lives, and *of course* those with the best connections and deepest pockets will often be the most successful at influencing it. The question is, what created this situation, and what should we do about that? The critics of inequality tell us that the problem is not *how much* arbitrary power the government has, but *whom* the government uses that power for. They say that by handing the government even more power, and demanding that it use that power for the sake of "the 99 percent" rather than "the 1 percent," everyone will be better off. We believe that only when the government is limited to the function of protecting our equal rights can people rise through merit rather than government-granted privilege, and that the cure for people seeking special favors from the government is to create a government that has no special favors to grant.

But as important as it is to identify what's wrong with America today, we also need to identify what's *right* with America today. Whatever our problems, we still have a substantial amount of freedom and we're still using that freedom to improve the world around us. Modern life, as a result, is amazing. We're living longer, healthier, richer lives than at any time in history. We have more ways than ever to learn, travel, create, and communicate. And more and more people are gaining access to this amazing world: among *poor* Americans today, nearly 75 percent have at least one vehicle, 50 percent have cell phones, two-thirds have cable or satellite TV, half have at least one personal computer, and 43 percent have access to the Internet.[28] And for anyone who wants to make something of his life, there are still abundant economic opportunities available. The Internet alone has dramatically lowered the barriers to gaining new knowledge and skills, to finding work, and to launching new business ventures.

None of this is to deny the real struggles millions of Americans face, or to suggest that we can't do better. On the contrary, the reason it's vital to talk about these achievements is so we can learn what made them possible and put those lessons to work. But all too often the critics of economic inequality *don't* want to talk about these achievements, because, as we'll see, the forces that have made modern life possible go hand in hand with *enormous economic inequality*. Only when people are free to act without arbitrary interference by the government and to amass great fortunes do we get an innovative, prosperous, opportunity-rich society. Silicon Valley wasn't built by paupers and ascetics.

Given this link between opportunity and economic inequality, some commentators have proposed that we make a distinction between *good* inequality—the inequality that arises from unequal achievement—and *bad* inequality—the inequality that arises from expropriation and other forms of government favor-seeking.

Obviously, the distinction between earned wealth and unearned spoils is vital, but those who suggest distinguishing "good inequality" from "bad inequality" miss the larger point. There is no rational reason to put such a distinction in terms of "inequality." We don't admire innovative entrepreneurs because they create "good inequality" and we don't despise frauds, thieves, and lobbyists because they create "bad inequality." (Nor do we condemn a bum who robs a doctor because he creates "bad equality.") What's relevant is the nature of their actions—not whether the outcomes of those actions make people more or less equal. Before we go about trying to distinguish between different kinds of inequality, we should ask why we should care about relative differences in economic condition in the first place. If what we're concerned about is opportunity, then the answer is: we shouldn't care.

That, anyway, is what we aim to show. In the next chapter, we'll look in depth at the case *against* economic inequality, and see that the story told by the critics—that the American Dream flourishes when we fight inequality and flounders when we don't—simply does not add up.

In Part 2, we'll discover the real key to the American Dream: political equality and the freedom it unleashes. To the extent a society is free, those at the top have neither the incentive nor the power to exploit those below—they can gain only through productive achievement and mutually beneficial voluntary exchange. In a country in which the government acts as the guardian of our equal rights, the door is open to merit and closed to political privilege, regardless of differences in wealth or income.

In Part 3, we will see how disturbingly far we've moved away from that ideal. The government is making it harder and harder for anyone to rise by their own effort—especially if they're starting at the bottom—and it's making it easier and easier for everyone—rich, poor, or anywhere in between—to obtain unearned benefits at the expense of their neighbors. Although the American Dream is far from dead, it is also far from healthy—and fighting economic inequality will only make things worse.

Finally, we will discover what's behind the crusade against inequality. The critics of inequality are attempting a bait and switch: in claiming we must fight economic inequality in order to protect the American Dream, they are in reality attempting to get us to substitute the goal of fighting inequality *for* the American Dream. The American Dream was of the opportunity to rise as far as a person's ability and ambition would take him. In condemning inequality and proposing to bring down those at the top, the inequality critics are seeking to punish those who *epitomize* the American Dream and to move America further in the direction of the European regulatory-welfare states the inequality critics admire.

There is a reason *America* became the land of opportunity, and it was not because we modeled ourselves after the Old World. It was because we did something unprecedented: we liberated human ability and celebrated human achievement. Our future will be determined by whether we recommit ourselves to the ideal of opportunity—or whether we abandon that ideal in the name of waging war on economic inequality.

CHAPTER TWO

EXAMINING THE INEQUALITY NARRATIVE

IS INEQUALITY REALLY THE KEY TO EVERYTHING?

The inequality critics have a story to tell. When the government lets inequality get out of control, the American Dream suffers; when the government fights inequality, the American Dream flourishes—and our problem today is that the government has been hijacked by "the rich," who are using the power of the state to *promote* economic inequality. According to Bill Clinton's former labor secretary, Robert Reich:

> The old view was that anyone could make it in America with enough guts and gumption. We believed in the self-made man (or, more recently, woman) who rose from rags to riches: inventors and entrepreneurs born into poverty, like Benjamin Franklin; generations of young men from humble beginnings who grew up to be president, like Abraham Lincoln. We loved the novellas of Horatio Alger and their more modern equivalents—stories that proved the American dream was open to anyone who worked hard. . . .
>
> A profound change has come over America. Guts, gumption, and hard work don't seem to pay off as they once did—or at least as they did in our national morality play. Instead, the game seems rigged in favor of people who are already rich and powerful—as well as their children.

Instead of lionizing the rich, we're beginning to suspect they gained their wealth by ripping us off.[1]

According to this narrative, America's "Golden Age" came in the era following World War II, when America enjoyed high mobility and "shared prosperity," thanks to government efforts to promote economic equality— high marginal tax rates, strong pro-union laws, a relatively high minimum wage, a burgeoning welfare state—and a social ethic that kept pay at the top in check. But then something changed.

In the late 1970s, "the rich," with the aid of their ideological apologists on the political right, launched a concerted campaign to assert their interests. By the time Reagan was elected, the narrative goes, "the rich" were well on their way to rigging the system in their favor, shifting the tax burden onto the middle class, undoing the gains made by unions, and dismantling the regulatory-welfare state. Meanwhile, any qualms "the rich" once had about taking home ostentatious paychecks dissolved, and executives started using their influence over boards of directors to take home pay that simply couldn't be justified on the basis of performance. The result was rising inequality, falling mobility, stagnation at the bottom, a devastating recession, and slower economic growth across the board.

"Perhaps a hundred years ago," Joseph Stiglitz concludes, "America might have rightly claimed to have been the land of opportunity, or at least a land where there was more opportunity than elsewhere. But not for at least a quarter of a century. . . . Americans are coming to realize that their cherished narrative of social and economic mobility is a myth."[2]

You can call this the Inequality Narrative. By no means does everyone who is worried about inequality subscribe to this narrative, but it is far and away the prevailing view. It places the blame for rising inequality and declining opportunity squarely at the feet of "the 1 percent," and implies that the solution is to tax them, regulate them, and curtail their political influence. According to this story, we're not keeping up with the Joneses, and the fault lies with the Joneses.

What's the evidence for this narrative? A key element is statistical data compiled by French economist Thomas Piketty. Building on research he conducted with economist Emmanuel Saez beginning in the early 2000s, Piketty uses tax data from the IRS to trace the path of income inequality

over the last century. As we can see in Figures 2.1, 2.2, and 2.3, he finds
that, after declining during the post–World War II era, income inequality
has been rising for the last forty years, driven primarily by the top 1 percent
of earners. In addition to income inequality, which refers to differences in
the amount of money that people earn on a regular basis, such as their annual salaries, Piketty also found a rising wealth inequality, which refers to
differences in people's net worth.[3]

For our purposes, the details of these trends aren't important. What
the inequality critics stress is the U-shaped nature of the curves. Inequality,
they point out, is high before World War II (a period they call "the Long
Gilded Age"), falls during the post-war era ("the Great Compression"), and
rises again around the late 1970s ("the New Gilded Age"). In their telling, it
was only during the Great Compression, when the government successfully
fought inequality, that the American Dream came close to being realized.

These statistics have been challenged to varying degrees. Although
Piketty's graphs give the appearance of rigorous finality, this disguises the
fact that there are enormous challenges in assessing the extent of inequality

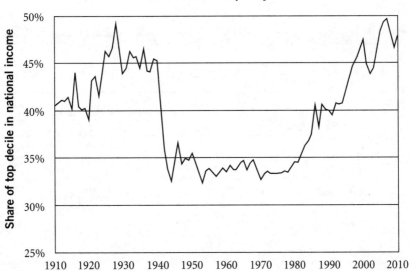

Figure 2.1
US Income Inequality

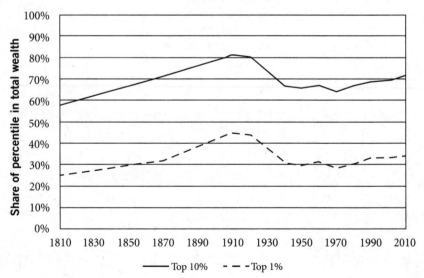

Figure 2.2
US Income; Decomposition of Top Decile

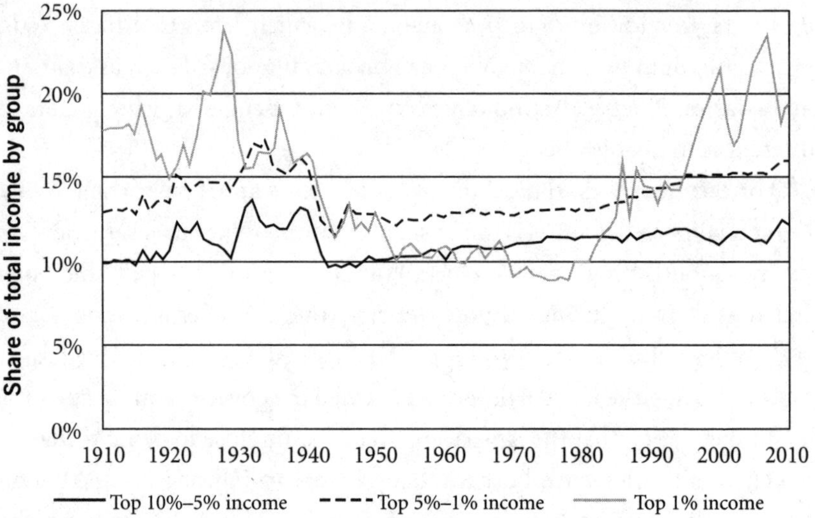

Share of total income by group

Top 10%–5% income   - - - Top 5%–1% income   Top 1% income

Figure 2.3
US Wealth Inequality

Share of percentile in total wealth

Top 10%   - - - Top 1%

and how it has evolved over time.[4] Not only are the data sometimes sketchy, but there are many options in deciding which data to use. For instance, if we are trying to assess income inequality, what do we count as income? Do we count pre-tax income or post-tax income? What about government handouts (usually referred to as "transfer payments")? What about non-monetary forms of income, such as health care benefits? And how do we adjust for inflation and for demographic changes, such as the aging of the population or a rise in divorce rates, which can impact inequality data in misleading ways? Different choices on these and other matters can lead to very different results.[5]

When it comes to measuring wealth inequality, the problems are magnified, in part because the historical data are far less reliable. It's no accident that while there is general agreement that income inequality has been increasing, there is nothing like a consensus when it comes to wealth inequality. Although Piketty shows wealth inequality increasing in the United States since around 1970, other researchers, including critics of inequality, have found that wealth inequality has remained stable or even declined.[6]

We'll have more to say about Piketty's data, and the theoretical conclusions he draws from the data, later. But even if we concede the accuracy of these trends, the Inequality Narrative still does not hold up. It misrepresents the past and it distorts the present.

HOW GILDED WAS THE "GILDED AGE"?

"[M]iddle-class America didn't emerge by accident," writes economist Paul Krugman. "It was created by what has been called the Great Compression of incomes that took place during World War II, and sustained for a generation by social norms that favored equality, strong labor unions and progressive taxation."[7] We'll come back to what exactly Krugman means by "middle-class America" in chapter 7. But one thing is clear: Americans were prospering long before the post-war era. Inequality may have been high, but the vast majority of Americans were living better and better lives.

Start with wages. Not only were wages rising throughout the nineteenth and early twentieth centuries, but they were rising at an *accelerating* rate (see Figure 2.4).[8] This was at a time before the government was

Figure 2.4
Index of Real Wages for Unskilled Labor

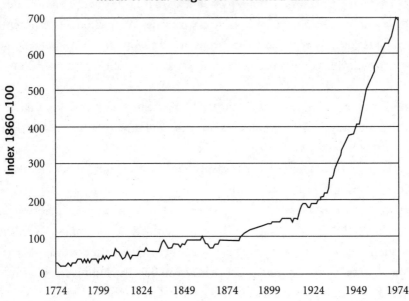

doing anything to fight economic inequality. There were no laws supporting unions, union membership was very low, and there was no minimum
wage. Wages were set by the market, and as workers became more productive, they saw their wages rise.

But even this striking growth in wages does not capture all the gains
made by Americans. Consider, for instance, the unprecedented increase
in longevity that took place during this era, which is one solid measure
of standard of living. Life expectancy from birth rose from 38 in 1850 to
nearly 60 by 1925, driven by advances in medicine, sanitation, and economic progress generally.[9]

Another good measure of progress is number of hours worked. As
workers earn more, they tend to take some of their remuneration in the
form of more leisure time—that is, they work less because they can afford to work less. In 1870, Americans worked, on average, 61 hours a week,
which, subtracting time off, amounted to 3,069 hours a year. By 1913, that
had fallen to 53.3 hours a week and only 2,632 hours a year. And by 1938,

TABLE 2.1

Year	Work-week (hours)	Work-day (hours)	Work-week (days)	Annual Hours (paid)	Vacation (days)	Holidays (days)	Other Time Off (days)	Annual Hours Worked
1870	61.0	10.2	6.0	3,181	0.0	3.0	8.0	3,069
1890	58.4	9.7	6.0	3,045	0.0	3.0	8.0	2,938
1913	53.3	8.9	6.0	2.779	5.0	3.5	8.0	2,632
1929	48.1	8.0	6.0	2,508	5.5	4.0	8.0	2,368
1938	44.0	8.0	5.5	2,294	6.0	4.5	8.0	2,146
1950	39.8	8.0	5.0	2,075	6.5	6.0	9.0	1,903
1960	38.6	7.7	5.0	2,013	7.0	7.0	9.0	1,836
1973	36.9	7.4	5.0	1,924	8.0	7.5	9.0	1,743
1990	34.5	7.3	4.7	1,799	10.0	11.0	9.5	1,584
1996	34.4	7.3	4.7	1,794	10.5	12.0	10.0	1,570

that had fallen further still, with Americans working only 44 hours a week, or 2,146 hours a year.[10]

And none of these measures come anywhere near capturing the actual, day-to-day improvements in human life. During the so-called Gilded Age, the existential circumstances of life were improving by the day. Between 1835 and 1935, medicine advanced (anesthesia, antiseptics, insulin, penicillin, and pasteurization were all developed during this era, along with huge improvements in sanitation), transportation was revolutionized (the internal combustion engine spawned trucks, cars, tractors, and airplanes, while steam trains became far safer thanks to the development of the air brake), new means of communication connected the world (telegraph, telephone, radio), and entrepreneurs filled Americans' homes with electricity, incandescent lighting, sewing machines, washing machines, running water, indoor plumbing, air-conditioning, and a whole lot more. Whatever hardships they continued to face, people were eating better, dressing better, living better.

By no means were these improvements reserved for the very wealthy. In 1934, in the depths of the Depression, a survey of Pittsburgh found that

> . . . even in the poorest districts in the city, 98 percent of the dwellings had running water (only half had hot water), 91 percent had electricity

or gas for lighting, 75 percent had indoor water closets, and 54 percent had a shower or bathtub. This study and others indicate that working-class families of the 1930s had increasing access to utilities and appliances that made housework easier.[11]

Commenting on these changes, one contemporary observer from the nineteenth century, statistician and social activist Carroll D. Wright (whom no one would have accused of being an apologist for the rich), railed against the notion that only "the rich are getting richer," calling the expression a "wandering" phrase

> ... without paternity or date; it is not authority but familiarity that has given it weight. . . . To the investigator the real statement should be, The rich are growing richer; many more people than formerly are growing rich; and the poor are better off. If the sum total of wealth were stationary, any increase in the wealth of the rich would be an exploitation of the poor. . . . But the sum total of wealth is not stationary; it increases with great rapidity, and while under this increase the capitalistic side secures a greater relative advantage than the wage-earner of the profits of production, the wage-earner secures an advantage which means the improvement of his conditions.[12]

Even most critics will admit that, alongside growing economic inequality, there was enormous improvement in the general standard of living during the nineteenth century. "The nineteenth century saw perhaps a doubling of measured material standards of living in the United States," writes inequality critic J. Bradford DeLong, "perhaps a tripling once proper account is taken of the impact of new technologies like the railroad and the telegraph, and the expanded range of technological capabilities. Nineteenth century growth was itself remarkably fast: people christened the nineteenth century the 'industrial revolution' because it was remarkable compared to what had happened before."[13] Krugman himself acknowledges, "[T]he growth of the U.S. economy during the Long Gilded Age benefited all classes: Most Americans were much better off in the 1920s than they had been in the 1870s."[14]

THE POST-WAR ERA

There is no question that in the post–World War II economy, wages increased at an unprecedented rate. But why? The Inequality Narrative credits government efforts to fight inequality and suggests that this was an era dominated by government control over the economy: above all, high taxes, pro-union laws, a burgeoning welfare state.

What was responsible for the post-war boom in wages is a complicated question, and there is no consensus among economic historians. One thing that's important to note is that the dramatic acceleration of wage growth actually started during the 1920s, and probably reflects the fact that Americans were enjoying productivity gains made possible by the accumulation of capital, infrastructure, technology, and human capital that had been built up during the nineteenth and early twentieth centuries.

But it is also relevant that we're talking about the post-*war* era: Europe was in shambles, and although that was a tragedy that in the long run made us all worse off economically, it also meant that there was an enormous demand for industrial production, and the United States was the only game in town. As a National Bureau of Economic Research study explains, "At the end of World War II, the United States was the dominant industrial producer in the world. With industrial capacity destroyed in Europe—except for Scandinavia—and in Japan and crippled in the United Kingdom, the United States produced approximately 60 percent of the world output of manufactures in 1950, and its GNP was 61 percent of the total of the present (1979) OECD [Organisation for Economic Co-operation and Development] countries. This was obviously a transitory situation."[15] It was also a period in which the United States clamped down on immigration, and so the supply of U.S. workers was restricted at the very moment that the demand for U.S. labor was high. Basic economic theory would predict that these forces would result in rapid wage growth.

That's not something to celebrate. What we care about is not wage rates per se, but our actual standard of living, and there is no question that war and restrictive immigration policies *lower* our standard of living. World War II not only destroyed an incalculable amount of wealth, both at home and abroad, but it also robbed countless individuals of their *lives*.

Immigration, meanwhile, not only allows foreigners to share in the American Dream, which is something we should value for its own sake, but may also fuel economic growth.[16] Low-skilled workers tend to bid down wages for low-skilled work, which sounds bad until you remember that this lowers the cost of the products we all buy. And high-skilled workers bring us all the benefits of their ability, which includes starting new businesses (see the careers of Andrew Carnegie, PayPal's Elon Musk, Intel's Andy Grove, and Google's Sergey Brin, among many others).

But we should not paint a one-sided picture. Although the inequality critics highlight the restrictions on economic liberty of the post-war era (more on that shortly), in many ways it was an era of growing economic freedom. This is difficult to quantify, but the best attempt to date comes from economist Leandro Prados de la Escosura, who has constructed a Historical Index of Economic Liberty (HIEL) similar to indexes produced by the Heritage Foundation and the Fraser Institute that try to measure economic freedom today. HIEL gives us very rough measures, but it can at least give us a sense of the extent to which government was intervening in the economy. Looking at four aspects of economic freedom—property rights, sound money, international trade, and regulation—de la Escosura finds that, after declining sharply during the New Deal and World War II period, economic freedom expanded in the post-war period as significant parts of the New Deal regulatory regime were rolled back, and continued to expand until the early 1970s when it once again contracted.[17]

Regardless of what one thinks of de la Escosura's index, however, there is no justification whatever for attributing the rapid growth of the post-war era to the policies enshrined by the Inequality Narrative: pro-union laws, high tax rates, and a growing welfare state.

UNIONS

First of all, it's important to distinguish between unions, which can be valuable organizations, and pro-union legislation, which gives unions coercive power at the expense of employers and non-unionized workers. Employees who freely choose to join a union (which their employer freely chooses to deal with) can benefit from collective bargaining. But, economist Henry Hazlitt warns, "it is easy, as experience has proved, for unions, particularly with the help of one-sided labor legislation which puts compulsions solely on employers, to go beyond their legitimate functions, to act irresponsibly, and to embrace shortsighted and antisocial policies."[18]

Unfortunately, that is precisely what happened during the mid-twentieth century. Labor laws such as the National Labor Relations Act of 1935 (usually called the Wagner Act) gave unions coercive powers they would not have had in a fully free society. Among other provisions, the Act forced companies to recognize and bargain with labor unions and simultaneously allowed a majority vote to force *all* employees into the union, even if some preferred not to join. "In practice," notes our former colleague Doug Altner, "the Wagner Act allows unions to make unreasonable demands, and forces business leaders to choose between caving in to some of these demands and facing costly and time-consuming litigation."[19] With this political power in their pocket, unions were able to raise wages *artificially high.* And who paid the price? The companies on whom the unions depended, for one, but also *non-union workers,* who faced fewer job opportunities and higher prices.

In fact, one of the perverse effects of unions was that, by raising the costs of the products they sold, their short-term gains often came at their own long-term expense. In the coal industry, for instance, the United Mine Workers won higher pay for their workers between 1925 and 1960. But this caused many buyers to switch from coal to oil, reducing employment in the coal industry, and decimating many of the communities built around coal mining.[20] In the auto industry, to take one more example, the United Automobile Workers' union succeeded in raising compensation for its workers. But, as Krugman admits, the auto companies were able to "pass on the higher costs [of union benefits] to consumers."[21] As a result, American autos were unable to compete with more affordable imports. Economist Thomas Sowell describes the results:

> As of 1950, the United States produced three-quarters of all the cars in the world and Japan produced less than one percent of what Americans produced. Twenty years later, Japan was producing almost as many automobiles as the United States, and, five years after that, more automobiles. By 1990, one-third of the cars sold in the United States were made in Japan. . . . All this of course had its effect on employment. During the 1980s, the number of jobs in the American automobile industry declined

by more than 100,000. By 1990, the number of jobs in the American automobile industry was 200,000 less than it had been in 1979.[22]

This is the larger point about unions. While they can raise wages for some people, they can only do so temporarily and at the expense of other people. They cannot raise wages in general without raising costs and, thereby, the prices that we all have to pay—which sort of defeats the purpose.

TAXES

Although the top income tax rate was high in the post-war era, it applied to a very small number of people, and there were so many loopholes that the effective tax actually paid by the most successful Americans was not the 91 percent top rate but actually between 50 and 60 percent.[23] (This is potentially misleading, however, since that era saw a higher corporate tax rate than today, although scholars continue to debate the degree to which that tax fell on the wealthiest Americans.[24])

But the real question is, How are high taxes supposed to *promote* prosperity? All else being equal, taxes discourage production and prosperity. Not only do they dampen the incentive to produce, but they also tend to reduce the capital accumulation that funds new buildings, machinery, R&D, and jobs. As we'll see in chapter 4, those forces are instrumental in fueling progress. If there are countervailing economic forces that cause high taxes to foster progress, the Inequality Narrative certainly doesn't specify what they are. At best, all the inequality critics can claim is that, under the unique economic conditions that prevailed during the post-war years, higher tax burdens on the wealthy existed alongside relatively high rates of economic growth. But would there have been even faster progress if the tax burden had been lower? On that issue, the Inequality Narrative has nothing to say.

THE WELFARE STATE

To credit the welfare state with creating a growing middle class requires us to ignore some basic facts of history. Until 1965, when Lyndon B. Johnson

TABLE 2.2

Year	Social Security Recipients	Percent of U.S. Population
1945	1,288,107	0.9%
1955	7,960,616	4.8%
1965	20,866,767	10.7%

launched his so-called Great Society programs and the "War on Poverty," the only significant welfare program was the Social Security Act of 1935, and it wasn't until the end of the post-war era that a substantial number of Americans were receiving Social Security retirement checks.[25]

Moreover, the money paid out by Social Security could not have created or even expanded the middle class since Social Security payments were mainly financed by taxes *on* the middle class. It was a redistribution not from the rich to everyone else but mostly from middle-class workers to middle-class retirees.

In the portrait painted by the Inequality Narrative, the only period in which there was widespread prosperity in America came in the thirty years after World War II, thanks to major government efforts to intervene in the economy and reduce inequality. This view, as we've seen, is simply not defensible. Equally indefensible is the narrative's depiction of the last forty years, when America supposedly returned to the unrestrained capitalism of the "Gilded Age"—and paid a steep price.

THE FREE MARKET MYTH

When the critics of economic inequality tout the expansion of government during the prosperous post-war era, they usually leave out the fact that the Forties, Fifties, and Sixties were followed by the Seventies. Long before economic inequality began to increase, and long before the supposed abandonment of the anti-inequality policies the critics admire, America hit on hard times.

Brought on by the incredible surge in government spending that started in the 1960s, inflation was rampant for much of the 1970s. American industry struggled to remain competitive. The stock market, as measured

by the Dow Jones Industrials, was basically flat from 1965 to 1982. Productivity growth, the main driver of wage growth, slowed as early as the
mid-1960s and with a few brief exceptions remained sluggish until the
1990s.[26] Economic growth was non-existent, with repeated recessions and
high unemployment during the 1970s. And because the combination of inflation, stagnation, and unemployment was a phenomenon unanticipated
by mainstream Keynesian economists, a new term was coined: stagflation.
Jimmy Carter expressed the bleakness of the time in his famous "malaise"
speech, claiming that America was suffering from "a crisis in confidence."

Instead of sharing Carter's sense of defeat, Americans rebelled. The
rebellion began with a tax revolt. In 1978, California voters passed Proposition 13, a severe limit on property taxes, by a margin of 2 to 1. Journalists
John Micklethwait and Adrian Wooldridge describe Proposition 13 as the
beginning of "a peasants' revolt that swept across the country. . . . It re-
minded Americans that their country was founded by a tax revolt, and that
politicians were the public's servants, not its masters."[27]

Then came the presidency of Ronald Reagan. "It is time to check and
reverse the growth of government," Reagan told Americans, summing up
the theme of his candidacy. The country was facing a crisis, and the problems were "parallel and . . . proportionate to the intervention and intrusion
in our lives that result from unnecessary and excessive growth in government."[28] Americans agreed, and elected Reagan in a landslide.

How do the inequality critics describe these developments? Seldom do
they mention the stagnation and malaise of the 1970s. Instead, they claim
"the rich" organized to protect their interests and launched a well-funded
campaign to influence politicians and dupe Americans into supporting
what journalist Hedrick Smith calls the "laissez-faire philosophy of the
past three decades [which] promised that deregulation, lower taxes, and
free trade would lift all boats."[29] The rich bought the government and suck-
ered the public into supporting their self-serving agenda, the inequality
critics say. Only then did problems in the economy emerge, as we became
less equal and less productive.[30]

Although it is true that Americans rebelled against the left's failed policies during the 1970s, it is wrong to say that the last forty years have in any
way marked what left-wing author Thomas Frank labels a "laissez-faire
revival."[31] The truth is that the free-market rhetoric of the right did not

match its behavior once in power. To be sure, the Reagan administration and conservative legislators did repeal some of the disastrous interventions strangling the economy (a trend actually started by Carter). They lessened our crushing tax burden, rolled back a few of the most crippling regulations, undid some of the most destructive controls, and helped curb inflation—all of which helped improve the economy. But if we look at the overall picture, what we see is that throughout the era of "cowboy capitalism," government grew enormously in size and scope. As shown by Figure 2.5, for example, federal government spending as a percentage of GDP increased dramatically over the course of the twentieth century, with no significant decline after 1980, except for a slight dip during the Clinton administration.[32]

If we zoom in to the last forty-five years, and look at spending at all levels of government (Figure 2.6), we see that it hovers around 35 percent of GDP, again declining a bit during Clinton's administration.[33]

However, most of Clinton's cuts came from reduced military spending following the end of the Cold War, as shown in Figure 2.7.[34]

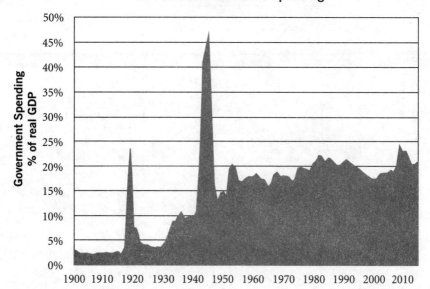

Figure 2.5
US Federal Government Spending

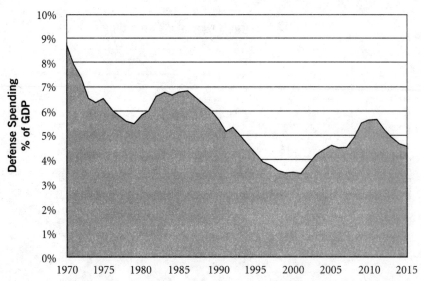

Figure 2.6
Recent US Total Government Spending

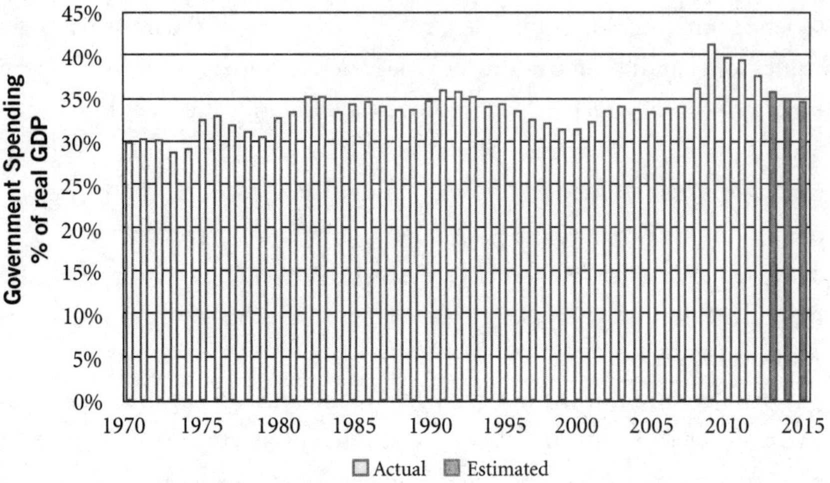

Government Spending
% of real GDP

☐ Actual   ■ Estimated

Figure 2.7
Recent US Defense Spending

Defense Spending
% of GDP

Figure 2.8
US Pensions and Health Care Spending

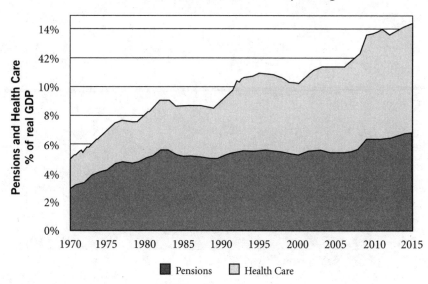

Meanwhile, as Figure 2.8 shows, government spending on pensions and health care—driven mainly by the largest welfare state programs, Social Security, Medicare, and Medicaid—grew.[35]

The picture is a bit more complicated for spending on other welfare programs. Spending rises and falls, but—when you look at the data—it becomes clear that it rises and falls depending on how the economy is performing. As Figure 2.9 shows, welfare spending declines when the economy is doing better because fewer people sign up for welfare, and it rises when the economy is doing poorly because more people call on it—not because free-market ideologues cut welfare programs. In fact, the only substantial cut to welfare spending came with Bill Clinton's 1996 Welfare Reform Act, which is widely credited with helping move people off the welfare rolls and into the labor force.[36]

On the regulatory side of things, the trend is the same. The budgets and staffing of U.S. federal regulatory agencies grew enormously between 1960 and 2013. According to economist Pierre Lemieux, "Over those 53 years, the federal regulatory budget has jumped seventeen-fold in constant

Figure 2.9
US Welfare Spending Trends

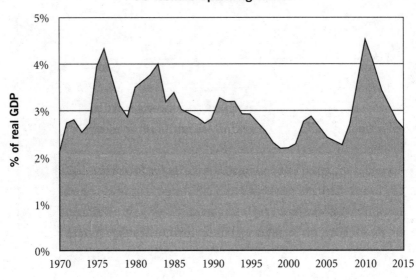

dollars, while the staffing of federal regulatory agencies has increased five-fold."[37] Another proxy of regulatory growth is the number of pages of the *Code of Federal Regulations* (CFR), which catalogs all federal regulations. The CFR has seen almost constant growth, starting at 19,335 pages in 1949 and growing to 134,261 pages by 2005.[38] Patrick McLaughlin of the Mercatus Center points out that if you made reading the CFR your full-time job, it would take you three years to finish.[39] And this is only for the federal government. One economist estimates that state regulations amount to 150 percent of the CFR.[40]

Finally, let's take a look at one industry that is most often cited as a glaring example of the dangers of rampant deregulation, the financial industry. At the national level alone (not counting state regulatory agencies), the U.S. financial system was subject to *eight* different regulatory authorities during the supposed era of deregulation. They were:

1. U.S. Securities and Exchange Commission (SEC)
2. Financial Industry Regulatory Authority (FINRA)
3. Commodity Futures Trading Commission (CFTC)

Figure 2.10
Regulation over Time

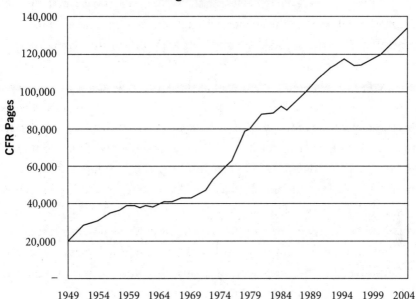

4. Federal Reserve (Fed)
5. Federal Deposit Insurance Corporation (FDIC)
6. Office of the Comptroller of the Currency (OCC)
7. National Credit Union Administration (NCUA)
8. Office of Thrift Supervision (OTS)

All of these agencies were enormously active during the so-called laissez-faire era. As the former CEO of BB&T Bank John Allison notes, "Government spending alone . . . on financial regulations (not company bailouts) increased, in adjusted dollars, from $725 million in 1980 to $2.07 billion in 2007."[41] Meanwhile, between 1980 and 2009, for every one instance of financial deregulation, there were four instances of new financial regulation.[42] It is one thing to claim that regulators didn't do their job during the last few decades, or that the government should have placed even more regulatory restrictions on the financial industry—all that is debatable—but it is quite another thing to describe the last few decades as a time when financial markets were deregulated, let alone unregulated.[43]

The Inequality Narrative tells a seductively simple story: when the government intervenes in the economy to fight inequality, a nation prospers; when the government takes a hands-off approach to the economy, "the rich" gain at the expense of everyone else. This simplicity is deliberate: it is an attempt to short-circuit the need to think carefully about the source of prosperity and the effects of government intervention. America has always had both elements of freedom and elements of government control—with the element of government control becoming more and more dominant starting with the New Deal. When thinking about economic issues, we need to always keep in mind the fact that America is not a fully free society but a *mixed economy*. This means that we cannot automatically attribute problems to the free element or positives to the controlled element. We have to think carefully about which element is responsible for what outcome.

And we have to think carefully about what the outcomes are. Just as inequality critics wrongly paint the last forty years as an age of laissez-faire freedom, so they wrongly paint it as an age of middle-class stagnation.

THE AGE OF STAGNATION?

"If the rich were growing richer," writes Joseph Stiglitz, "and if those in the middle and at the bottom were also doing better, that would be one thing, especially if the efforts of those at the top were central to the successes of the rest. We could celebrate the successes of those at the top and be thankful for their contributions. But that's not what's been happening."[44]

What has been happening, according to the critics of economic inequality? Incomes for the poor and middle class have stagnated. Citing census data, Stiglitz states that "the income of a typical full-time male worker has stagnated for well over a third of a century."[45] As for low-income workers, "over the last three decades those with low wages (in the bottom 90 percent) have seen a growth of only around 15 percent in their wages."[46] Piketty and Saez reach similar conclusions. Looking at IRS tax data, they conclude that between 1979 and 2007, 60 percent of income growth was achieved by the top 1 percent, whereas the average income growth of the bottom 90 percent was only 5 percent.[47]

We need to dig into these claims, but before turning to the statistical data, let's start by getting a big-picture view of how most Americans have done over the last forty years. To anyone who was around in the 1970s, it's obvious we've come a long way since then. The sheer abundance and quality of things like housing, cars, medicine, food, and electronics today makes it utterly implausible that we've stagnated over the last four decades. The popularity of $4 lattes, $10 craft beers, $120 tennis shoes, $400 cell phones, and $20,000 SUVs suggests that Americans have more disposable income than ever. General observations can be deceiving, of course, but in this case other evidence is overwhelmingly consistent with the conclusion that life has improved for the vast majority of Americans.

George Mason University economist Donald J. Boudreaux and University of Michigan-Flint economist Mark J. Perry point to three useful measures of well-being: life expectancy, spending on "basics," and the goods and services middle-income Americans can actually consume. On all fronts, they argue, the picture is not one of stagnation, but advance. Life expectancy at birth has increased by five years since 1980, from seventy-four to seventy-nine. Spending on basics—food, housing, transportation, clothing, utilities, etc.—"fell from 53 percent of disposable income in 1950 to 44 percent in 1970 to 32 percent today." And when it comes to consumption, many of us are enjoying what were once considered luxuries (if they existed at all): air travel, cell phones, personal computers, eBook readers, and much more.[48]

The data on consumption is particularly striking, and is worth a closer look. One way to think about improvements in consumption is to compare how many hours of work it takes the average American worker to purchase an array of different goods today versus in the past. Table 2.3 presents some figures collected by Perry, comparing the cost of various household appliances in 1973 and in 2013.[49]

The real prices of most of the goods we buy today are far lower than they were in the 1970s, contributing to a dramatic rise in the average American's standard of living. Yet these numbers actually understate that rise, since they don't take into account improvements in *quality*. Today's TVs, dishwashers, and vacuum cleaners are far superior to their 1973 counterparts. And even products that don't last as long as their predecessors more than make up for their shorter lifespan with markedly lower prices.[50]

TABLE 2.3

Household Appliances	Retail Price 1973	Hours of Work @ $3.95	Retail Price 2013	Hours of Work @ $19.30
Washing Machine	$285	72.2	$450	23.3
Clothes Dryer (gas)	$185	46.8	$450	23.3
Dishwasher	$310	78.5	$400	20.7
Refrigerator	$370	93.7	$432	22.4
Freezer	$240	60.8	$330	17.1
Stove (gas)	$290	73.4	$550	28.5
Coffee Pot	$37	9.4	$70	3.6
Blender	$40	10.1	$40	2.1
Toaster	$25	6.3	$37	1.9
Vacuum Cleaner	$90	22.8	$130	6.7
Color TV	$400	101.3	$400	20.7
Totals	**$2,272**	**575.2**	**$3,289**	**170.4**

It's also important to keep in mind that many of the advances we've enjoyed over the past forty years do not even show up in economic statistics. Statistics do not capture the *value* of products, only their price. But how would you quantify the value of being able to sing your daughter to sleep while you're away from home using a free video conferencing technology like Skype or FaceTime? Or of never having to worry about getting lost, thanks to GPS devices like Google Maps? Or of being able to find the answer to almost any question at the touch of a button, thanks to sites like Wikipedia? Or of being able to gain instant access to any book, song, or movie? These and countless other advances *matter,* and the fact that economists can't quantify them doesn't mean that we can ignore them when making pronouncements about our standard of living.

All of this good news calls for some caveats. First, it ignores the fact that some important costs have risen substantially in recent decades, such as the costs of health care and education. (As we explain in chapter 5, however, these rising costs are largely the consequence of government intervention.) Second, more middle-class families now have two earners, as many women have chosen to enter the workforce rather than become stay-at-home mothers. On the whole, that's a good thing. But it does complicate the picture, since it means that some amount of this improvement in our standard of living is owed not to pure economic progress, but to more people working. (That said, women constitute only 9 percent more of the workforce than they did in 1970—nowhere near enough of an increase to account for the gains American households have seen.[51]) Finally, some of these improvements may be a consequence of Americans taking on irrational levels of debt, which is not a sustainable path to growth. (Although the best evidence suggests that, in actuality, Americans have not significantly increased their debt-to-income ratios in recent decades. Instead, notes economist Steven Horwitz, "The debt has taken a different form, being somewhat more geared to credit cards rather than other types of loans, particularly store credit and buying consumer durables in payments, but the overall burden is not much greater."[52])

What we can say at this point is that there has been substantial economic progress made over the last forty years. Less progress than there could or should have been, perhaps, but Americans have made real gains.

So how then do we make sense of the claims of stagnation? The impression the inequality critics give is that they are just telling us the facts. But those "facts" are in truth controversial interpretations of murky statistics.

There are two main sources for income data: the Current Population Survey (CPS), tracked by the U.S. Census Bureau, and IRS tax records. Each has advantages and disadvantages. The major limitation of household surveys, apart from the question of whether respondents give true and accurate answers, is that they don't provide reliable information for top income earners. Even a large sample of the population will capture too few of these earners to accurately assess trends.[53] The major limitation of IRS tax data, on the other hand, is that it doesn't provide reliable information about income for those *below* the top, because it leaves out significant sources of their income, including government transfers (e.g., Social Security), some non-wage forms of market income (e.g., non-taxable capital gains, employer benefits that include health insurance and pension contributions), and income from other members of the household (if they file separately).[54] Given these limitations, the Congressional Budget Office has created a source that combines both data sets. And while this source is arguably superior, drawing conclusions about the data remains enormously difficult, as we'll discuss shortly.

To get a sense of how important the choice of the data source is, consider this: According to the approach taken by Piketty, the median U.S. income in 2007 was $30,000. The CPS data puts it at $52,650. And the CBO data gives us $77,200—more than double Piketty's number.[55] As we'll see in a moment, none of these numbers can be taken at face value. The lesson so far is simply that when we hear about claims regarding stagnation, we need to know the source from which they are being drawn, and we need to keep in mind the limitations of that source.

Regardless of which data set you use, there are many factors that can alter what conclusions you reach about changes in income over time. Here we'll highlight some of the most important factors. Then we'll look at how these factors lead different analysts to reach fundamentally different conclusions about middle incomes over the last forty years.

The aggregate problem. Statistics by their nature deal with statistical categories, but these categories can often conceal what is happening to real-life individuals. Asking what's happening over time to "the 1 percent" or the "bottom 20 percent" ignores the fact that the composition of these groups is constantly changing. Something that needs to be kept in mind at all times, then, is that when we're talking about middle incomes over time, we are not talking about the incomes of the same individuals. The claim that the middle class has stagnated since 1979 does not mean that someone who started working in 1979 is making the same amount of money today. That is seldom true.

There are basically two ways to measure what happens to individuals over time. One way involves using what's called cohort data. Using this method, we can look at what people between the ages of, say, 20 to 30 earned in 1979 and compare that to what 48- to 59-year-olds earned in 2007. When economist Stephen J. Rose compared incomes for married couples using this method, he found that the median household income rose from $55,600 in 1979 to $81,000 in 2007 (both in 2007 dollars).[56] We get similar results when we look at longitudinal panel data—that is, studies that follow the same individuals over long periods of time. Examining the first such study, the Panel Study on Income Dynamics, which started in 1968, Rose found that for "those who started aged 20–31 years old, median incomes rose 44 percent over the ensuing 28 years."[57] In other words, the experience of most real-life individuals is that their incomes have grown significantly over time.

The defenders of the stagnation thesis generally don't deny this (although they don't usually go out of their way to point it out). However, they attribute virtually all of these gains to what are called life-cycle gains, i.e., the fact that people generally make more as they age through skill and career advancement. The question the stagnationists are asking is whether the gains from *economic progress* are impacting those below the top. In other words, is the typical median-income household today doing better than a similarly situated household forty years ago? Has the rising tide that is the American economy lifted all boats—or just a few yachts?

The challenge is that answering that question forces us to rely on data about statistical categories, and those categories can easily disguise what's been going on in the economy, as we're about to see.

Household composition. One factor that can alter income estimates is a change in household composition. If there is a rise in divorce or if couples wait longer to get married, this will tend to make people look worse off, even if their actual standard of living has stayed the same or increased. For example, imagine a household in which a married couple each earns $25,000 a year, for a total household income of $50,000. Now let's say they get divorced. Even if they both get a substantial raise, say to $35,000 a year, the change in households will drag down median household income: instead of one household making $50,000 there are now two households making only $35,000 a year. Everyone is better off financially, and yet it appears they're doing worse. Given that divorce rates rose dramatically during the 1970s, the effects of this factor alone could be profound. What's more, household sizes have fallen in recent decades as people have had fewer children, which means that, all else being equal, a given income provides for a higher standard of living today than it did in the past.[58]

Immigration trends. Over the past forty years, millions of low-skilled immigrants have entered the U.S. workforce. Immigrants now make up about 13 percent of the population, versus only 5 percent in 1965, and they are twice as likely to be poor as native-born Americans.[59] The effect of this influx of immigration on income statistics is enormous. Imagine that you had a party with ten guests, each of whom was 5'10". Now imagine that a few hours later, ten more guests arrived who were only 5'. The average height of the guests in the room would suddenly plunge from 5'10" to 5'5"—even though no one got shorter. The same thing is true when immigrants come and take jobs that, by American standards, are low-paying. We can appear to stagnate or get poorer—even if every flesh-and-blood individual is better off.

Employer benefits. Since the 1970s, the proportion of our compensation that comes in the form of employer benefits, including health insurance and pension or 401(k) contributions, has risen from about 10 percent to 19 percent.[60] If we look only at income, we can miss out on a significant part of a person's actual compensation. Other, less tangible benefits can be almost impossible to measure. If employers become more flexible with hours or working arrangements, or offer more pleasant working conditions, this can entice employees to accept lower wages: they'll seem poorer even though on net they're better off.

Inflation adjustments. A dollar earned in 1979 is not worth the same as a dollar earned in 2015, and analysts try to adjust for these changes. But there are several different methods for adjusting for price inflation, none of which is perfect, and you can reach very different results depending on which method you use. The Consumer Price Index, or CPI-U, is the main measure of price inflation the government uses to make adjustments. But it's generally recognized that the CPI-U overstates inflation and so tends to underestimate how much better off people are over time. As a result, even though most stagnation claims are based on CPI-U adjustments, most researchers prefer more accurate measures, such as the Consumer Price Index Research Series Using Current Methods (CPI-U-RS), or the "chain-weighted" CPI, which takes into account the fact that people's purchasing decisions change when prices change.[61] Even these methods, however, probably overstate price inflation.

Taxes and transfers. People do not live on their so-called market income. The government both takes money from us (taxes) and gives money to us (transfers). In analyzing incomes, it makes a huge difference whether the analysis is pre-tax, pre-transfer or post-tax, post-transfer, or some other combination. Different studies take different approaches, and it's critical to be clear which approach is being taken and why.

Changes in the tax code. Changes in the tax code can alter how individuals, especially high earners, report income. This means that using IRS data to track high earners' incomes over time (as Piketty does) can be misleading. Economist Alan Reynolds, for instance, estimates that "more than half of the increase in the top 1 percent's share of pretax, pretransfer income since 1983, and all of the increase since 2000, is attributable to behavioral reactions to lower marginal tax rates on salaries, unincorporated businesses, dividends and capital gains."[62]

The economic unit. Finally, it makes a huge difference what unit is used to assess income: the individual, the household, or the tax unit. It might seem that the best unit is the individual, but in fact this produces incredibly misleading results. In a four-person household in which one parent works, treating the individual as the unit of well-being would show one well-off individual, and three people living in dire poverty. The tax unit, which is what IRS tax data measures, is slightly better, but it too can produce misleading results. Imagine, for instance, a college student, who lives at home and works part time for some extra cash, filing a tax return. His actual standard of living may be very high, but based only on his tax return, his income will appear to be very low. Or take what is perhaps a more widespread phenomenon: cohabitating couples. If what we're trying to assess is a person's standard of living, a non-married couple living together, each making $75,000 a year, is, all else being equal, able to consume more than are two individuals who live alone and make $75,000 a year. The cohabitating couple gets to enjoy economies of scale: saving on rent, utilities, food, and many other expenses. The final economic unit is the household, i.e., people living under one roof. The main drawback here is that unless you adjust for household size, you can misleadingly equate households that have radically different standards of living (e.g., a childless couple making $100,000 and a family of ten making $100,000). Indeed, one of the more quirky facts of the inequality debate is that *most people have household incomes above the median.* It sounds bizarre, but it's simply a product of the fact that higher-income households tend to have more people in them than lower-income households.

What difference do these various factors make? In a 2011 paper, Richard V. Burkhauser, Jeff Larrimore, and Kosali I. Simon demonstrated that

TABLE 2.4
COMPARING THE TOTAL GROWTH FROM
1979 TO 2007 USING EACH SHARING UNIT,
SIZE-ADJUSTMENT, AND INCOME SERIES COMBINATION

	Tax Unit	Household	Size-Adjusted Tax Unit	Size-Adjusted Household
Pre-tax, pre-transfer	3.2%	12.5%	14.5%	20.6%
Pre-tax, post-transfer	6.0%	15.2%	17.0%	23.6%
Post-tax, post-transfer	9.5%	20.2%	25.0%	29.3%
Post-tax, post-transfer + Health Insurance	18.2%	27.3%	33.0%	36.7%

they can make a big difference. Drawing on CPS data, the three econo-mists created the table above, showing different measures of median in-come arrived at by changing just a *few* of the factors we've talked about. As Table 2.4 shows, depending on which measures you use, you can ar-rive at totally opposite conclusions: that the middle class is stagnating (3.2 percent growth since 1979) or that it has seen strong if not extraordinary growth in income (36.7 percent since 1979).[63]

We can see the same effect if we look at the CBO's data. Depending on which factors we consider, the results will be dramatically different. In-equality critic Jared Bernstein uses the CBO data to conclude that between 1979 and 2010, household wage and salary income *declined* by 7 percent. However, Bernstein conceded, that's pre-tax, pre-transfer. If post-tax, post-transfer income is considered, household income for the middle fifth rose 36 percent during that period.[64] This dispels the myth of middle-class stag-nation, but it also makes it sound as if the only things keeping the middle class from stagnating are handouts from the government. But as Manhat-tan Institute scholar Scott Winship explains, these results are deceiving. "The figures [Bernstein] is citing, like those of Piketty, combine retirees and members of working-age households." What happens if you exclude retirees from the data?

> Wages and salaries only detract from middle-class income growth (that is, they only decline) for elderly households. Rather than constituting

91 percent of income growth, taxes and transfers only account for 54 percent of income growth among nonelderly households. . . . [In fact, middle-class] households with children had earnings $7,000 to $13,000 higher in 2010 than in 1979 (after accounting for the rise in the cost of living), a gain of 14 to 23 percent. If one adds other forms of pre-tax and -transfer income, the increase was over $15,000, or 25 percent. Childless nonelderly households also saw significant gains in pre-tax and -transfer income ($8,000, or 20 percent).[65]

For all the disagreements, this much is indisputable: the *only* numbers that support the middle-class stagnation thesis are pre-tax, pre-transfer wages that don't include all forms of market compensation, that don't take into account the changing composition of households and the workforce, and that don't adjust accurately for inflation. By every other conceivable measure, there has been substantial progress—the only debate is over exactly how much.[66] Unsurprisingly, even some critics of inequality reject the stagnation thesis. Economist James Galbraith, for instance, points out that:

The typical story is that median wages peaked in 1972 and have been stagnant and falling since then. As a result, it must be the case that people who are working now are much worse off than they were ten, fifteen, twenty years ago. That's not an accurate story—at least not up until the crisis in 2008—because over that period the labor force became younger, more female, more minority, and more immigrant. All of these groups start at relatively low wages, and they all then tend to have upward trajectories. So there's no reason to believe that life was getting worse for members of the workforce in general. On the contrary, for most members of the workforce it was still getting better. Plus they had the benefit of technical change and improvement in the other conditions of life.[67]

Given all of the challenges involved in assessing economic well-being, it would be a mistake to rely on any single statistic. But when common-sense observation, big-picture data about living standards, and most reasonable interpretations of statistical data all point in the same direction, we believe it is hard to conclude anything other than that an overwhelming majority of Americans today are far better off than they were in the 1970s—not only because of life-cycle gains, but because economic progress has in fact lifted most if not all boats. Inequality is increasing (probably), yet most Americans are doing better.

A WAY FORWARD

The Inequality Narrative claims to provide an explanation of how we've abandoned the American Dream and how we can revive it. It tells us that when the government fights economic inequality, we flourish, and when the government doesn't, we don't.

But that story simply will not hold up. It doesn't explain the past and it misrepresents the present. America has always been a mixture of freedom and government control, and the last forty years have seen a mixture of good and bad news. The key is to identify which forces are responsible for the good news and which are responsible for the bad.

To do that, we cannot start by looking at the *distribution* of wealth. We have to examine the *production* of wealth and, more broadly, the conditions that make the pursuit of success and happiness possible.

PART TWO

DISCOVERING THE AMERICAN DREAM

CHAPTER THREE
THE LAND OF OPPORTUNITY

THE PURSUIT OF HAPPINESS

America is known as the land of opportunity. But what exactly does that appellation mean? Opportunity, broadly speaking, refers to conditions that are favorable to the achievement of success and happiness. To appreciate the way in which America has fostered those conditions, consider a place where opportunity is almost totally absent: communist Cuba.

Prior to the communist revolution, Cuba was an autocratic regime riddled with corruption and oppression, and at least a third of Cuban citizens were abysmally poor. But things would become infinitely worse after Castro seized power in 1959, promising to level down the rich and ensure economic equality for all. According to one Cuban, who was eleven when the communists took over and who goes by the name "John B.," "Castro promulgated class warfare as a wedge once he took power, [saying], 'We're going to give all the poor people money, and redistribute the wealth.'"[1] The communists would take over banks, factories, small private businesses—"Even the boxes of shoeshine boys were seized," notes Cuban blogger Yo-ani Sánchez—and redistribute wealth on a massive scale. The economy quickly began to deteriorate, despite billions of dollars in aid from the Soviet Union.[2] As John recalled, "Food became scarce because the [collectivized] farms weren't producing. . . . [E]verything was rationed, and nothing was available the way it had been. . . . People are paid the equivalent of about ten dollars a month. They justify the low salaries because, well, there's nothing to buy. What do you need money for?"[3]

In pursuing a program of economic equality, the communists rejected any concern for political equality. Political elites were given free rein over the economy, and while they did indeed grind most Cubans down into equal poverty, they also used their power to enrich themselves at the population's expense. While most Cubans were regularly interrogated and frisked by police to make sure they hadn't gotten their hands on black-market cheese or cooking oil, the politically powerful enjoyed privileged access to well-stocked stores, palatial homes, foreign luxuries, and other extravagances unavailable to the public. "There is nothing in Cuba," said a Cuban schoolteacher after escaping to America in 1980. "You cannot express what you feel. The only ones who have a good social life are the Communist leaders. They have cars, nice houses. In the last couple of years, there has been a lot of hunger, little clothing. Sometimes we don't get soap for three months."[4]

It was possible for regular Cubans to get their hands on occasional "luxuries," such as televisions or refrigerators—but only by gaining a special favor from the state. According to Sánchez, "Everything you received above and beyond the norm was not due to your own efforts or talent." Instead, "it was a perk, a reward for obedience" to the communist party.[5]

When the Soviet Union collapsed and its aid to Cuba was shut off, things began to deteriorate even faster. As journalist and Cuban resident Mark Frank describes it, "The lights were off more than they were on, and so too was the water. . . . Food was scarce and other consumer goods almost nonexistent. . . . Doctors set broken bones without anesthesia. . . . Worm dung was the only fertilizer."[6]

Today things are marginally better, thanks in part to minor extensions of freedom, a burgeoning black market, and the Cuban tourist industry. But an individual who wants the chance to make something of his life will find precious few opportunities in Cuba, where the government not only controls all economic activity but even institutes a *maximum* wage: $20 a month for most jobs, $30 if you manage to become a doctor or a lawyer.[7] Cubans aren't just barred from rising: they are victims of an egalitarian system that seeks to stamp out even their *desire* to rise. As Sánchez observes:

[S]ince the 1970s there has been an attempt to shape a kind of person whose aspirations would not exceed the ceiling that the state had set for him: individuals who would have a self-perception that they could not compete, men and women who should feel satisfied, and even grateful, with what little could be given to everyone equally. Mediocrity began to be called modesty, while self-confidence was branded as arrogance. Amid a widespread lack of material things, the true revolutionary embraced the austerity that labeled the slightest weakness for fashionable clothing as extravagance, while consumerism and any desire for the new was considered as unpardonable.[8]

To the extent there is any opportunity for Cubans to make something of their lives, it comes from only one of two paths. The first is to be one of the lucky few who manage to get a job in the tourist industry (less than 1 percent of the population), where tips from foreign visitors can give a hotel maid an income far higher than that of a heart surgeon. The second is to flee—which tens of thousands of Cubans do every year, often risking their lives in the process. As one U.S. Coast Guard authority told the *New York Times* in 2014, "We have seen vessels made out of Styrofoam and some made out of inner tubes. These vessels have no navigation equipment, no lifesaving equipment. They rarely have life jackets with them. They are really unsafe."[9]

John B.'s family was one of the lucky ones. A few years after the revolution, they were able to immigrate to America by plane. "When we arrived in Miami in 1962, we had thirty-five pounds of clothing, and nothing else. No money. No property."[10] But, John said, "This country had so many opportunities when I came here in the Sixties. If you worked, you could make yourself whatever you wanted."[11] In America, even the poorest worker makes more in a day than most Cubans make in a month, and millions are able to rise out of poverty every year—with a significant minority even rising from rags to riches.

What explains the difference between America and Cuba? Why is it that few people thought of Cuba after its revolution as a land of opportunity, but millions of people during the nineteenth century and to this day think of America as a land of opportunity? In Cuba, most doors are closed to you as an individual, and the only way to open them is to get on your knees and beg your rulers for a favor, or bring others to their knees by scrambling to become one of the rulers. In the U.S., by contrast, each individual is free to pursue his happiness, to succeed or fail according to merit, neither ruling others nor being ruled by others.

That such a stark difference exists between the two nations should not be surprising. Both the Cuban government and the American government were established by ideologically driven political revolutions, and the ideologies behind those revolutions could not be more opposed. Cuba's ideological foundation is *collectivism*—America's is *individualism*.

Collectivism holds that an individual is fundamentally part of a group, the way that your individual cells are fundamentally part of your body. Morally, therefore, the group and its welfare are held to be superior to the individual. As philosopher Ayn Rand explains, collectivism, in its most consistent form, says "that the individual has no rights, that his life and work belong to the group . . . and that the group may sacrifice him at its own whim to its own interests."[12] According to collectivism, your hopes, dreams, convictions, and values are subordinate to the desires and commands of society, and your primary duty is to serve society by obeying the edicts of society's representative: the state. If the state decides that the business you want to start, or the prices you want to charge, or the book you want to write, or the investment you want to make is not in the "public interest," then it has every right to stop you by using physical force.

In its purest form, collectivism implies totalitarian control over the individual, as in Cuba. Collectivism isn't always applied consistently, however. Before the creation of the United States, most political systems were collectivist to one degree or another. Although some nations extended certain protections and liberties to the individual, the guiding principle was that the welfare of society trumped the interests of the individual. As Rand explains:

> Under all such systems, morality was a code applicable to the individual, but not to society. Society was placed *outside* the moral law, as its embodiment or source or exclusive interpreter—and the inculcation of self-sacrificial devotion to social duty was regarded as the main purpose of ethics in man's earthly existence.

Since there is no such entity as "society," since society is only a number of individual men, this meant, in practice, that the rulers of society were exempt from moral law; subject only to traditional rituals, they held total power and exacted blind obedience—on the implicit principle of: "The good is that which is good for society (or for the tribe, the race, the nation), and the ruler's edicts are its voice on earth."[13]

The United States, by contrast, was established on the principle of *individualism*. This was embedded in the nation's founding documents, which stated that the purpose of government was to protect political equality by securing the inalienable rights of each individual to life, liberty, and the pursuit of happiness. This entailed the abolition of the initiation of physical force from human relationships. If each man was to be free to pursue his own happiness, then others could not use force to stop him from pursuing his own happiness. And if someone did resort to force, the government's job was to uphold the rights of the individual by employing retaliatory force against the aggressor. This, in theory if not always in practice, was the foundation of America. In Rand's formulation:

All previous systems had regarded man as a sacrificial means to the ends of others, and society as an end in itself. The United States regarded man as an end in himself, and society as a means to the peaceful, orderly, *voluntary* coexistence of individuals. All previous systems had held that man's life belongs to society, that society can dispose of him in any way it pleases, and that any freedom he enjoys is his only by favor, by the *permission* of society, which may be revoked at any time. The United States held that man's life is his by right (which means: by moral principle and by his nature), that a right is the property of an individual, that society as such has no rights, and that the only moral purpose of a government is the protection of individual rights.[14]

Individualism is widely misunderstood. Individualism, we often hear, assumes that people derive no benefit from working together in groups. But individualism isn't atomism. Individuals can and should cooperate—but only on terms each individual voluntarily agrees to. Individualism, we hear, implies indifference to other people. But individualism isn't misanthropy. Individuals can and should care about other people—but they shouldn't be forced to sacrifice their hopes and dreams for other people. Individualism, we hear, is the view that only money matters. But individualism isn't materialism. Individuals can and should pursue all of the values that contribute to a happy and successful life—spiritual as well as material. In short, individualism means, as Rand says, "that man is an independent entity with an inalienable right to the pursuit of his own happiness in a society where men deal with one another as equals in voluntary, unregulated exchange."[15]

It is America's commitment to individualism that, at the deepest level, explains why John B. and hundreds of thousands of other Cubans risked their lives to make it to the United States. In a land that treats the individual as sovereign over his own existence, they are free to live self-supporting, self-directing lives. And it is only by leading a self-supporting, self-directing life that human beings are able to flourish.

In this chapter, we'll see how an individualist approach to government provides the widest possible opportunity for people to pursue happiness, regardless of whether they start out rich or poor. We will also see the kind of person who is attracted to a land of opportunity—and the kind of person who is not.

THE MEANING OF SUCCESS

In *Into the Wild,* Jon Krakauer recounts the true story of Christopher Johnson McCandless, who journeyed into the Alaskan wilderness to get away from modern society and "live off the land for a few months." McCandless doesn't leave behind all modern conveniences. He brings along a shotgun, a machete, and a few other tools, and even ends up taking shelter in an abandoned van. In the end, it's not enough.

Within three months, and even though game animals are abundant, McCandless is starving and trapped behind a raging river. He leaves a note on the van: "S.O.S. I need your help. I am injured, near death, and too weak to hike out of here. I am all alone, this is NO JOKE. In the name of God, please remain to save me. I am out collecting berries close by and shall return this evening." The note is found a month later by some locals, but it's too late. McCandless has starved to death.[16]

Nature doesn't give us what we need to survive. As McCandless discovered the hard way, we don't live in a Garden of Eden in which our desires are satisfied automatically and effortlessly. To live we need to *think* and to *act*. Alone in the wilderness, we need to figure out what food is edible and take action to get it, whether by picking berries off the ground or hunting down a moose. To secure shelter we need to figure out how to build a hut and then go out and do it. Nature doesn't automatically fulfill our needs, but what it does give us is a virtually limitless supply of raw materials that we can transform through ingenuity and effort into *wealth*, i.e., all of the material values that we need in order to live and enjoy life.

The same thing is true in an advanced economy with a division of labor, in which we cooperate with other producers. Working with other people enables us to be far more productive, and it gives us access to a far greater number of goods and services, but it doesn't change the essential issue: to acquire wealth, we have to think and produce *as an individual.* This is true whether the individual is the car mechanic who has to learn how to diagnose and repair a broken alternator, or a doctor who has to learn how to diagnose and repair a clogged artery, or the manager who has to learn how to diagnose and repair a broken business process. Regardless of the productive endeavor we choose to pursue, the creation of human values requires individual thought and effort. That's not some regrettable fact about nature—that is precisely *how* human beings pursue success and happiness.

We often equate success with money, and while money is certainly not irrelevant to success, it is not the whole story. By almost every measure, one of the most successful individuals in recent memory was Steve Jobs, and he was very clear on what he thought about the issue. In an interview for the PBS documentary *Triumph of the Nerds,* he explained: "I was worth about over a million dollars when I was 23 and over 10 million dollars when I was 24, and over 100 million dollars when I was 25 and it wasn't that important because I never did it for the money."[17] What did he do it for? As he would later put it in his famous Stanford University commencement address: "You've got to find what you love. And that is as true for your work as it is for your lovers. Your work is going to fill a large part of your life, and the only way to be truly satisfied is to do what you believe is great work. And the only way to do great work is to love what you do. If you haven't found it yet, keep looking. Don't settle."[18]

To live, each of us has to produce the material values our lives require, and the bulk of our time will be spent devoted to that task. Success is first and foremost an issue of finding a vocation that makes the days and hours of our life both materially and *spiritually* rewarding. We're happiest when we are able to engage our minds fully, to expand our knowledge and capabilities, to rise from achievement to achievement, doing work that we regard as interesting and worthwhile. For some of us, that can involve creating earth-shaking innovations that make us billions of dollars, but for others that can include educating children or managing a restaurant. What's important is not the scale of our achievements or the size of our incomes. What's important is that we constantly learn, grow, face, and overcome new challenges in a career that we love. Yaron, for instance, has a Ph.D. in finance, and no doubt could have made far more money on Wall Street than as the head of an educational non-profit. He chose the latter route because championing the ideas that he believes in is what gives him the deepest sense of purpose and satisfaction. Whether you want to be a teacher, an accountant, an actor, or an entrepreneur, to be a success is to find a productive endeavor that you love and do all that you can to be the best you can be.

This is not to slight the contribution of money to a successful life. In a division of labor economy, producing *means* working to earn money. We work, we earn money, and we use that money, not only to put food in our stomachs, but to help us realize *all* of our dreams and aspirations. Whether your dream is to live near the beach, travel the world, send your kids to college, or launch a new business venture, money is a tool that can help you achieve it. Just as you can't live too long or be too happy, so you can't have too much money. But money's value depends on its overall role in your life. It makes a vital difference how you obtain it and how you spend it. Living a successful life requires earning money *productively*. Unearned money cannot make up for lacking a fulfilling productive purpose. If you have a fulfilling productive purpose, however, and if you give careful thought to how best to use the money you earn to achieve your well-being, then the more money the better.

This remains true even in cases in which people earn more than they could ever spend on their own personal consumption. Noting that Amazon CEO Jeff Bezos's estimated fortune amounted to $22 billion, columnist R. J. Eskow wrote, "That's a lot of net worth for one individual. Granted, Bezos is much smarter than most of his peers. He's got skills and he's worked hard. Why shouldn't he be rich? It's the American way, after all. But does he need to be that rich?"[19] But what drives innovators is not buying up more of the goods that currently exist—it's pioneering the next great thing. Not *consuming,* but *creating.* We would never think to ask why J. K. Rowling continues to write books, even though she has a billion dollars in the bank from writing the Harry Potter series. We understand that it is the *writing* of the books that drives her. That same motivation applies not only to artists, but to innovators and entrepreneurs as well. They don't seek wealth in order attain a life-long goal of stagnating. They are committed to life-long growth, and they view wealth as a tool for expanding what they can achieve. In Bezos's case, he has not only continued to expand Amazon, but he has also started a side venture, Blue Origin, to pioneer private space travel. This is one of the values of having a fortune that far surpasses what you could spend on your personal consumption. A fortune this vast opens up new vistas of achievement, so that you can potentially solve problems that would be impossible to tackle with fewer resources.

VOLUNTARY TRADE:
THE GUARDIAN OF OPPORTUNITY

To pursue success and happiness is to live the life of a producer, who supports his own existence and lives by his own independent judgment. This is why the United States, and not Cuba, is the land of opportunity. In Cuba, the collectivist creed of the communists means that the road is closed to productive ability and independent thought. In America, our individualistic creed means that—to the extent we live up to that creed—each individual is free to exercise his mind, choose his path, deploy his talents, earn a living or a fortune, and pursue his dreams. If opportunity refers to conditions that are favorable to the achievement of success and happiness, then America has always supplied those conditions in spades: the freedom to think, choose, and produce—and the chance to live among other producers, whose ever-growing sum of knowledge, wealth, and achievements magnifies what we can achieve.

In America, we have the opportunity to work with entrepreneurs like Bill Gates and Mark Cuban—or to become one of them. We have the opportunity to use new technologies pioneered by innovators like Steve Jobs and Peter Thiel—and to create our own. We have the opportunity to gain access to capital from banks, venture capitalists, and other investors—and to become a capitalist. We have the opportunity to take advantage of the services of first-rate doctors, electricians, home builders, and chefs—and to become first-rate in whatever field we choose. We have the opportunity to buy an increasingly wide array of goods, of increasingly good quality, at an ever-declining cost. And the price for all of this is not bowing down to some political authority, but rising up to the challenge of producing wealth.

In a free society, the government doesn't give you a ration card that entitles you to something for nothing. Everything you get, you have to earn through production and *voluntary trade* with other producers. Whether you want a job or a thriving business or a loan or an iPhone, the passkey is your own achievement, which you trade for the achievements of others. No one owes you a living. "A trader," Rand writes,

> is a man who earns what he gets and does not give or take the undeserved. He does not treat men as masters or slaves, but as independent equals. He deals with men by means of a free, voluntary, unforced, uncoerced exchange—an exchange which benefits both parties by their own independent judgment. A trader does not expect to be paid for his defaults, only for his achievements. He does not switch to others the burden of his failures, and he does not mortgage his life into bondage to the failures of others.[20]

The institution of voluntary trade is the guardian of opportunity. The reason no one can exploit you or prevent you from succeeding is precisely because you get to decide the terms on which you'll deal with others—and if you and they can't come to mutually agreeable terms, you're all free to go your own separate ways. And by the same token, the reason that you can succeed, whatever your background or starting point, is because it is in the interests of other producers to deal with anyone who has value to offer. No one cares whether the person who fixes his car or performs his brain surgery or applies for a job at his company is male or female, Indian or Pakistani—he wants to know whether they are competent. And if he *does* care about irrelevant factors like sex or race, he is the one who suffers for his irrationality. He has no power to prevent others from patronizing or hiring the best.

The inequality critics often tell us that economic transactions shouldn't be classified as voluntary just because the government refrains from interfering. Instead, they say, those with enormous resources are able to exploit those who have fewer, rendering economic transactions involuntary. The guys at the top have all the power, and they'll use that power to profit at the expense of those at the bottom, both by paying workers less than they deserve and by charging customers more than can be justified. This view is based on a profound philosophic error: the conflation of political and economic power.

Political power is the power of the gun—the power to use physical force to get what you want. Political power is what Castro's goons used to strip people of their land and throw them in jail for speaking out against communism. It is the power possessed by the government. The government has a monopoly on the use of physical force: its laws are not offers, enticements, or suggestions. They are commands, and the failure to obey them is met with physical coercion.

Economic power is the power of trade—you can offer your resources in exchange for the resources of others. It's the power of Apple to offer its phone for sale at a price it chooses (and it's your power to spend your money elsewhere). It's the power of Amazon to offer its incredible platform to authors and publishers willing to accept its terms (and it's their power to refuse those terms and live with the consequences). Economic power is not the power to harm people, exploit people, or rob them of their rights—it's the power to offer rewards or not. As philosopher Harry Binswanger puts it, "A business can only make you an offer, thereby expanding the possibilities open to you. The alternative a business presents you with in a free market is: 'Increase your well-being by trading with us, or go your own way.' The alternative a government, or any force-user, presents you with is: 'Do as we order, or forfeit your liberty, property, or life.'"[21]

No employer, regardless of his economic power, can force someone to accept a job at his establishment. He can only make an offer, which the prospective employee is free to accept or reject. And since there are always competitors bidding for workers, a lowball offer is very likely to be rejected, which is why only a small percentage of the workforce earns the minimum wage. (And even if employers did somehow manage to underpay employees, they wouldn't be able to pocket the gains: competition would force them to pass on the savings to customers in the form of lower prices.)

But what about the rare cases in which a potential worker has very few options? Even here, the fact that a prospective employee may have to choose between taking a low-paying job and unemployment doesn't make his choice involuntary. It still remains true that the would-be employer is *expanding* the possibilities open to him—not restricting them. To call low pay "wage slavery" is to insult both employers and slaves. As economist George Reisman notes:

> The difference between freedom and slavery is as sharp as day and night, even when a worker must work to avoid the pain of hunger. For even in this case it is not the capitalist employer who *causes* the worker's hunger. On the contrary, he provides the means of *satisfying* the worker's hunger. The worker works for the capitalist always in order to receive a positive—his wages. The difference between a free worker and slave can always be seen in this: A slave is someone who is kept at his work against his will: by chains, whips, and guns—i.e., by physical force applied by other people. In the absence of such things, he would run off. A free worker, on the other hand, is someone who works of his own choice and who, more likely, can be *kept from* his work only by means of physical force.[22]

Even in today's tough economic climate, there are so many opportunities to earn an income that Americans aren't faced with such dire alternatives. But how should we think about the extremely low pay earned by workers in poor countries? Poverty, we need to keep in mind, is the given. We're born without resources, and have to create them. But why do so many people remain poor in a world that is so rich? Often there is an injustice involved: individuals are oppressed through political power, and, as a result, they live in abject poverty, subsisting on as little as a dollar a day.

This is tragic because it is so unnecessary. In countries like Afghanistan, Cuba, and Sudan, individuals who aspire to a better life have almost no hope because they have almost no freedom. But what is astonishing is that it is not *these* individuals whom the inequality critics point to as "exploited" and "oppressed." Instead, they point to workers in *developing* countries who are rising out of poverty thanks to increasing freedom. Workers in places like China and India are said to be working for "slave wages" in "sweat shops," and American companies like Apple are maligned for "profiting off their backs."

No American would want to work in a Chinese factory eleven hours a day for $1.50 an hour. But that is because we have better opportunities available. The reason thousands of Chinese willingly flock to these "sweat shops" is because these *are* better opportunities than the alternatives that are open to them.

Journalist Leslie Chang spent two years getting to know female assembly line workers in China, learning firsthand about their experiences, frustrations, and aspirations. She was struck by the fact that certain "subjects came up almost never, including living conditions that to me looked close to prison life: ten or fifteen workers in one room, fifty people sharing a single bathroom, days and nights ruled by the factory clock. Everyone they knew lived in similar circumstances, and it was still better than the dormitories and homes of rural China." Chang acknowledged that "the factory conditions are really tough, and it's nothing you or I would want to do," but concluded that, "from their perspective, where they're coming from is much worse, and where they're going is hopefully much better . . ."

Again and again, Chang documents how these jobs provided the young women she talked to not only with more money than they could have earned elsewhere, but a sense of purpose, a sense of pride, and opportunities for education and upward mobility that simply would not exist absent their so-called enslavement. This led Chang to conclude, "Chinese workers are not forced into factories because of our insatiable desire for iPods. They choose to leave their homes in order to earn money, to learn new skills, and to see the world."[23]

Research by economist Benjamin Powell supports Chang's experience. As shown in Figures 3.1 and 3.2, Powell found that "sweat shops" typically deliver a far higher standard of living than is available elsewhere in developing countries—sometimes as much as *three times* the average national income.

Even more striking, Powell found that those who worked in "sweat shops" that had been criticized *by name* in the U.S. news were usually better off—often much better off—than most people in their country.[24]

The lesson, Powell stresses, is that we can't evaluate work opportunities in a given economy according to how they compare to the opportunities *we* have. We have to compare them to the next best alternatives that are *actually available* in those countries. Powell recounts how, in one famous 1993 case, "U.S. senator Tom Harkin proposed banning imports from countries that employed children in sweatshops. In response a factory in Bangladesh laid off 50,000 children. What was their next best alternative? According to the British charity Oxfam, a large number of them became prostitutes."[25]

Pay isn't low in developing countries because of the economic power of "greedy" employers. Those employers have to compete for workers the

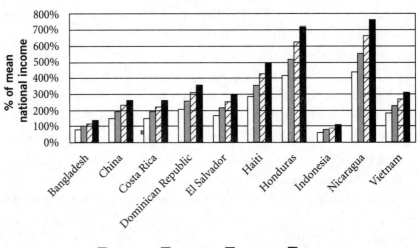

Figure 3.1
Apparel Industry Wages

Figure 3.2
Mean Protested Sweatshop Wages

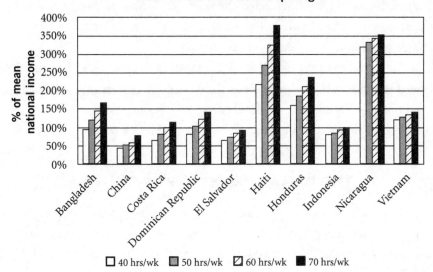

☐ 40 hrs/wk   ▨ 50 hrs/wk   ▨ 60 hrs/wk   ■ 70 hrs/wk

same way their American counterparts do. To the extent a business lacks political power, it can't use its economic power to pay whatever wages it wants—it has to pay enough to lure potential workers away from their next best alternative. But, at the same time, it cannot pay a worker more than he adds to the company's profits. Those are the boundaries that determine compensation in the developing world, just as they do in the developed world. The problem, as Powell explains, is that, "Wages are low in the third world because worker productivity is low (upper bound) and workers' alternatives are lousy (lower bound)."[26] The same thing, of course, was true in the United States a hundred fifty years ago, before we amassed the enormous capital that makes even low-skilled American workers incredibly productive.

What some regard as offensively low pay in fact reflects voluntary, win/win transactions—with one giant caveat. None of the countries we are talking about are anywhere close to fully free. To the extent people's rights aren't being protected by the government—to the extent individuals *are* subject to political power—they are not being treated fairly, and we are right to protest in the name of safeguarding their liberty. First and foremost we should fight for their freedom to immigrate to the United States if they wish. But we should also champion the protection and expansion of freedom in their home countries, so that they can continue to enjoy the same gains from economic progress that we enjoy.

In a land of opportunity, we are *free*—free to produce and to rise by our productive ability. But to flourish in a land of opportunity is not easy or effortless. Opportunity is demanding, and the question each of us faces is whether we will choose to live up to those demands, or not.

THE DEMANDS OF OPPORTUNITY

A while back, Don talked to Susan Petersen, an entrepreneur who was featured on the show *Shark Tank*, about how her business got started. Susan said she had taught herself how to make stylish baby moccasins and decided to turn her talent into a business. The problem was, she didn't have any money to buy the supplies she needed to get started. But instead of lamenting her lack of opportunities, she asked her brother, who installed windows for a living, if she could follow him around for the summer and keep the aluminum frames of discarded windows. She spent three months knocking the glass out of old window frames and, at the end of the summer, sold the scrap aluminum for $200, which she used to buy the leather she needed to create the shoes. Today, her company, Freshly Picked, is a success.

Susan's story illustrates a crucial fact about opportunities: their value depends on our willingness to spot them and capitalize on them. The only reason that Susan's brother's business represented an opportunity was because she chose to turn her talent into a business, spent time thinking about how to solve a critical problem, and then put in the sweat equity to carry out her plan.

Even opportunities that may come to us without effort on our part—affluent parents, valuable personal connections, a good education—require enormous effort to capitalize on. Going to an excellent school doesn't do us any good if we don't study. In his runaway bestseller *Outliers,* Malcolm Gladwell makes much of the fact that successful people have encountered these sorts of "lucky breaks" at one time or another. The young Bill Gates, for instance, benefited from having access to computers when few people did. But the salient fact about Gates is not that he *had* this opportunity (which thousands of others in his situation did), but that he acted to capitalize on it, spending countless hours learning to program computers, and eventually launching a software company that would aim to put "a computer on every desk and in every home." It was only in light of these chosen goals, and of his focused determination to achieve them, that the computers in Gates's high school represented an opportunity.

In a free society, opportunities are abundant, but we have to exercise thought and effort in order to transform them into achievements. In fact, many of the opportunities that allow us to succeed are opportunities that we *create* through our own choices. Andrew Carnegie, for instance, arrived in America as a twelve-year-old Scottish immigrant. With barely a penny to his family's name, and with only five years of formal education behind him, he went to work at a textile mill, twelve hours a day, for $1.20 a week. His first major break came when he was hired by the Pennsylvania Railroad. Why was he hired? Because at his previous job, Carnegie came in before his twelve-hour shift started so he could learn how to send and receive telegraph messages. Eventually, he was able to take telegraph messages by ear rather than by transcribing the Morse code—a feat only two other people in America could perform.[27] Although the scale of Carnegie's achievement is unique, the fact is that any time we acquire knowledge or develop a skill or achieve something of value, we open up new opportunities that were previously unavailable to us.

To thrive in a land of opportunity, you can't coast. You have to be committed to learning, improving, making tough choices, and setting aside immediate gratification in order to achieve long-range goals. A successful life is something you have to build. You have to be willing to stand on your own two feet and take responsibility for every aspect of your life: decisions about your career, your relationships, your health, your finances. A land of opportunity requires a person to live a self-supporting, self-directing life—a life where there is no limit to what you can achieve, but where you bear full responsibility for achieving it. It is no accident that America appealed to those who were willing to assume that responsibility. Recall the poster calling for Irish immigrants to the United States we quoted in chapter 1: "In America, *a man's success* must altogether rest with himself—it will depend on his *industry, sobriety, diligence* and *virtue;* and if he do not succeed, in nine cases out of ten, the cause of the failure is to be found in the *deficiencies* of his own character."[28]

Many commentators have expressed puzzlement at the fact that the United States was one of the last advanced nations to adopt a welfare state. But that's no coincidence. Opportunity seekers don't want to be "taken care of." They want to be free so they can build for themselves the kind of life they want. They know that the flip side of "someone is looking out for you" is "someone is deciding for you." Even Franklin D. Roosevelt, the man who created the American welfare state, understood this, observing that "in this business of relief we are dealing with properly self-respecting Americans to whom a mere dole outrages every instinct of individual independence."[29]

Not everyone values "individual independence," however. Some people have no intention of making anything of their lives and, as a result, they do not desire the freedom needed to do so. They desire to have their needs fulfilled without thought or effort, which means: they desire the *unearned*.

This desire can take different forms and exist in varying degrees. At its extreme, there are people who literally dream of sitting around the house and watching TV, as they mooch off relatives or the state, and there are criminals, who satisfy their desire for the unearned by resorting to theft or fraud. Much more common is the person who is willing to work, but who doesn't approach his career or his life thoughtfully or ambitiously. Although he may show up on time and do what's required of him, he is essentially passive and believes that changing conditions should never require him to learn more or change his routine. ("If my uneducated grandfather could earn a middle-class wage working at the local factory, then why can't I?") Then there are the political favor-seekers who actively pursue riches, but do so, not through productive achievement, but through feeding at the public trough. Whatever their differences, one thing remains the same: their ideal world is a Garden of Eden where all of their wants and needs are satisfied automatically and effortlessly, and where they aren't responsible for exerting the thought, judgment, and effort that success and happiness require.

This is precisely what the regulatory-welfare state advocated by the inequality critics claims to provide. You don't have to learn how to become more valuable if you want to earn more—the government will mandate a minimum wage. You don't have to think about how to save and invest—the government will provide you a guaranteed old-age pension. You don't have to bother setting aside an emergency fund—the government will guarantee you unemployment benefits. You don't have to think about whether a product is useful or safe—the government will judge for you. You don't have to investigate whether a bank is making prudent decisions—the government will insure your deposits. You don't have to think about how to educate your children—the government will decide what ideas and values they should be taught. You don't continually have to innovate to stay ahead of the competition—the government will protect your company or industry from competition. You will be guaranteed security without having to bother using your mind.

Of course an opportunity seeker cares about economic security—he knows that bad things can happen. But he also understands that genuine security comes from having his rights protected so that he is free to deal with life's challenges and unknowns as he judges best: to save and invest for the future, to purchase insurance, to keep his skills up-to-date so he doesn't end up unemployed. His goal is to be free to deal with the demands of nature—not to have the government free him from nature's demands.

The worst evil of the paternalistic regulatory-welfare state is that, in attempting to protect people who *don't* take responsibility for their lives from the consequences of their own passivity, it sacrifices the responsible individual, who is no longer free to make his own decisions and live on his own terms. If the government gets to decide what the minimum wage is, *you* don't get to decide that it's in your interest to accept a lower wage. If the government gets to decide that you have to cough up 12.4 percent of your income for Social Security, you don't get to decide what to do with that money or how to plan for your retirement. If the government gets to decide what products are useful and safe, then you don't get to disagree—say, by trying a potentially life-saving drug the FDA has yet to approve. If the government gets to decide which companies and industries deserve protection and support, then you don't get to challenge the status quo (at least not without a severe handicap). Government-guaranteed "security" necessarily means *limited opportunity.*

And the government can't even provide actual security. Genuine security comes from knowing that you are in control of your own life and that you have made provisions for contingencies. The only thing the government can do is give the *appearance* of security. But when our alleged security is based, not on our own work and our own judgment, but on government handouts and government dictates, we are at the mercy of bureaucrats and voters. Consider the fact that because our so-called entitlements are facing unfunded liabilities on the order of $100 trillion, the government will inevitably have to slash Social Security and Medicare at some point. When? By how much? No one can say. Some security.

If you want to understand what makes America—and Americans—unique, it is the extent to which we have embraced the demands of living in a free society. In 1952, *Reader's Digest* published a short statement from the politician Dean Alfange entitled "An American's Creed" that eloquently captures the American spirit.

> I do not choose to be a common man. It is my right to be uncommon—if I can. I seek opportunity—not security. I do not wish to be a kept citizen, humbled and dulled by having the state look after me. I want to take the calculated risk; to dream and to build, to fail and to succeed. I refuse to barter incentive for a dole. . . . I will not trade freedom for beneficence nor my dignity for a handout. I will never cower before any master nor bend to any threat. It is my heritage to stand erect, proud and unafraid; to think and act for myself, enjoy the benefit of my creations, and to face the world boldly and say, this I have done. This is what it means to be an American.[30]

This is the kind of person opportunity appeals to: the person who desires to *earn* success by his own choice and effort—not someone who desires the unearned. And apart from a small minority who are severely handicapped, and necessarily depend on the support of those who aren't, earning success is a challenge all of us can meet.

RISING FROM NOTHING

A free society eliminates barriers to success by securing our rights. But success is never easy—particularly for those who start with nothing. What's important to understand is that, so long as men are left free, success is *possible* to anyone willing to exert the thought and effort it requires.

Consider the story of Ben Carson.[31] Carson, a black man, was raised in a poor household by a single mother whose own education ended in the third grade. Despite his inauspicious start, Carson decided at an early age that he wanted to become a doctor.

It would not be easy. Carson was not a naturally gifted student, and starting at the bottom of his class, he set an ambitious goal—to become the top student. He cut the amount of TV he watched, diligently studied, and used his free time to read widely. "Bennie," his mother told him, "if you can read, honey, you can learn just about anything you want to know. The doors of the world are open to people who can read."[32] Within two years Carson had achieved his goal—he was the top student in his class.

But his focus began to slip a few years later as he entered high school and started paying more attention to being "one of the guys" than earning high marks. When he realized that his grades had dropped, Carson reevaluated his priorities. His mother had taught him he was the one "ultimately responsible" for his own life. As he pondered his low grades, he writes, "I began to realize that I had myself—and only myself—to blame. The in-group had no power over me unless I chose to give it to them."[33] He once again put his energy into his school work.

Eventually, thanks to his top grades and high SAT scores, Carson was able to attend college at Yale and later enter medical school at the University of Michigan. Once again he struggled, and once again he took responsibility for improving:

> During my second year . . . I got out of bed around 6:00 a.m. and would go over and over the textbooks until I knew every concept and detail in them. . . . All during my second year, I did little else but study from the time I awakened until 11:00 at night. By the time my third year rolled around, when I could work on the wards, I knew my material cold.[34]

Shortly thereafter, Carson fell in love with neurosurgery, and chose it as his specialty. "*I have to know more,* I'd find myself thinking. Everything available in print on the subject became an article I had to read. Because of my intense concentration and my driving desire to know more, without intending to I began to outshine the interns."[35] He started taking over the responsibilities of the medical interns and residents, who would hand Carson their beepers and go nap in the lounge. Carson didn't mind—it gave him a chance to learn.

Ultimately, Carson's intense focus, ambition, and relentless commitment to learning would lead him to become a top neurosurgeon at Johns Hopkins. Reflecting on his path, Carson concluded:

> These young folks need to know that the way to escape their often dismal situations is contained within themselves. They can't expect others to do it for them. Perhaps I can't do much, but I can provide one living example of someone who made it and who came from what we now call a disadvantaged background. Basically I'm no different than many of them.[36]

This is the kind of tenacity and dedication to a productive purpose that anyone can emulate and that can enable one to triumph over seemingly insurmountable obstacles to success. No, not everyone can become a surgeon. We have to set goals commensurate with our abilities (although we should be careful not to underestimate our abilities). But if we do that, then it is entirely possible to overcome our disadvantages and build a career for ourselves that is financially and spiritually rewarding.

Take someone who, despite his best efforts, struggles with academic work. There are still enormous opportunities for skilled blue-collar work—for mechanics, electricians, plumbers, welders, and the like. These are well-paying jobs that can be deeply fulfilling, and yet millions of such jobs are going unfilled right now because there aren't enough workers trained to do them. As former *Dirty Jobs* host Mike Rowe has argued, the main reason for this is that "our society [has] waged . . . a sort of cold war on [blue-collar] work. . . . [L]ook at the way those industries are portrayed in pop culture. Show me a plumber, and I'll show you a 300-pound guy with a giant butt crack and a tool belt. He's a punch line."[37] But it's the plumber who gets the last laugh: the fact is that with only a couple years of training, a junior plumber can earn between $40,000 and $50,000 a year, and an experienced plumber can earn upward of $70,000.[38]

Even the low-skilled service-sector jobs at places such as McDonald's and Walmart have been unfairly maligned as "dead-end jobs." A low-skilled, low-paying job is not a limit on opportunity—it's a stepping-stone to greater opportunity. Or it is if you choose to make it one. Most employers today are *desperate*, not just for great employees, but even for good employees—competent workers who show up on time and stay until the job is done. Anyone who does that *can* advance. And many people do. After studying fast-food workers from Harlem's ghetto, sociologist Katherine Newman found that about a third of the workers she followed had climbed their way out of poverty over the course of eight years—sometimes through internal promotion, sometimes by leaving the fast-food industry for higher-paying jobs elsewhere, and sometimes by going to college or trade school. (And, as she also shows, many of those who didn't escape poverty were held back by their own choices.)[39]

One of the worst things we can do for people who want to advance out of low-paying jobs, Newman points out, is to demean those jobs as mindless or degrading. As she writes in her book *No Shame in My Game*, even though many low-paying workers employ talents similar to those used by their white-collar counterparts—"memory skills, inventory management, the ability to work with a diverse crowd of employees, and versatility in covering for fellow workers when the demand increases" among many other skills—such workers are "limited by the popular impression that the jobs they hold now are devoid of value." Newman is particularly disturbed by the fact that "when journalists want to call upon an image that connotes a deadening, routinized, almost 'skill-free' job, they routinely invoke the fast-food burger flipper as the iconic example. Writers interested in championing the cause of the de-skilled worker have also contributed to this image problem" by suggesting that "there is no skill left in the job" and that "any worker with half a brain [would run] for the door."[40] We live in a culture that has denigrated honest work, and the inequality critics share no small part of the blame. Instead of recognizing the dignity in a job well done, they equate dignity with a job well-compensated (or, absent that, a welfare check).

Overcoming poverty or a bad education and making something of your life is a heroic achievement. An even more heroic achievement, however, is building a successful life for yourself when your friends, family, and neighbors do not nurture your talent and ambition, but actively *dis-courage* you in your pursuit of a better life. Tragically, that is the reality faced by millions of young people today—particularly in America's poorest communities.

"You don't travel very far in the ghetto," writes *New York Times* reporter Jason DeParle, "without hearing a crab-pot story, of someone who tried to get ahead but was dragged down by family and friends—a resentful boyfriend, an addicted sister, a brother headed for jail. Stories of ghetto success often involve a moment of physically breaking away, to school, the army, or merely the asylum of an outside mentor."[41]

In his moving account of gifted inner-city students, *And Still We Rise*, *Los Angeles Times* reporter Miles Corwin describes an example of this "crab-pot" phenomenon—named after the behavior of crabs in a pot, who try to escape, only to be caught and pulled back down by other crabs—in which people who make an effort to rise are dragged down by pressure from their peers:

> In the ghetto, where teenage machismo is venerated in rap songs and music videos, where athletes and gangbangers gain the most attention in the school hallways, an affinity for academics is something to camouflage, not celebrate. The serious student often is regarded as effete, as a sellout, as someone who has disdained his culture.

In his book, Corwin describes the experience of a young man named Sadi, who "had participated in class discussions and tried to articulate his opinions" only to have other students "mock him or shout: 'Stop trying to act white.'" The head of the school's gifted program, Scott Braxton, explained to Corwin that many students would rather quit the gifted program than face such ridicule: "[E]very year a number of boys come by my office, begging to get out. They feel that by going the academic route, they just can't fit in. The pressure gets to them. They just get dragged down by this strong undercurrent in the neighborhood against carrying books, against studying, against striving to succeed in school."[42]

The problem is broader than outright hostility toward ambition and achievement. Growing up in a broken home, surrounded by crime, racial prejudice, drug addiction, alcoholism, and shiftlessness all work against a young person's ability to develop the values and character that make success possible, and—as recent work by researchers such as Charles Murray and Robert D. Putnam has persuasively argued—many of these problems are on the rise in poor communities.[43]

Success is always hard, even when you have everything going for you. But to set ambitious goals and remain dedicated to them when your family, your neighbors, your community are all pushing you in the opposite direction takes an exceptional amount of courage and independence, and is an immense moral achievement. But as millions of Americans have shown, it *is* possible. It is patronizing to conclude, as many people do, that a bad environment absolves an individual of responsibility for making something of his life. You can see this attitude most clearly in one of the most influential works on inequality in American history, Michael Harrington's 1962 work *The Other America: Poverty in the United States*. In it, Harrington claims that poor people are helpless in the face of the challenges that come from living in impoverished neighborhoods.

> The drunkenness, the unstable marriages, the violence of the other America are not simply facts about individuals. They are descriptions of an entire group in the society who react this way because of the conditions under which they live. . . . The other Americans are those who live at a level of life beneath moral choice, who are so submerged in their poverty that one cannot begin to talk about free choices. . . . [S]ociety must help them before they can help themselves.[44]

This is far different from acknowledging the fact that it is enormously difficult to grow up in the ghetto, or that in forming a moral judgment of someone it's relevant to consider whether he is surrounded by good role models and plentiful resources or by destitution and lowlifes. It says people are *helpless* in the face of such influences and *blameless* for their bad decisions. This is one of the most troubling strains in the economic inequality critique: the implicit, and sometimes explicit, suggestion that Americans *can't* succeed through their own effort. "The status of your children, your grandchildren, your great grandchildren, your great-great grandchildren will be quite closely related to your average status now," says University of California Davis economist Gregory Clark.[45] In the face of such alleged facts, we should not expect people to struggle over obstacles in order to succeed—and we certainly shouldn't hold them accountable for choices that undermine success, such as choosing to use drugs, or commit crimes, or to have children they can't afford to support. That, writes *Salon*'s Elias Isquith, would be "blaming the victim" and conveying the message that "a person's inability to provide herself with the material comforts of a modern life stems from her own shortcomings, rather than the failure of the social and economic system at large."[46]

This represents a ludicrous false alternative: it says that either individuals are always at fault for where they end up, or that they are never at fault. And it ignores the far more pressing question: what should a person do about his circumstances going forward? Whether or not it is a person's *fault* that he's failed to achieve success, achieving success is still his *responsibility*. Responsibility, in this context, isn't about condemnation, but empowerment: it means even if you've been victimized, you don't have to live as a victim—you can rise above your circumstances. Even in today's world, in which too many communities are hostile to success, and in which too many government policies make success more difficult to achieve, success *is* possible—but only if an individual doesn't accept the role of a victim, doesn't wait around for society to cure all its social and economic ills, and instead fights to make something of himself.

Don's friend Jeremiah is a testament to the power of individual responsibility. Growing up in some of the roughest neighborhoods in Connecticut, Jeremiah spent his early years living in motel rooms, housing projects, and homeless shelters, all while living in fear of an abusive father. "He was an alcoholic. He was into drugs. He has a jail record that goes back to the Seventies. My most vivid memories of my father were of him coming home angry and my being in trouble. . . . He was a terror." Many evenings, Jeremiah and his sisters were left alone while his parents partied. The next day, the kids would have to sit silently in bed for hours, until their parents woke up in the afternoon. Sometimes this meant that Jeremiah missed school. That was particularly rough: there was seldom enough to eat at home, and he often went hungry. "When I lived at home my sisters and I would dream about the day when we would run away. I know one of my favorite stories was *The Boxcar Children,* because that was my dream. I would take my sisters and we would find an empty boxcar somewhere and figure out how to live." He never did run away, but eventually Jeremiah was put into the foster care system, which was a step up from the hell that came before, but just barely.

If anyone ever had an excuse for thinking of himself as a victim, Jeremiah certainly did. Instead, he viewed himself as better than his surroundings, and regarded it as his responsibility to overcome them. "I had certainly concluded by the time I was fourteen that if I was going to do anything I needed to do it myself. [I thought,] 'I am not going to wait for other people to get things done for me.'" He became "fiercely independent. If it needed to be done, I was going to do it. And when I do it, it's going to get done."

Whether it was at school or on the jobs he held throughout his teens and early twenties, Jeremiah cultivated a savage work ethic. At school he regularly made honor roll, and when it came to work, whether he was filing papers at a business office, or selling shoes at a department store, or washing dishes at a pizza joint, his attitude was always the same: "If you're going to do anything, then just be the best at doing it. . . . I wasn't going to just wash dishes, I was going to be the best dishwasher they had."

His hard work would pay off. Although life remained tumultuous throughout his teens, Jeremiah ultimately enrolled in college and, after graduating with a degree in literature, built a successful career for himself. Today he teaches grammar and literature to middle school students. "I wanted to teach people about the world around them. . . . The world of education is thrilling to me, in that it has that potential to raise people from the cave, so to speak."[47]

The fact is that Americans are not helpless, and it is not compassionate but *immoral* to tell them that they are. Preaching a philosophy of victimhood only creates more victims, and encourages precisely the kinds of environments that are hostile toward ambition and success. When people are taught that they *cannot* succeed through their own efforts, those who accept that notion will naturally come to resent those who *try* to succeed through their own efforts, creating the crab-pot phenomenon that drags so many people down. One of the subjects in sociologist Katherine Newman's study of poor fast-food workers explains it this way:

> Tiffany, also a teen worker in a central Harlem Burger Barn [a fictional name for a nationwide hamburger chain], thinks she knows why kids in her community who don't work give her such a hard time. They

don't want her to succeed because if no one is "making it," then no one needs to feel bad about failing. But if someone claws her way up and it looks as if she has a chance to escape the syndrome of failure, it implies that everyone could, in theory, do so as well. The teasing, a thinly veiled attempt to enforce conformity, is designed to drag would-be success stories back into the fold.

"What you will find in any situation, more so in the black community, is that if you are in the community and you try to excel, you will get ridicule from your own peers. It's like the 'crab down' syndrome. . . . If you put a bunch of crabs in a big bucket and one crab tries to get out, what do you think the other crabs would do now? According to my thinking, they should pull 'em up or push 'em or help 'em get out. But the crabs pull him back in the barrel. That's just an analogy for what happens in the community a lot."

Keeping everyone down protects against that creeping sense of despair which comes from believing things could be otherwise for oneself.[48]

We should be compassionate toward those who face daunting challenges. But we should also respect them enough to insist that they take responsibility for overcoming those challenges and acknowledge that they are able to overcome them. And, given the huge obstacles the government has put in the way of their success (see chapter 5), we should fight for a freer America, so that everyone has the greatest possible opportunity to rise by his own effort.

THE "EQUALITY OF OPPORTUNITY" RUSE

Today it is fashionable to speak, not of opportunity, but of *equality* of opportunity. This phrase is seldom defined, and comes in a variety of flavors, but the most influential conception of equality of opportunity comes from the late egalitarian philosopher John Rawls. For Rawls, equality of opportunity does not refer simply to the absence of legal barriers to success (e.g., Jim Crow laws), but to *equality of initial chances of success* as well. In the race of life, according to the Rawlsian view, everyone should have a fair shot at success; just as a track meet would be unfair if some people started halfway to the finish line, so it's critical that the government help even out the opportunities we encounter in life—to level the playing field by taking away advantages from the fortunate (e.g., huge inheritance taxes) and giving advantages to the less fortunate (e.g., government provision of health care and education).[49]

This idea of equality of opportunity is appealing to many people, even those untroubled by unequal economic outcomes. As the authors of *The Spirit Level* point out, "Unlike greater equality itself, equality of opportunity is valued across the political spectrum, at least in theory."[50] The reason it's so appealing is that it taps in to our sense of fairness: in any game, we want everyone to play by the same rules.

But life is not a game, and achieving equality of initial chances means forcing people to play by *different* rules. Trying to equalize initial chances of success in life requires the government to treat people unequally: in order to ensure an equal material and educational starting point, the government has to take earned money from well-to-do parents and give unearned money and education to less well-to-do parents. But even that doesn't achieve equality of initial chances. Taken seriously, the egalitarian notion of equality of opportunity would mean that you would not be allowed to provide your child with any opportunities—a better school, a better computer, a better book collection, a trip abroad—if other people's children did not have the same opportunities. One philosopher recently mused that it might even be wrong for parents to read to their children since it could give them an "unfair advantage" in life.[51]

If that agenda is obscene, the premise it's based on is absurd. The fact is that life is *not* a race: success in life isn't determined by how well you do compared to other people. It's determined by whether you are able to achieve whatever hopes and dreams you set for yourself: to build a great company, to write a great book, to excel as a computer programmer, to be a great teacher or a great plumber. None of that requires besting others; the favorable circumstances they enjoy can't hold you back. Exactly the reverse is true. Part of the reason people flock to the United States is precisely because it is a land in which other people are wealthier, better educated, and more productive than in their home countries. It is infinitely easier to prosper as a cab driver in the Hamptons than in Havana. If life was actually a race in the sense that the egalitarians suggest, then instead of foreigners immigrating to America, Americans should be immigrating to places like

Mexico and India, where they would be among the wealthiest and best educated people in the country. The reason this doesn't happen is because we know in some terms that we aren't locked in a zero-sum battle for success, where we have to conquer opponents in order to achieve victory. In reality, we succeed by producing values and trading them with other producers, in exchanges where *both* sides win—and the more others have to offer, the easier our success becomes.

All of us are born with certain advantages and certain challenges, and our happiness depends on maximizing our advantages and overcoming our challenges. Will the struggle upward be harder for some than for others? No question. If your parents are loving, rich, educated, and well-connected, you'll probably have an easier time building a successful life than if you're born a poor orphan. This is one reason parents work so hard to provide their children with opportunities. But the only way to equalize opportunities would be to deprive some people of the opportunities that are rightfully theirs. Our focus should be on making the most of our own lives, regardless of whether we start at the bottom or the top—not on envying the advantages and achievements of others.

And it is the freedom secured by *political equality* that allows us to make the most of our lives. When we're equal before the law, no one can use the power of the government to gain special privileges that hold us back or exploit us. Black or white, rich or poor, we all have the same rights: to think, produce, and trade freely with other people. In this sense, a free society *does* provide a level playing field. Everyone can participate in the opportunity provided by a free society, because we all play by the same rules.

It was the ideal of political equality that, to the extent we lived up to it, made America, America. The reason millions have left the countries of their birth to come to America's shores, the reason they thought of this as the land of opportunity, was not because they would have *equal* opportunity, but because equality of rights meant they would be *free*—and because this freedom would allow them to participate in the greatest wave of progress in human history. In their home countries, other people could *stop* them from making the best of their circumstances by restricting their freedom and confiscating their property. In America, no one can.

What made America great—and the reason it continues to be the place to which people flee in search of opportunity—is the extent to which we have the liberty to rise by means of our own thought and effort, regard-less of where we start. Whereas collectivist ideologies such as communism appeal to people's sense of envy and the desire for the unearned, America appeals to the best in people: their desire to earn their way to a better life, whatever the obstacles. As John B., the Cuban immigrant we met earlier, put it:

> I went to school, worked, and progressed through life to where I was secure. I'm retired now, but I did reasonably well. This country allows us to do that. There were no restrictions, no class systems. . . . Nobody ever gave me anything special, nor did they take anything away from me. I competed on my own merit, and did everything on my own.[52]

The economic inequality critics regard this attitude as naïve. Opportunities, they maintain, must be equal. And, they add, opportunities can't be equal, so long as *outcomes* are unequal. "Inequality of outcomes and inequality of opportunity reinforce each other," writes Joseph Stiglitz.[53] Every time a person achieves a successful outcome, such as finishing college, that opens up a new range of opportunities—opportunities not enjoyed by those who haven't achieved the same outcome. When parents rise from poverty to become affluent, their outcomes translate into unequal opportunities for their children, who can now enjoy better health care, go to better schools, and afford to take prestigious but low-paying internships. "What it all comes down to," writes Paul Krugman, "is that although the principle of 'equality of opportunity, not equality of results' sounds fine, it's a largely fictitious distinction. A society with highly unequal results is, more or less inevitably, a society with highly unequal opportunity, too." And so, argue the critics, to achieve genuine equality of opportunity, the government needs to equalize results: in education, in health care, in wages, in wealth. "If you truly believe that all Americans are entitled to an equal chance at the starting line," concludes Krugman, "that's an argument for doing something to reduce inequality."[54]

If we genuinely care about opportunity, we need to reject the egalitarian concept of equality of opportunity, and put the focus squarely back on equality of rights and the freedom it gives us to take advantage of life's limitless opportunities.

CHAPTER FOUR
THE CONDITIONS OF PROGRESS

OUR AMAZING WORLD

Economic progress is at the heart of the American Dream. The optimism so characteristic of Americans comes from the conviction that life will be better in the future than it was in the past. But what makes progress possible?

Although we often take progress for granted, it is a startlingly new phenomenon. For most of human history, the world looked pretty much the same at the end of your life as it did at the beginning. Life was cyclical, not progressive. For more than two million years, mankind's most advanced technology consisted of a few stone tools. *Two million years.* Imagine if Apple didn't update the iPhone for two million years! But it's not that our ancestors were stupid. It's that gaining new knowledge and creating new technologies are the most difficult things human beings do. What should astonish us is not how long it took our ancestors to emerge from the cave, but how far we've come since they did.

But forget the caveman—just look at how far we've come in the last hundred years or so. By historic standards, Americans in 1900 were already the wealthiest people in history, having virtually eliminated two of mankind's most dire adversaries—disease and famine. And yet, by every measure you can think of, human life has improved beyond our great-grandparents' wildest dreams. Let us share with you some research compiled by the Cato Institute's Human Progress project. Cato is a free-market-leaning think tank, but none of this research is controversial. Start with life expectancy from birth, which has risen from just over thirty-five to nearly eighty in the United States in just two hundred years (Figure 4.1).[1]

In the United States, infant mortality has declined from 26 out of every 1,000 births in 1960 to only 6 out of 1,000 in 2011 (Figure 4.2).[2]

For most of human history, our most pressing problem was getting enough food. Now food is abundant and affordable. In Figure 4.3, for instance, we see that wheat yields have increased dramatically while the price of wheat has fallen.[3]

What about living standards? One interesting measure of our standard of living is the percent of our income we spend on life's basics. In 1929, over 54 percent of our income went to essentials such as food and housing. By 2011, that had plummeted to 32 percent (Figure 4.4).[4]

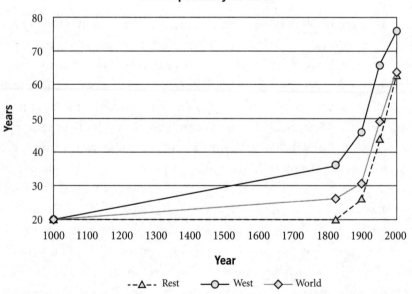

Figure 4.1
Life Expectancy at Birth

Figure 4.2
U.S. Infant Mortality Rate

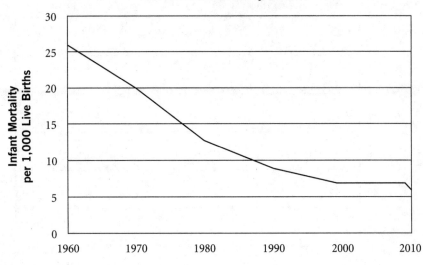

Figure 4.3
U.S. Wheat

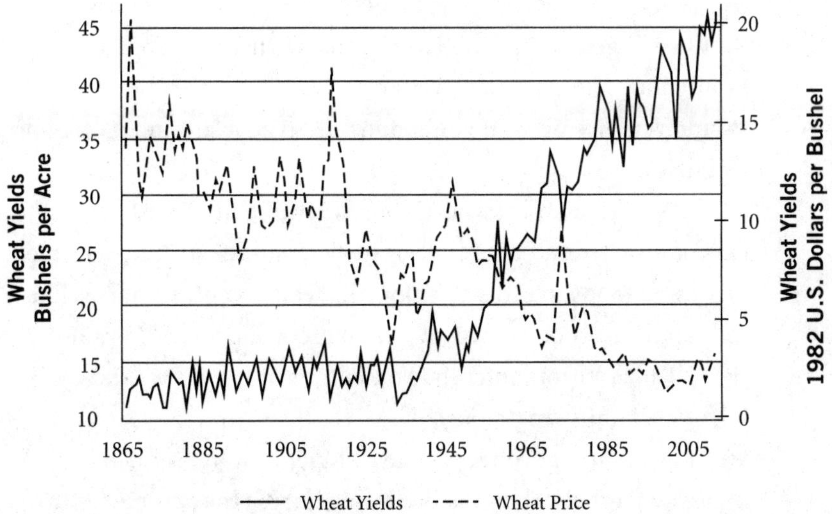

Figure 4.4
U.S. Spending on Essential Goods and Services

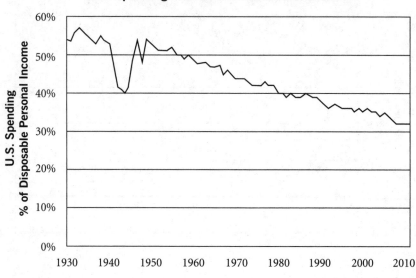

But all of this data is almost beside the point. To see how far we've progressed, just ask yourself:

- Would you give up your job for fourteen grueling, dangerous, and monotonous hours a day on a farm?
- Would you give up your car and instead trudge around on foot or by horse?
- Would you give up your nutritious, tasty diet filled with tender cuts of meat, fresh fruits and vegetables, and cheap and convenient processed foods in order to enjoy nineteenth-century staples like milk-and-bread dinners? How about giving up your TV, radio, iPod, iPad, and computer in favor of four or five books and relentless family sing-alongs?
- Would you give up your spacious, temperature-controlled home, in favor of a shack that was sweltering during the summer and freezing during the winter (unless you were willing to fill your house with the noxious smoke from your fireplace)? And where

your trash wasn't whisked away by a garbage truck, but piled up on your sidewalk? And where you or your spouse would have to spend most of the week performing the tasks now handled by clean-burning stoves, automatic coffeemakers, dishwashers, and washing machines?

- Would you give up modern medicine and return to a time when an infection often meant amputation or worse, when childbirth often meant death, and a trip to the dentist always meant torture? (Okay, some things never change.)

From a long-term historical perspective, more of us are living longer, safer, richer lives than ever before. No, we don't live in a Garden of Eden, where the things we need are automatically supplied by nature. But we do live on a Glorious Earth, where we can make life amazing. And it can be amazing for *everyone*, because it turns out that the way we improve our lives—ingenuity and effort—is not a fixed-sum game, where we battle over a static amount of wealth. We *produce* wealth, and there is no limit to how much wealth we can produce.

WHO CREATED THE MODERN WORLD?

In his autobiography, Apple cofounder Steve Wozniak, or Woz, as he's usually called, describes how his dad, an engineer, would explain to the four-year-old Woz how electronics worked. "I remember sitting there and being so little, and thinking: 'Wow, what a great, great world he's living in,'" Woz recalls. "I mean, that's all I thought: 'Wow.' For people who know how to do this stuff—how to take these little parts and make them work together to do something—well, these people must be the smartest people in the world. . . . I could see right before my eyes that whatever my dad was doing, whatever it was, it was important and good."[5]

By the time Woz was ten, he was telling his father that he wanted to be an engineer.

I wanted to put chips together like an artist, better than anyone else could and in a way that would be the absolute most usable by humans. That was my goal when I built the first computer, the one that later became the Apple I. It was the first computer to use a keyboard so you could type onto it, and the first to use a screen you could look at. The idea of usable technology was something that was kind of born in my head as a kid, when I had this fantasy that I could someday build machines people could use. And it happened![6]

But it wasn't easy—it was the climax of a lifetime of work and study. Woz spent his childhood building gadgets, such as an electronic tic-tac-toe machine that was programmed to never lose a game and, in eighth grade, an electronic calculator that could add and subtract. In high school, Woz discovered computer programming, which was still at a primitive stage. When other kids his age were off dating and playing sports, he stayed home and created computers.

I'd take [computer] catalogs of logic components, chips, from which computers are made, and a particular existing computer description from its handbook, and I'd design my own version of it. Many times I'd redesign the same computer a second or third time, using newer and better components. . . . Because I could never afford the parts to build any of my computer designs, all I could do was design them on paper. Typically, once I started a design, I'd stay up very late one or more nights in a row, sprawled on my bedroom floor with papers all around and a Coke can nearby. Since I could never build my designs, all I could do was try to beat my own designs by redesigning them even better, using fewer parts. I was competing with myself and developed tricks that certainly would never be describable or put in books.[7]

In 1975, when he was only 25 years old, Woz found out about the microprocessor, and realized that "all those minicomputers I'd designed on paper" in high school and college "were pretty much just like this one"—only "now all the CPU parts were on one chip. . . . It was as if my whole life had been leading up to this point." The idea for the personal computer was in his head. "[I]t was that very night that I started to sketch out on paper what would later come to be known as the Apple I," he said.[8] In 2000, the invention of that first personal computer would land Woz in the National Inventors Hall of Fame, which honors "the women and men responsible for the great technological advances that make human, social and economic progress possible."[9]

Who creates wealth? On one level, all of us. We all go to work and help create the goods and services that make up today's amazing world. Maybe you write code for software. Maybe you teach music to middle-schoolers. Maybe you fix cars or perform brain surgery or, God help you, write books on inequality. Whatever it is, you do productive work in exchange for money, which you use to buy the dizzying array of things that other people produce.

But that's only part of the story. Not all work is equally productive. Some of us create a little wealth. Some of us create a lot. A tiny handful, like Steve Wozniak, create so much that their names go down in the history books.

Think of some of the things that make your life wonderful. Your cell phone, your computer, the Internet? You can thank Robert Noyce and Jack Kilby, who invented the integrated circuit. The car that took you to work? You can thank Henry Ford, who transformed the automobile from a curiosity of the rich into a mass-market product. The radio you listened to on the way to work? You can thank Guglielmo Marconi. The airplane that took you to your best friend's wedding? You can thank the Wright brothers. The big screen TV you can easily afford? You can thank Sam Walton. The electricity that lets you watch that TV? You can thank Thomas Edison and Nikola Tesla. The penicillin that easily cured you of an infection that was fatal a hundred years ago? You can thank Alexander Fleming. This book? You can thank Johannes Gutenberg—unless you're reading this on an iPad, in which case you can thank Steve Jobs.

Many other people contributed to these discoveries in one way or another, of course. That's not the point. The point is that of all the billions of people who have walked this earth, we can thank a few hundred for virtually everything that makes our lives so much more safe and enjoyable than that of our ancestors.

What distinguishes these individuals from the rest of us? Well, obviously it's not muscles. No doubt any longshoreman could have taken Steve Jobs in a fight. Nor is it effort or virtue alone. To be sure, all of these individuals exercised enormous effort and virtue in achieving what they did. But sign on to Netflix and watch some old episodes of *Dirty Jobs*—you'll see plenty of electricians, janitors, and zookeepers who work thoughtfully and diligently, and while they deserve our admiration and respect, they aren't changing the world.

No, the crucial fact about all these individuals is that they contributed new *ideas*. The key to understanding our amazing world is to understand that the production of wealth is fundamentally an intellectual project. Wealth creation is first and foremost *knowledge creation*. And this is why you can add to the list of people who have created the modern world, great *thinkers:* people such as Euclid, Aristotle, Galileo, Newton, Darwin, Einstein, and a relative handful of others.

Whether we're making a spear out of sticks and stones or making a skyscraper out of steel and glass, all human production amounts to taking the raw materials of nature and rearranging them for a human purpose. Finding those materials, figuring out their potential uses, discovering new ways to put them together, and conceiving of the purposes they are to serve—all of that requires thought. The biggest breakthroughs in human well-being are breakthroughs in knowledge: they involve someone discovering a new, important idea, which is then put into productive practice.

Aristotle discovers the essentials of logical thinking and makes possible all the later achievements of science. Newton discovers the laws of motion and universal gravitation and invents calculus, laying the foundation for classical mechanics, which among other achievements got us from the Earth to the Moon. Thomas Newcomen discovers how to make the first practical steam engine and launches the machine age. Henry Ford discovers how to dramatically lower costs through mass production and puts millions of Americans behind the wheel of a car. Louis Pasteur discovers the principles of vaccination and saves untold millions of lives. Norman Borlaug discovers ways to make major improvements in agriculture, saving over a billion people from starvation.

The source of human progress is human ability, which means *intellectual* ability. The greatest contributors to production are not those who supply physical labor but those who contribute ideas—new theories, inventions, tools, businesses, and methods—to the productive process. We can see this most clearly when we look at the role of the entrepreneur.

The entrepreneur seeks out new profit opportunities, often introducing new products, new services, or new ways of doing business. Entrepreneurs like Bill Gates (Microsoft), Elon Musk (PayPal), and Richard Branson (Virgin) are the risk takers and trailblazers who start new businesses and even new industries. The word "entrepreneur" comes from the French word *entreprendre,* which means to "undertake" and is thought to have been coined by the French economist Jean-Baptiste Say. According to Say, the entrepreneur is the "master-agent." He sets a business enterprise in motion, often risking his own wealth along with that of other investors. The success or failure of the enterprise rests on his shoulders.

Consider the case of Steve Jobs. Jobs didn't design the Apple I or the Apple II—that was Woz's achievement. But, as Woz puts it, if he was the builder, Jobs was the businessman.[10] It was Jobs who was responsible for recognizing that Woz's creation belonged not in a hobbyist's garage but in every American's home. According to Woz, "I would never have been able to explain to the world, 'Here's why you should have computers in your home, here's why they are good for society and good for the world.'"[11] That was Jobs's achievement: to take Woz's brilliant creation and transform it into a successful consumer product. Starting with $1,300 in working capital, and working out of parents' home, Jobs would soon turn Apple into the most successful computer company in the world and, eventually, one of the most successful companies in history, transforming the way we live and work.

What's true of the entrepreneur is equally true of the other crucial roles people play in the economy: it is human intelligence that fuels prosperity. To see this, let's look briefly at three of those roles: management, finance, and labor.

Management. The vast majority of the innovations that have improved our lives were not innovations in products but innovations in *processes:* how to organize a company, how to structure a supply chain, how to use resources efficiently, how to find and keep great employees. The key figure here is the manager. The manager oversees the use of capital and labor in order to ensure that the company's goals are being met and that its resources are being used as efficiently as possible. Managers, from the frontline supervisor to the CEO, plan and manage the firm's resources. While workers are focused on individual projects and tasks, the manager's job is to take a broad view of the organization. The top manager—the CEO—takes the widest perspective and the most long-range time frame.

In Apple's case, Steve Jobs would eventually come to play this role as well. Jobs had been forced to resign from the company he helped to create in 1985, but after a string of bad managers put Apple on the brink of bankruptcy, he returned to the company in 1997 and assumed the position, first, of interim CEO, and then of CEO. Many people at the time thought Apple was done for, its market share torn to shreds by Microsoft. Jobs disagreed.

In Jobs's view, Apple had been destroyed by its previous leaders' "bringing in corrupt people and corrupt values" and abandoning its commitment to "making great products."[12] To save Apple, Jobs would enact vast changes on both fronts. As biographer Walter Isaacson explains, "Jobs immediately put people he trusted into the top ranks at Apple" and, at the same time, worked "to stop the hemorrhaging of [existing] top Apple employees."[13] As for the products, Jobs started by diagnosing the problem: "The products *suck!* There's no sex in them anymore!"[14] Jobs decided that one of the problems was a lack of focus: Apple had too many products, and too many versions of each product. He started cutting product lines until he zeroed in on what he thought would save Apple. Isaacson describes a key product strategy session:

> He grabbed a magic marker, padded to a whiteboard, and drew a horizontal and vertical line to make a four-squared chart. "Here's what we need," he continued. Atop the top columns he wrote "Consumer" and "Pro"; he labeled the two rows "Desktop" and "Portable." Their job, he said, was to make four great products, one for each quadrant. "The room was in dumb silence," [one participant] recalled.[15]

Jobs made thousands of other key decisions in those early days. According to Isaacson, "He got involved in all aspects of the business: product design, where to cut, supplier negotiations, and advertising agency review." Jobs even replaced practically the entire board of directors.[16]

His first public initiative as CEO was Apple's famous Think Different campaign, which centered on a commercial that attempted to sum up the Apple philosophy:

> Here's to the crazy ones. The misfits. The rebels. The troublemakers. The round pegs in the square holes. The ones who see things differently.

They're not fond of rules. And they have no respect for the status quo. You can quote them, disagree with them, glorify or vilify them. About the only thing you can't do is ignore them. Because they change things. They push the human race forward. And while some may see them as the crazy ones, we see genius. Because the people who are crazy enough to think they can change the world are the ones who do.[17]

It was with this hymn to human ability that Apple started on the path that would, indeed, change the world, guided throughout by human intelligence—starting at the top.

Finance. Finance involves acquiring financial capital and directing it to productive uses. It is made up of the investors, shareholders, bankers, brokers, traders, and speculators who together supply capital to the economy. They take savings—unconsumed wealth from prior acts of production—and put them into the hands of the entrepreneurs and managers who create all of the goods and services that make up our amazing world.

This is no easy task. At any time, there are countless people seeking capital investment, from the immigrant who wants to start a dry cleaner's to the college dropout who wants to pioneer a new technology. But capital is limited. Put capital into the wrong hands, and you could destroy it. Put it into the right hands, and what you can achieve is limitless. The capitalist is the one who makes these decisions.

In *The Birth of Plenty,* William Bernstein observes that "the lion's share of Western society's prosperity originates in the minds of a few geniuses." But, "[t]ranslating their ideas into economic reality requires . . . staggering amounts of capital."[18] This was true in Apple's case. To grow beyond Jobs's parents' garage, Apple needed capital—lots of it. But who would be willing to risk hundreds of thousands of dollars on two inexperienced kids who wanted to bring an untested good to the market in an industry that didn't even exist? Jobs approached several potential investors and was roundly rejected. Then he met Mike Markkula. Described by Jobs's biographer as "cautious and shrewd," Markkula saw the enormous potential of Apple. "We're going to be a Fortune 500 company in two years," he told Jobs. "This is the start of an industry." Markkula offered Jobs and Woz a $250,000 line of credit. Later Jobs would recall, "I thought it was unlikely that Mike would ever see that $250,000 again, and I was impressed that he was willing to risk it."[19] Without Markkula's vision and his willingness to risk his money in the name of that vision, Apple might never have been born.

Labor. Labor, for lack of a better term, is what carries out the vision of entrepreneurs and the plans of managers, using the resources supplied by capitalists. It includes pilots, restaurant hostesses, car salesmen, coal miners, construction workers, TV writers, and accountants, among thousands of other examples. It stretches from unskilled workers performing manual labor to roles that require every bit as much thought as that required of a company's leaders.

At Apple, for instance, one of the key workers was Jony Ive, head of the design team. By the time Jobs returned in 1997, Ive was ready to quit, frustrated that Apple had long ago abandoned its commitment to great products. Jobs assured him it was a new day. Jobs would later describe Ive as "a spiritual partner." Both men shared a deep commitment to creating products that were simple and elegant, with thought given to every aspect of their design. "What I really despise," says Ive, "is when I sense some carelessness in a product." There was no carelessness in Ive's work. He recognized that achieving the simplicity he and Jobs sought required an enormous amount of thinking. "It involves digging through the depth of the complexity. To be truly simple you have to go really deep. For example, to have no screws on something, you can end up having a product that is so convoluted and so complex. The better way is to go deeper with the simplicity, to understand everything about it and how it's manufactured. You have to deeply understand the essence of a product in order to be able to get rid of the parts that are not essential."[20]

Whether you're an administrative assistant, a car mechanic, a mid-level manager, or the chief designer at Apple, what enables you to excel? What determines how productive you are? It's not your muscles—even athletes know that brute strength is only a small part of what makes them successful. Nor is it even how "hard" you work, in the sense of how much physical effort you exert or how much discomfort you endure. The core of what enables you to achieve your career goals is your knowledge, skills, judgment, and *intellectual* effort. That's true no less of janitors than jet pilots: the difference between a good janitor and a bad one is in large part determined by the former's superior knowledge of how to clean well, quickly, and efficiently. In any field, it's your *mind* that makes you indispensable.

So who created the modern world? *Thinkers,* of every level of ability, with the most credit going to the men and women of extraordinary ability. One of the most disturbing features of the debate over inequality is the almost deafening silence on the issue of human ability. More often than not, those who condemn inequality don't discuss ability. And when they do, it is usually to accuse the greatest wealth creators of being greedy exploiters. But the men and women of extraordinary ability aren't exploiters—they are the great benefactors of anyone who is willing to produce wealth.

THE HARMONY OF INTERESTS
AMONG PRODUCERS

When someone pursues *unearned* wealth, he can do so only at the expense of other people's interests. They do the work, he seizes the rewards. But when people deal with one another as traders, on mutually beneficial terms or not at all, they enjoy a *harmony of interests.* And this is true regardless of their level of income or ability. In fact, it is those with *less* ability who benefit the most from this arrangement: the productive efforts of those at the top raise everyone else's standard of living.

This isn't what is sometimes disparagingly called "trickle-down economics," the theory that wealth will magically trickle down from rich people to poor people in a free market. What actually happens when trade is voluntary is that those with greater ability radically magnify the productivity of everyone, especially those with less ability. This is what Ayn Rand calls the Pyramid of Ability. The higher the most able producers rise, the more they contribute to the productivity of the less able.

A factory worker makes a real contribution: he helps turn a pile of parts into a TV or a toaster. But the end product of his work goes no further. It provides particular goods destined for particular customers. But the man who supplies an idea is able to raise the productivity—and the standard of living—of an unlimited number of other men. It was his contribution that *created* the factory, that *invented* the television, that *designed* the assembly line, and that thereby made it possible for a factory worker of modest ability to produce TVs, earn a wage, and live better than kings did a few hundred years ago. As Rand explains:

> In proportion to the mental energy he spent, the man who creates a new invention receives but a small percentage of his value in terms of material payment, no matter what fortune he makes, no matter what millions he earns. But the man who works as a janitor in the factory producing that invention, receives an enormous payment in proportion to the mental effort that his job requires of *him*. And the same is true of all men between, on all levels of ambition and ability. The man at the top of the intellectual pyramid contributes the most to all those below him, but gets nothing except his material payment, receiving no intellectual bonus from others to add to the value of his time. The man at the bottom who, left to himself, would starve in his hopeless ineptitude, contributes nothing to those above him, but receives the bonus of all of their brains.[21]

In her journals for *Atlas Shrugged*, Rand develops this point, taking the example of a worker who "makes a hundred pairs of shoes a day with the help of a machine":

> He gets paid on the basis of having produced a hundred pairs of shoes (the share of the factory owner, inventor, etc., being taken out); but left on his own (without the machine, the management, etc.) he would be able to produce, say, only ten pairs of shoes a day. His productive capacity has been raised by the inventor of the machine. Yet neither of the two men robs the other one; it's a fair exchange; but the worker gives to the inventor less than the inventor has given to him.[22]

The Pyramid of Ability is not simply an issue of the most able producers supplying the machines that make us more productive. Whether it is Aristotle instructing us on how to think logically or Steve Jobs showing us what it means to set uncompromisingly high standards of excellence, the men and women of extraordinary ability are among our greatest *teachers:* to paraphrase George Washington, they raise a standard to which the rational and productive can repair. Far from their interests being in conflict with ours, the more they achieve, the more we can achieve.

Now you might think there are plenty of counter-examples here, cases in which the interests of producers do seem to clash. For example, it seems self-evident to many people that the interests of labor and management clash. A worker wants higher compensation; an employer wants to keep costs down. The error here is to take too narrow a view of people's interests. Although a worker and an employer may disagree over compensation, both sides have an interest in setting pay within the range that is both profitable to the company (otherwise it'll go out of business) and that is competitive with other opportunities open to the worker (otherwise he'll go elsewhere). More broadly, both sides share an interest in being *free* to arrive at an employment agreement that is satisfactory to both sides. If the government can override their judgment, both sides lose.

If you keep in mind the big picture, it's clear that there is no conflict of interest among productive people with different levels of ability. When we deal with one another as traders, all of us can improve our lives by exercising thought and effort. Life is not a race, in which some have to lose so that others can win. It's not a contest at all. Your well-being doesn't depend on being *better* than others—it depends on being *good,* which means being competent, hardworking, eager to learn and to grow.

To be sure, there is competition in an economy, but it's not a zero-sum game in which some have to lose so that others can win—not in the big picture. If you don't get selected for a job, or if you start a company that goes out of business when Walmart comes into town, you don't get shipped off to Siberia: you're free to look for another job or start a new business. All the while you're better off living in the kind of prosperous, dynamic economy that results from people being free to compete for jobs or customers.

Economic competition is really competition to find your place within the division of labor—to find a role that is best for you and for the people who deal with you. If you want a sports analogy, the closest parallel is trying out for a Little League baseball team. Everyone can make the team and everyone will get to play. Competition is really a discovery process, in which each person finds a role in which he has a comparative advantage. The difference is that, in an economy, no one can *put* you into a position you don't want, and there are new tryouts every day.

How did men rise from the Stone Age to the Digital Age? Thanks to the contributions of countless individuals, above all those of exceptional ability, we expanded our understanding of reality and discovered new and better ways to rearrange natural elements to improve human life. The result has been a revolution in human relationships. Instead of equally poor hordes battling over scraps, everyone is able to prosper at the same time. In America today, even those who are poor relative to their neighbors are among the richest people in history.

Unfortunately, some have not benefited from human progress, namely the people who live in those parts of the world that have not industrialized. In some tragic cases, they have been victims of invasion and colonial exploitation. But this is not the *cause* of their poverty, nor was colonization the main source of the West's prosperity. The West's prosperity came from creating the conditions under which individuals could think, create, trade, and prosper. Today, more and more of the world is following our lead, with the result that billions around the globe have been liberated from poverty in recent decades: since 1981, the fraction of the earth's population living on less than a dollar a day has dropped from over 40 percent to only *14 percent*.[23]

This is an incredible achievement. Yet most of the people who wring their hands over economic inequality have been inexcusably silent about this feat. Our intellectual leaders should have taught us to celebrate this triumph and should have explained the political and economic conditions that made it possible. Imagine if mortality from cancer had declined from 40 percent to 14 percent in California's hospitals. We would expect medical researchers to investigate what was responsible for that magnificent achievement—and we would be outraged if we discovered that they had ignored it. What some of the people alarmed by inequality have done is worse. They haven't simply been silent about the global escape from poverty; they have condemned it for *increasing inequality*— which is akin to condemning those hospitals for increasing cancer survival inequality.[24]

It's time to celebrate the escape from poverty—in the West, starting two and a half centuries ago, and in the rest of the world today—and to investigate the political, economic, and moral conditions that made it possible.

HOW REASON AND FREEDOM
UNLEASHED HUMAN PROGRESS

Today's trend of constant progress really began during the 1700s, starting in Holland, spreading to England and (later) to the United States. What changed in these countries during this time period to put them on the path to prosperity? Consider where they started.

During the Middle Ages, virtually all individuals were *subjects*—they owed obedience to religious and political authorities who controlled almost every element of their lives, including their economic lives. This was the ultimate rigged system. Under English feudalism, for instance, your status was determined by your birth. Ability did not matter. If your parents were nobles, you were a noble. If your parents were peasants, you were a peasant. If you hated farming and longed to get an education or become, say, a smith, you were basically out of luck. It didn't matter how hard you worked or how eager you were to learn and grow. You were tied to your lord's land, and your job was to perform the same monotonous routine that your father had. Those at the top lived large—by the standards of the day, anyway—by exploiting those at the bottom.

The oppression of the individual invariably went hand in hand with poverty and stagnation. The feudal system was an incredibly poor and unproductive system because it left no room for individual thought and ability. Individuals were taught that it was their duty not to question authority, but to conform to tradition and custom—and if they did question authority, they would be stopped by the iron fist of those in authority, who could employ physical force to extract obedience. Absent physical coercion, nothing can stop someone from thinking, producing, and innovating. Individuals are always free to choose to passively conform, but only coercion can *make* them conform. During this period, force was an omnipresent fact of life. Take the economic life of towns during this era. According to economic historian Nathan Rosenberg and legal scholar L. E. Birdzell, Jr.:

> Within the towns, most lines of industry and trade were the exclusive monopolies of the guilds. The church's notion of a "just price" and a "just wage" gave moral sanction to guild regulations covering prices, wages of apprentices and journeymen, standards of product quality

and workmanship, admission to the trade, and a duty to ply one's trade at established prices and wages. The guilds had the political authority to make binding rules and to judge, fine, and punish violations of their rules.[25]

The rise of the West was made possible by the death of feudalism and the weakening of its all-encompassing regulation of economic life. But the West really came into its own during the Enlightenment. After witnessing the Scientific Revolution, epitomized by Isaac Newton's epic achievements, Enlightenment thinkers came to see reason, not revelation, as the key to unlocking the secrets of the universe. The individual was no longer viewed as helpless in the face of an unknowable reality ruled by incomprehensible supernatural forces. He was a rational creature, competent to understand the world, set his own goals, make his own choices, and support his own life. It was this pro-reason, pro-individual perspective that gave birth to the ideal of political equality. As beings possessing reason, men "are all equal, and *equals can have no right over each other*," wrote seventeenth-century English politician Algernon Sidney.[26] Viewed from an Enlightenment perspective, individuals were not subjects who had a duty to bow to political and religious authorities. They were autonomous beings who possessed equal rights and should therefore be left free to think, to work, to trade, to pursue happiness and success here on earth.

"During the Enlightenment," writes Princeton University economist Angus Deaton, "people risked defying accepted dogma and were more willing to experiment" with new scientific, medical, and commercial techniques. This meant that "[h]appiness could be pursued by using reason to challenge accepted ways of doing things, including obedience to the crown and the church, and by finding ways of improving one's life, including both material possessions and health."[27] By exercising reason, human beings could continuously expand their understanding of the world and put that knowledge into productive action in order to improve human life.

That is how the West grew rich. The rise of individualism, and its glorification of reason and freedom, made it possible for individuals to use their reason to reshape the earth into a place progressively more hospitable to human life and happiness. Just as freedom leaves the road open to individual ability, so it creates the conditions of human progress. But how does this process work? How specifically does freedom translate into progress? The short answer is: freeing human reason unleashes limitless technological innovation.

THE LIBERATED ECONOMY

A few years ago, one of us (Don) was visiting San Francisco with his wife, Kate, and although they had driven up from Southern California without any difficulty, they were warned by the hotel staff not to bother trying to drive around the city. Searching for parking in San Francisco is like trying to find chastity in a brothel. Anyway, it turns out that there are only about four cabs in the entire city, and on their first outing, Don and Kate found themselves standing around for close to an hour before they could hail a taxi, which was driven by an irritated cabbie who reeked of cigarette smoke. Then they discovered Uber.

Within seconds of logging into the Uber iPhone app, Don got a message on his phone: a car was on its way. Using the app, Don could also see the driver's name, photo, license plate number, and reviews from other passengers. Two minutes later, a cheerful driver in a shiny black sedan pulled up, opened the door, and offered Kate and Don bottles of ice-cold water. When the ride was over, Don didn't have to hand over his credit card—the app took care of the payment automatically. He just thanked the driver, got out, and was on his way. The cost was a bit higher than a typical cab ride, but as Don and hundreds of thousands of other passengers have found, Uber was worth every penny.

Uber is an incredible innovator. Before it came along, consumers had to choose between expensive limo services, which usually required advanced booking, and unreliable taxi cabs. Uber discovered a way to provide customers with a relatively inexpensive luxury car service, accessible by an easy-to-use smartphone app. Later, with its UberX service, it even managed to undercut most taxi cab rates.

Like all innovators, Uber is disruptive: its business model threatened the profits of the taxi industry. But Uber was also disruptive in another sense. For decades, the taxi companies it competes with have been protected from competition in most locales by laws that limit the number of taxi medallions, which give drivers the right to drive a cab. If you think that taxis are expensive, unpleasant, and hard to find, you aren't free to solve the problem yourself by latching an "In Service" sign to the roof of your car and trying to outdo them. First, you would have had to spend tens of thousands, perhaps hundreds of thousands, of dollars to get one of those medallions. Uber has attempted to get around these restrictions by positioning itself as a limo service rather than a cab company. But the taxi cab drivers have fought back, lobbying the government to shut Uber down.

Whether Uber succeeds or fails will depend not only on its ability to outcompete its rivals by offering its customers great service at a price they're willing to pay, but also on whether it will have the *liberty* to compete—or whether the government will use its coercive powers to hobble or stop Uber from competing.

Human progress is fueled by *innovation*. Innovation is the source of our prosperity and rising standard of living: it's the primary way in which human ability improves our lives and fosters economic growth. We don't just do more of the same things our ancestors did (grow more wheat, construct more horse-drawn carriages, etc.). We use reason to create new products, new tools, new organizational forms—we make things better, faster, and cheaper.

From wood and bricks to concrete and steel. From animal power to fossil fuels to nuclear energy. From the shovel to the bulldozer. From the telegraph to the telephone to the Internet. From record players to cassette tapes to CDs to MP3s. From snake oil to newer and better lifesaving medicines. From the abacus to the calculator. From mainframes to minicomputers to PCs to cell phones that have more computing power than the machines that sent us to the moon. These are only a handful of the innovations that have revolutionized the way we live—to say nothing of the countless smaller innovations that steadily improve the world around us.

But we don't see widespread innovation in every society or in every historical era. Instead, we see it only in places that *value* innovation and that protect the *process* of innovation. In many societies, innovation is seen as a threat to the established order, and these societies often use political power to stifle and suppress such advances, the way the taxi industry is attempting to use the government to stop Uber. For innovation to flourish, individuals need (1) the freedom to challenge old ideas and adopt new ones, (2) the freedom to put new ideas into practice, (3) the freedom of others in society to adopt or reject the innovator's ideas, and (4) the freedom of the innovator to profit from successful innovations. This is what political equality protects, above all by guaranteeing to every individual freedom of thought and speech, freedom of contract, and private property rights (including intellectual property rights).

Freedom of thought and speech protect the individual's ability to adopt and advocate any idea he wants, without interference. No pope, king, mob, or dictator can stop an innovator from challenging conventional wisdom.

Freedom of contract protects the individual's ability to enter into whatever economic relationships and transactions he judges to be in his interest. An innovator doesn't need to ask anyone's permission to enter a new field, offer a new product, or charge what he thinks the market will bear. (By the same token, he cannot force anyone to invest in his business, work for his company, or buy his product, which would violate their freedom of contract.)

Private property rights protect the right of producers to earn and use property. This is crucial for innovation in two basic ways: it gives people the *ability* to innovate and the *incentive* to innovate. Without property rights, independent action is impossible. Most new ideas fail, and most of the ideas that eventually succeed were once considered foolish by the mainstream. When Google first launched, many commentators asked, "Who needs another search engine?" The only reason an innovator such as Larry Page can start an untested company is because he's free to use his resources as he judges best (and to enlist the help of anyone he can convince to voluntarily support him). And the only reason an innovator *will* take on the huge risk of starting an untested company (and the only reason he can convince others to risk their time and money in his undertaking) is because there is an opportunity for huge rewards. Private property rights ensure that whatever gains an innovator makes, he gets to keep.

We can now see why innovation as a way of life arose only in the modern West. Political inequality had always meant that the concerns of the powerful trumped the autonomy of the individual. It was only when the West made a commitment to political equality that it was slowly able to remove those shackles. As Rosenberg and Birdzell explain:

By the mid-nineteenth century, Western societies had given their enterprises certain rights which can be viewed either as a grant of authority to make a number of decisions which had been made by political or religious authorities in most other societies, or as a grant of freedom from many common types of political or religious control. Four of these rights set the stage for economic growth based on innovation. First, individuals were authorized to form enterprises, with less and less political restriction. The formation of enterprises was extensively restricted by lack of money, lack of talent, or both, but not by lack of license from the political authorities, nor by lack of ecclesiastical blessing. Second, enterprises were authorized to acquire goods and hold them for resale at a profit or loss, again with little or no restriction. Third, enterprises were authorized to add activities and to switch from one line of activity to another that seemed more promising, again with little restriction. Political or religious restriction arose only at the outer bounds of the numerous economic choices open to the enterprise: that is, the products or services it would make, how it would make them, the extent to which it would make them or buy them from other enterprises, how it would sell them, and the prices it would charge. Finally, while the assets of the enterprise and such profits as it accumulated from its activities might be taxed at predetermined rates, its property came to be regarded as immune from arbitrary seizure or expropriation by the political authorities.[28]

Economic historian Deirdre McCloskey sums up the results: "By adopting the respect for deal-making and innovation and the liberty to carry out the deals that Amsterdam and London pioneered around 1700, the modern world was born."[29]

America would soon follow, going further than any other nation toward protecting the freedom to innovate. The "sum of good government," said Thomas Jefferson, is "a wise and frugal Government, which shall restrain men from injuring one another, shall leave them otherwise free to regulate their own pursuits of industry and improvement, and shall not take from the mouth of labor the bread it has earned."[30] Although the United States never fully limited itself to this sum, it did approach it, and men "free to regulate their own pursuits of industry and improvement" innovated on a scale the world had never seen.

In 1854, an English observer noted that "there is not a working boy of average ability in the New England states, at least, who has not an idea of some mechanical invention or improvement in manufactures, by which, in good time, he hopes to better his position, or rise to fortune and social distinction."[31] During the nineteenth and early twentieth centuries, America went through what can only be called an age of invention. Alexander Graham Bell introduced the telephone. Elias Howe invented the sewing machine, later improved by Isaac Merritt Singer. Elisha Graves Otis invented a device to prevent elevators from falling, making it possible for William Le Baron Jenney and others to pioneer the skyscraper. John Roebling perfected the suspension bridge and undertook what would become the Brooklyn Bridge (a project that would be completed by his children after his death). George Westinghouse pioneered the life-saving railway air brake, among hundreds of other innovations. Willis Carrier introduced the first air conditioner. Thomas Edison's contributions included the quadruplex telegraph, the phonograph, the electric power plant, the incandescent lightbulb, the storage battery, and the motion picture camera, among countless others. And this, of course, barely scratches the surface.

Inventors, entrepreneurs, and other innovators weren't just tolerated in America—they were often glorified. Even the celebration of America's centennial in 1876 highlighted the nation's commercial achievements as much as its political achievements. At Machinery Hall in Philadelphia, "a profusion of mechanisms seduced the eye: power looms, lathes, sewing machines, presses, pumps, toolmaking machines, axles, shafts, wire cables, and locomotives."[32] The *Times* (London) concluded that "The American invents as the Greek sculpted and the Italian painted: it is genius."[33]

Invention is only one aspect of innovation, and alongside this multitude of inventions came innovations in the organization and capitalization of productive enterprises. To create a beam of steel or to produce an automobile is one thing, but to supply a nation with steel and to put a car in every driveway is a staggering undertaking. American progress required enterprises far larger than anything that had ever existed. Only such large-scale organizations could mass produce the goods Americans wanted to buy at a price they were willing and able to pay.

The key development in this regard was the rise of the modern corporation, which could amass and deploy unprecedented amounts of capital investment.[34] Much of that capital was used to buy expensive tools of production—factories, power looms, steam engines, electric generators, cranes, blast furnaces—which, thanks to the economies of scale made possible by mass production, slashed production costs. By using these economies of scale, Andrew Carnegie, for instance, was able to reduce the cost of making steel from about $100 a ton to only $12 a ton, while John D. Rockefeller was able to cut production costs of a gallon of kerosene from 1.5 cents a gallon to .45 cents a gallon.[35]

By dramatically lowering their costs and expanding their output, American industrialists were able to reap increasingly large profits even though they were selling their goods at lower and lower prices. As Carnegie supplied the country with increasingly affordable steel, for example, he saw his profits rise from $2 million in 1888 to $40 million in 1900.[36] And what did innovative industrialists like Carnegie, Rockefeller, and Ford do with their profits? Overwhelmingly they plowed them back into their enterprises, continually expanding their productive capability and America's overall rate of progress.

This same process, it's worth pointing out, is what explains the steadily rising wages of workers that we noted in chapter 2. By making their businesses more and more capital-intensive, industrialists made their workers more and more productive. They gave them better tools to work with, so that, for example, an autoworker was able to triple the number of wheels he could attach to a chassis each day. And when workers became more productive, their compensation increased to reflect this. Why? Because employers have to compete for workers, the same way businesses have to compete for customers. The more productive a worker is, the more he will add to a company's bottom line, and the higher an employer will be willing to bid for his services.

That's what happened at Ford, for example. In 1914, Henry Ford famously raised his starting wage to $5 a day (nearly $120 in today's dollars). He had to: turnover at Ford in 1913 had been 370 percent.[37] In order to find and keep the workers who were assembling his increasingly profitable cars, Ford had to be willing to outbid his competitors (which included not only other car makers, but every other employer bidding for his prospective employees).

If America was unique in the extent to which it protected the freedom of innovators, it was also unique in how its inhabitants embraced the constant flow of change unleashed by innovation. The great nineteenth-century British machinist Joseph Whitworth wrote with admiration of "the readiness with which [American workmen] cause new improvements to be received and the impulse which they thus unavoidably give to that inventive spirit."[38] Although there was always some resistance to change, especially by those who saw their skills, technologies, and businesses made obsolete, overall Americans accepted these challenges as the price of progress. "Like no other people," concludes economic historian Jonathan Hughes, "Americans have conditioned their society and their plans for the future in terms of economic change. It is a greatly rewarding life in material terms. It is also a life of uncertainty and continuous social and economic upheaval. It is not a simple way to live."[39]

In many ways, this remains true of America today. Although upstarts like Uber can no longer take for granted their freedom to challenge entrenched industries, we continue to see new companies overtake old stalwarts: Walmart overtakes K-Mart. Amazon overtakes retail bookstores like Borders and (to a large extent) Barnes and Noble. Google overtakes Yahoo! Facebook overtakes MySpace. The United States remains a world leader in innovation—and that is why we continue to enjoy the fruits of economic progress.

INEQUALITY AND PROGRESS

The fact that economic progress goes hand in hand with economic inequality is undeniable. If men like Edison, Carnegie, and Jobs are not free to earn, enjoy, and invest enormous fortunes, the result will not be equal prosperity, but equal misery. Every country that experiences steady economic progress also has enormous levels of inequality, including so-called low-inequality countries, such as those in Scandinavia. They may have less inequality than the United States, but there are nonetheless huge gaps between what the majority of citizens make and what the most successful earn. Trying to eliminate those inequalities would wipe out economic progress.

If we want a laboratory experiment to test that claim, we can do no better than the contrast between East Germany and West Germany. From the end of World War II until the collapse of the Berlin Wall in 1989, East and West Germany were separated not only by bricks and mortar shells but by economic doctrines. People who shared a history, a language, and an environment took radically different approaches toward human freedom—and achieved radically different results.

While retaining various forms of wealth redistribution and economic interventionism, West Germany's economy was relatively free after the war. Freedom of speech was protected. Most property was privately owned, and prices and wages were for the most part determined by the voluntary decisions of individuals. People were free to rise by their own productive efforts, even if this made them far richer than their neighbors. East Germany, however, conformed to Soviet-style totalitarian rule, economic central planning, and an egalitarian ideology that "stressed uniformity in outcomes, irrespective of individual differences in ability or effort."[40] The Socialist Unity Party of Germany oversaw virtually all production, most of the means of production were owned by the state, and prices and wages were placed under centralized control. The government dictated what to produce, how to produce it, and how to distribute what was produced. Although it allowed for some income gaps, those gaps were far narrower than in West Germany.[41] But if we focus on living standards rather than income differences, it is clear that East Germany's economic equality went hand in hand with poverty and stagnation, and West Germany's economic inequality went hand in hand with prosperity and progress.

Here's one author's description of West Berlin circa the early 1960s.

West Berlin . . . was a bustling place, very much on the move, very much up-to-date, even in its outcroppings of nostalgia here and there. . . . Downtown, the Kurfürstendamm ("Ku'damm"), West Berlin's main thoroughfare, which lit up brightly at night, offered still another aspect of this unique frontier outpost. This broad boulevard, Fifth Avenue (as it once was) and the Champs-Élysées rolled into one . . . was flanked

part of the way, before its further reaches fizzled into urban ordinari-
ness, by elegant shops flaunting the latest fashions and chic travel goods
and by cafés blending old world *Gemütlichkeit* with state-of-the-art
ambience. Kempinski's offered the finest ice cream sundaes that side
of the Atlantic, though many who lounged in the sun on its Ku'damm
patio indulged instead in lush slabs of hazelnut torte capped with out-
sized dollops of snowy, outrageously rich *Schlagsahne*.[42]

And here is a 1963 report from *Time* magazine on East Germany:

East Germans are barely getting enough to eat. Their faces tend to
look grey because of the lack of citrus and other fresh fruits (the average consumer gets fewer than five oranges a year). With the exception
of bread, meal, some baked products and margarine, most foods are
rationed. In Saxony, for example, each person's theoretical weekly al-
lowance is one-half pound of meat, two eggs, one-half pound of hard
sausage, and about six ounces of butter. The favorite strategy for buying
up unrationed goods in short supply is to dispatch every member of the
family to stand in line at different shops. Prices are about four or five
times as high as in West Germany, and many families help make ends
meet by selling such scarce items as coffee ($10 per lb.) at a markup to
people who do not have the time to wait in line for hours.[43]

The differences were so stark that mere statistics can't fully capture the
East's impoverishment. In the West, for instance, 41 percent of Germans
owned cars in 1983; in the East, fewer than 20 percent did.[44] But the only
car available to most East Germans was the Trabant, a vehicle so pitiful
that Germans used to joke you could double its value by filling up the gas
tank.

In 1989, the Berlin Wall fell, and the world learned that even the pa-
thetic productivity claimed by the East Germans had been wildly exaggerated. When, in the early days of reunification, a desperate East Germany
offered a free factory to one Italian company in hopes of attracting investment, it was turned down. "The restructuring costs were so great," said the
chairman of the Italian company, "it did not make sense for us to take over
the East German operation, even though it was being offered to us free."

Such was the state of what had been, as the *New York Times* noted in 1990, "Communism's strongest economy."[45]

Of course, almost no one believes that turning America into East Germany will make us more prosperous. Even the critics of economic inequality usually concede that, as Thomas Piketty told economist Russ Roberts in a 2014 interview, "Inequality can actually be useful for growth." But Piketty went on to add, "The problem is when inequality of wealth and concentration of wealth gets too extreme, it is not useful anymore for growth."[46] Some economic inequality critics go further and contend that there comes a point at which inequality *undermines* progress—and, by and large, they believe the United States has reached that point today.

What do they base that conclusion on? There is no theoretical reason why differences in income or wealth should slow human progress. The notion that "spending drives the economy" and that rich people spend less than others isn't a view seriously entertained by economists, who on the whole recognize that savings, investment, and innovation are what make us richer.[47]

Instead, many inequality critics resort to statistically based empirical evidence that tries to draw correlations between high inequality and low growth and low inequality and high growth. But here, too, they are swimming against the tide. Most experts agree that, among advanced economies, the United States has the highest levels of income inequality. Yet, by almost every metric—per capita GDP, median standard of living, median disposable income, unemployment—it has also performed better over the last forty years than any other major Western nation.[48]

Nevertheless, some inequality critics point to studies like a widely touted report from the International Monetary Fund (IMF), which suggest that in *underdeveloped* countries, higher levels of inequality are correlated with lower rates of economic growth.[49] Citing the IMF study, Georgia Levenson Keohane, senior fellow at the left-wing group New America, says that the U.S. is a "North American banana republic" no better than some of its impoverished neighbors: "Our income inequality is worse than that of Guyana, Nicaragua, and Venezuela. When it comes to shared prosperity, we keep company with Iran and Yemen."[50] The conclusion, apparently, is that we should expect to see our economy head in the same direction.

This is like arguing that Walmart is destined to go out of business because KMart, Circuit City, and Montgomery Ward also offered steep sales discounts. The question is whether inequality lowers growth, and the mere fact that some low-growth economies also have high inequality doesn't answer that question. After all, these high-inequality, underdeveloped countries are also semi- or full-blown dictatorships, where the rulers use political power to exploit people for their own benefit and the benefit of their cronies. It would be ridiculous to draw conclusions about the merits of an economic inequality that emerges from freedom based on an economic inequality that emerges from theft.

What's more, those who cite studies like the IMF report ignore the fact that the literature concerning growth rates and inequality is vast, tentative, and contradictory: much of it shows that higher inequality is associated with *higher* growth, although these studies seldom make headlines.[51] Consequently, even many critics of economic inequality are hesitant to endorse the claim that inequality undermines growth. Paul Krugman, for instance, says that he is "a skeptic on the inequality-is-bad-for-performance proposition—not hard line against it, but worried that the evidence for some popular stories is weaker than I'd like."[52] Similarly, Jared Bernstein, in a study from the left-wing Center for American Progress, concludes that "there is not enough concrete proof to lead objective observers to unequivocally conclude that inequality has held back growth."[53] They are right. It is completely arbitrary to draw *any* conclusion from the academic literature on this question.

If the case that economic inequality undermines economic progress is hopelessly weak, the claim that the government can fight economic inequality without hampering economic progress is only slightly more feasible. The main evidence for this latter proposition is the success of Scandinavian countries such as Sweden and Denmark, which have some of the lowest levels of economic inequality in the developed world (thanks mainly to their massive welfare states) along with relatively high standards of living. But even here, the inequality critics have misanalyzed the facts and drawn the wrong conclusion.

First of all, it's important not to romanticize Scandinavia. It has its share of problems, including high rates of alcoholism, depression, suicide, violence, and no small number of economic challenges. In Denmark, one author explains:

> In addition to paying enormous taxes—the total bill is 58 percent to 72 percent of income—Danes have to pay more for just about everything. Books are a luxury item. Their equivalent of the George Washington Bridge costs $45 to cross. Health care is free—which means you pay in time instead of money. Services are distributed only after endless stays in waiting rooms. ([One resident] brought his son to an E.R. complaining of a foreign substance that had temporarily blinded him in one eye and was turned away, told he had to make an appointment.) Pharmacies are a state-run monopoly, which means getting an aspirin is like a trip to the DMV.[54]

This is not to deny these countries enjoy high standards of living. But those high living standards do not exist *because* these countries fight inequality—they exist *despite* the fact they fight inequality.

Overall, Scandinavian countries are comparable to other Western nations in the protections they give to human liberty: they have roughly the same degree of freedom of speech, freedom of contract, and private property rights as the United States, Canada, and Britain. When looking at nations that have a mixture of liberty and government control, it is enormously difficult to assess whether one country is, on the whole, more free than another. Scandinavian countries may have higher taxes and larger welfare states than the U.S., but the U.S. arguably has a more draconian regulatory regime and byzantine tax code, to say nothing of the myriad other factors that can affect how well an economy performs.

What is clear is that if we look at the history of Scandinavian countries, we find that they have prospered during periods in which they had more economic freedom (and higher inequality), and they have faltered in periods in which they had less freedom (and lower inequality). Take the case of Sweden, for example.

In the beginning of the 1800s, Sweden was among the poorest countries of Western Europe. By the mid-1900s, Sweden was one of the richest countries in the world. What made this possible? Freedom. Over the course of the first half of the nineteenth century, all major government

restrictions, regulations, and controls were removed and the basic institutions of capitalism were established: private ownership of the means of
production, freedom of competition, and free trade. The government was
small (spending around 10 percent of GDP), and taxes were low.[55]

The 1870s would mark the beginning of what is known in Sweden as
"The 100 Golden Years." Between 1870 and 1970, Sweden enjoyed some of
the highest economic growth, productivity growth, and wage growth in
the world. By 1970, it was the third-richest country in the world, in terms
of GDP per capita. At the end of the twentieth century, however, Sweden
was fighting to remain within the top 20.[56] Why? Because it abandoned its
commitment to liberty.

Between 1960 and 1980, the burden of government spending doubled,
rising from 30 percent of GDP to 60 percent of GDP.[57] To fund its growing
welfare state, taxes skyrocketed: the top marginal tax rate, for example,
hovered around 90 percent throughout the 1970s and 1980s.[58] As a result,
the rate of economic progress also slowed. In the 1950s and 1960s, the average growth rate was 3.5 to 4.5 percent per year. Between 1971 and 2001 the
average in Sweden was just over 2 percent per year. (By contrast, between
1971 and 2001 average OECD growth was 3.11 percent. The average for the
United States during the same period was 3.24 percent.)[59] Incidentally, it
was also during the 1970s and 1980s that Sweden achieved the lowest degree
of economic inequality of any advanced country in the modern world.[60]

What's happened since then? In 2006, Sweden started once again to
move in a freer direction. As the late Johnny Munkhammar, a member of
the Swedish Parliament, wrote, Swedes "have seen their borders opened for
more labor migration, they have seen still more state-owned companies
sold, and have seen their public authorities shrink in number. Stockholm
has also cut property taxes and abolished the wealth tax, and instituted a
new system of income-tax credits that lets working people with average incomes keep what amounts to an extra month of wages, after taxes, per year.
Today, the state's total tax take comes to 45% of GDP, from 56% ten years
ago." As a result, Sweden has no budget deficit and has reemerged as one of
Europe's fastest-growing economies.[61] (Inequality in Sweden, meanwhile,
has risen.[62]) Far from a counter-example, Sweden's history demonstrates
precisely what we've argued: that liberty and prosperity are inextricably
linked, and that economic inequality simply doesn't matter.

If we care about progress, our top concern should be protecting liberty and championing human ability. No society has yet had complete liberty, however. Even in America, there were important restrictions on freedom, including economic freedom, from the start. Slavery was the most glaring and vicious example, but hardly the only one. Today, meanwhile, although we have far more liberty than our feudal ancestors, there are countless ways in which the government restricts our freedom to produce and trade, including minimum wage laws, rent control, occupational licensing laws, tariffs, union shop laws, antitrust laws, government monopolies such as those granted to the post office and the education system, subsidies for industries such as agriculture or wind and solar power, eminent domain laws, wealth redistribution via the welfare state, and the progressive income tax.

Unfortunately, these burdens and controls are increasing—and *that,* not rising economic inequality, is what explains the sense that opportunity is under attack today. Our government is using its power in order to violate our rights, allowing some people to rise through political privilege, and preventing others from rising through merit. Although we are enjoying more opportunities than ever thanks to continued economic progress, the foundations of economic progress—political equality and economic freedom—are increasingly threatened.

The American Dream can be boiled down to one simple formula:

Ability and Effort + Freedom = Opportunity

To assess the state of the American Dream today, and to fully realize that dream, we first need to identify the ways in which the government is chipping away at our freedom to rise by means of our own ability (and *only* by means of our own ability). That will be our task in part 3.

PART THREE

THE BETRAYAL OF
OPPORTUNITY

CHAPTER FIVE
THE WAR ON OPPORTUNITY

THE MYTH OF MOBILITY?

According to the inequality critics, the American Dream has become a myth. "America used to be thought of as the land of opportunity," writes Joseph Stiglitz. "Today, a child's life chances are more dependent on the income of his or her parents than in Europe, or any other of the advanced industrial countries for which there are data."[1] According to President Obama, "[W]e were convinced that America is a place where even if you're born with nothing, with a little hard work you can improve your own situation over time and build something better to leave your kids. . . . The problem is that alongside increased inequality, we've seen diminished levels of upward mobility in recent years."[2]

The message? What you make of your life is largely out of your hands. If you're born wealthy, you'll probably stay wealthy. If you're born poor, you'll probably stay poor. In a country in which inequality is out of control, there is simply nothing much you can do to shape your future. "We may believe that anyone can succeed through hard work and determination," Paul Krugman writes, "but the facts say otherwise. . . . [I]n modern America, class—inherited class—usually trumps talent."[3] This is a depressing picture. But is it true? And if so, why and what should we do about it?

Most of these claims about the decay of opportunity are based on mobility statistics. The inequality critics typically conflate opportunity and mobility, but although the concepts are related, they are not identical. Opportunity, as we've seen, refers to conditions that are favorable to the achievement of success and happiness. Mobility is a narrower concept that refers to a person's ability to rise by merit from humble beginnings to the highest reaches of success. And mobility statistics, as we'll see in a moment, don't even measure *that*.

Mobility is important. It is a consequence of political equality, which makes it possible for innovators to come from anywhere. As James Truslow Adams argued in the book that introduced the term "the American Dream," the root of the "rampant optimism" that developed in America during the nineteenth century was "the complete absence of any legal class distinction. . . . In America, as contrasted with Europe, it was open to every man, theoretically at least, to rise from the very bottom to the top." He observed that "in the seething America of the 1830s and 1840s, both immigrant and old American felt that . . . fortune might be waiting for him around the corner. . . . Native or foreigner, rich or poor, learned or unlearned, the race was free for all, and the prizes were beyond the imaginations of the preceding generation or European magnates."[4] By the same token, the dynamism of a highly mobile society meant that, regardless of where you started, resting on your laurels would lead ultimately to failure. A popular saying at the turn of the last century was "Shirtsleeves to shirtsleeves in three generations." An innovator would build a fortune, leave it to children unable or unwilling to equal his achievement, and by the time the third generation came along, the fortune would be gone. Mobility is a by-product of the vitality of a free society: the only way to succeed over the long run is by continually exercising ability.

Is mobility alive and well in America today? That is not an easy thing to measure, and the approach taken by the inequality critics (and most everyone today) confuses more than it clarifies.

There are basically two ways researchers try to measure mobility. As Richard Wilkinson and Kate Pickett explain in their book *The Spirit Level*, "people can move up or down within their lifetime (*intragenerational* mobility) or offspring can move up and down relative to their parents (*intergenerational* mobility)." Note that when they say "move up and down relative to their parents," Wilkinson and Pickett don't mean simply that children make more money than their parents, so-called absolute mobility.

When it comes to absolute mobility, the overwhelming majority of Americans today live in households that have larger real incomes than their parents had at the same age.[5] What they are referring to is *relative* mobility: does someone make more money relative to his contemporaries than his parents made relative to their contemporaries? "If the correlation between parent's income and child's income is high, that means that rich parents tend to have children who are also rich, and poor parents tend to have children who stay poor."[6]

The problem with this approach is that mobility statistics don't measure mobility. More precisely, they don't measure whether people are *able* to rise, only how many *did* rise. That tells us nothing about whether, as Obama said, "with a little hard work you can improve your own situation" because mobility statistics lump together people who do work hard and people who don't, as well as people who don't advance for any number of other reasons. As economist Thomas Sowell observes:

> [S]ocial mobility—the opportunity to move up—cannot be measured solely by how much movement takes place. Opportunity is just one factor in economic advancement. How well a given individual or group takes advantage of existing opportunities is another. Only by implicitly (and arbitrarily) assuming that a failure to rise must be due to society's barriers can we say that American society no longer has opportunity for upward social mobility.[7]

Because mobility statistics don't distinguish between those who don't rise and those who can't, they are useless when it comes to assessing how healthy mobility is. Consider an estimate of American mobility from the U.S. Treasury (Table 5.1). Its 2007 report found that over the period 1996 to 2005, more than 50 percent of the poorest families moved up at least one quintile—and around 75 percent of middle-class families either stayed in the middle class or did even better.[8]

Is that a desirable amount of movement or not? There is simply no way to say. It is not true that if there is *any* relationship between where a person starts and where he ends up, that there are barriers to mobility. Even in a society in which everyone has the ability to rise, children whose parents are better educated, more affluent, or more attentive will generally find it

TABLE 5.1
INCOME MOBILITY 1996–2005

Fraction of households in each 1996 income category that had moved to the other income categories by 2005 (U.S. Department of Treasury)

	Lowest 20% (2005)	Second 20%	Middle 20%	Fourth 20%	Top 20%
Lowest 20% (1996)	42.4	28.6	13.9	9.9	5.3
Second 20%	17.0	33.3	26.7	15.1	7.9
Middle 20%	7.1	17.5	33.3	29.6	12.5
Fourth 20%	4.1	7.3	18.3	40.2	30.2
Upper 20%	2.6	3.2	7.1	17.8	69.4

easier to succeed. That's one of the reasons parents strive to earn money—to provide their children with opportunities. The question is whether there are barriers that *prevent* us from rising by means of ability, and mobility statistics cannot tell us that.

With that in mind, consider how the inequality critics use these statistics to support their agenda of propping up those at the bottom and bringing down those at the top. Citing mobility stats, they make two basic claims: (1) that as inequality has risen in the United States, U.S. mobility has declined, and (2) that mobility in the United States is lower than in countries with less inequality. Taken together, these claims allegedly prove that the very same policies that fight inequality—high taxes on "the rich" and a vast regulatory-welfare state—also promote mobility.

Even if these claims were true, the notion that you could create more movement among income categories by giving unearned gifts to some people and by seizing earned achievements from others wouldn't justify such actions. There's no value in movement as such. What we care about is whether individuals are able to rise *by merit*—and the fact is that many of the policies the inequality critics say will improve mobility actually make rising by merit much harder. The high taxes and regulatory burdens they favor have the effect of protecting established businesses. To accumulate a fortune requires earning a high rate of profit and continually reinvesting most of it in the business. The greater the tax burden, the harder this process becomes. In the same way that small investments can turn into big gains when compounded over time, even relatively small tax burdens can amount to enormous losses, since they too get compounded over time: the million dollars taxed away from a company today doesn't just cost it a million dollars, but all the income that million dollars would have generated had the business been free to reinvest it. Regulations, meanwhile, impose substantial compliance costs on a business—costs that an established business with a bull pen of attorneys can more easily meet, but which can stop upstarts in their tracks.

As if that weren't bad enough, it turns out that the critics' claims about inequality and mobility are no more reliable than the statistical claims we've seen them make about middle-class stagnation.

The first problem is that, as inequality critic Timothy Noah concedes, "the peak years of American mobility" were "the latter half of the nineteenth century and the early years of the twentieth, when the American industrial revolution was wreaking maximum creative destruction on what had previously been an agrarian economy." (Noah also notes that "mobility in [the] postwar era was no match for the mobility enjoyed by the generations of workers who lived during [Horatio] Alger's lifetime.")[9] And yet this was an era in which there was almost no regulatory-welfare state to speak of, in which taxes were mind-bogglingly low, and in which economic inequality was high.

Equally problematic to the claim that rising inequality leads to less mobility is a finding from the Equality of Opportunity Project that mobility in the U.S. has not decreased since 1971 (see Figure 5.1), even though inequality has risen. (The authors of the study, by the way, are themselves well-respected critics of inequality, including Thomas Piketty's occasional coauthor, Emmanuel Saez.)[10] It would be wrong to treat this finding as definitive. But it does raise the question of why the inequality critics often treat their claim of declining mobility as definitive.

The same goes for their claim that, as Richard Wilkinson and Kate Pickett put it in *The Spirit Level*, "the relationship between intergenerational social mobility and income inequality is very strong. . . . [C]ountries with bigger income differences tend to have much lower social mobility."[11] In one sense, that would be predictable but uninteresting. In a country with less inequality, relatively small changes in a person's

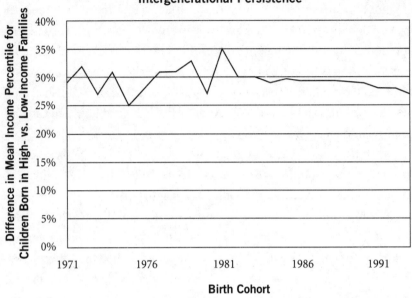

Figure 5.1
Intergenerational Persistence

income will improve his relative economic standing. Author Max Borders gives an apt analogy:

> Imagine you have two measuring sticks divided into fifths (or quin-tiles). One measuring stick reaches as high as the door knob. The other measuring stick goes up to the ceiling. Now suppose a friend and I are having a jumping contest. Suppose also that my friend is a former col-lege basketball player. If I'm using the door-knob measuring stick to measure my jumps, I am able to jump into the fourth quintile! My friend, using the ceiling length stick is only able to jump into the sec-ond quintile. Does that mean I jump higher than my friend? Of course not. It means we're using two different measuring sticks. People play the same kinds of tricks with data on income mobility.[12]

Unfortunately for the inequality critics, this is not the only problem with their claim that low-inequality countries enjoy higher mobility.

Wilkinson and Pickett's claims may already be outdated. The pair published their findings in 2009; recent studies have taken a more careful look at the data and reached very different conclusions. In addition to the challenge of comparing mobility in countries with different levels of inequality, one of the biggest problems with most of the earlier mobility studies is that they did not distinguish between upward mobility (the ability of a poor child to do relatively better than his parents) and downward mobility (the likelihood that a wealthier child will do relatively worse than his parents). The critics of economic inequality routinely equate lower mobility in the United States with less upward mobility. But a 2014 study by Miles Corak (University of Ottawa), Matthew J. Lindquist (SOFI, Stockholm University), and Bhashkar Mazumder (Federal Reserve Bank of Chicago) suggests that the lower overall mobility in the U.S. is almost solely the product of less *downward* mobility. Although the authors are careful to note that their results are not definitive, they conclude that, compared to Sweden and Canada, "we find almost no differences when we look at upward mobility from the bottom, despite the well-known concern that perhaps there are poorer prospects for upward mobility in the U.S."[13] Again, one study doesn't prove anything, but it says a lot about the credibility of the inequality critics that they typically only cite studies that support their views, and ignore any evidence that would undermine them.[14]

So if we can't rely on mobility statistics, how are we to assess the state of opportunity in America?

NOT BOUND TO RISE

Since, as we've seen, freedom allows us to rise by productive ability, the way to assess opportunity and mobility is by looking at government policies and whether they protect or restrict liberty. When we do that, what we see is that opportunity *is* under attack today, and the culprit isn't successful people earning huge paychecks. It is the labyrinth of obstacles the government puts in the way of everyone's success—and virtually all of these obstacles are *endorsed* by the critics of inequality.

What sorts of barriers does an ambitious young person who wants to make something of his life face today, thanks to state intervention? Probably the first and greatest obstacle he'll face is an abominable education system. We'll take a more in-depth look at education later in this chapter. For now, it's important to point out that the government has virtually monopolized the field of education, and then consigned millions of Americans to lousy and sometimes dangerous schools, from which only the affluent can afford to flee.

For the students who manage to make it through high school, the next challenge is college—above all, the challenge of paying for college. Thirty years ago, you could work your way through college even with a minimum-wage job, but today that's virtually impossible, thanks to skyrocketing tuition costs. And why have tuition costs grown so fast? A study from the Cato Institute finds that a main driver is government efforts to make college *affordable*: "One result of the federal government's student financial aid programs is higher tuition costs at our nation's colleges and universities." Although paradoxical, this result could have been predicted from basic economic theory: when students can come up with more money for college, thanks to the government's efforts, colleges can afford to increase their tuition. "The empirical evidence is consistent with that—federal loans, Pell grants, and other assistance programs result in higher tuition for students at our nation's colleges and universities."[15] It is rare for students to be able to make it through college without taking on huge debts, and the cost no doubt keeps many from even bothering.

For a young person who doesn't go to college and who lacks job skills and work experience, the surest way to succeed is to find a job, any job, and work his or her way up. Although service jobs at places such as Walmart or McDonald's are maligned, one of the values they provide is that they lay out a step-by-step path for people to advance—even people who lack a good education. As recently retired CEO Don Thompson pointed out, "Today at McDonald's 60 percent of our franchisees—those that own restaurants in the U.S.—started as hourly employees." (Thompson himself grew up in Chicago's notorious Cabrini-Green housing project, and started his rise working behind a McDonald's counter.)[16] The more common pattern, of course, is for unskilled workers to start at these low-skill, low-paying jobs, and use the skills and experience they acquire to find better jobs in other fields.

But what if a person can't get that first job? The biggest competitive advantage someone with limited education, skills, and work experience can offer is a willingness to work cheaply. When Andrew Carnegie came to this country as a young, uneducated immigrant, his first job was in a factory working for just over a dollar a week. But that job gave him the opportunity to show that he was able to work hard and learn fast, and very soon he found better jobs for better pay. But today the government prevents us from following this route to success, via the minimum wage.

We're taught to think of the minimum wage as a mechanism for helping people earn more. What it actually does is prevent people from deciding for themselves what pay to accept. If you can't find an employer to hire you at $7.25 an hour (the federal minimum wage as of this writing), then you are legally barred from accepting a lower-paying job. The minimum wage may raise pay for some workers, but at the price of stopping other people from working altogether. "[W]hat are the effects of increasing minimum wages?" asks Paul Krugman. "Any Econ 101 student can tell you the answer: The higher wage reduces the quantity of labor demanded, and hence leads to unemployment."[17]

The minimum wage obviously harms business owners. When Seattle recently increased its minimum wage, several restaurants that couldn't afford the higher labor costs had to shut down immediately.[18] But the biggest victims are the lowest-skilled workers. If the government raises the minimum wage, that higher wage can lure more skilled workers to compete for jobs they may have once avoided. A college student who wouldn't have taken a McDonald's job for $7.25 an hour may find it worthwhile at $10 an hour, leaving fewer opportunities for, say, an uneducated immigrant from South America. This doesn't faze some inequality critics. Sean McElwee of the left-wing public policy organization Demos declares that even if "some businesses [were] to fail, unemployment rose and prices increased, a higher minimum wage could still be an acceptable policy. We must ask ourselves whether we want to live in a society when the poorest working people cannot afford to purchase basic necessities."[19] Why should "we" get to decide that they are better off without jobs? McElwee doesn't say.

Today it is popular to cite studies that claim that the unemployment effects of the minimum wage are small or even nonexistent (ignoring the vast majority of studies that show the opposite[20]). But these empirical studies not only face the usual problem of examining a complex phenomenon, where cause and effect are elusive, they also run into two other major barriers. First, the wage increases they study have generally been relatively small, especially in comparison with the hikes proposed by the inequality critics. For example, the most widely cited study showing minimal unemployment effects of an increase in the minimum wage—the 1994 Card and Krueger study—looked at a modest increase from $4.25 to $5.05. When it comes to the minimum wage, size matters: a 16 percent increase is very different from the 30 and even 100 percent increases being proposed today.[21]

More important, though, is that these studies only show us what happens over the short run. Over the long run, minimum wage hikes can also lead companies to save money by replacing employees with technology, or by reducing employee perks and benefits. In other cases, higher labor costs may lead some companies not to expand, while other companies may never get started. Either way, fewer jobs for low-skilled workers.[22]

The point isn't to criticize the Card and Krueger study in particular. It's that it's wrong to take a single empirical study as gospel, and to extrapolate its results without great care. (Writing in 1998, Krugman found it "remarkable" that "this rather iffy result [from Card and Krueger] has been seized upon by some liberals as a rationale for making large minimum wage increases a core component of the liberal agenda. . . . Clearly these advocates very much want to believe that the price of labor—unlike that of gasoline, or Manhattan apartments—can be set based on considerations of justice, not supply and demand, without unpleasant side effects."[23] Later Krugman would come out in favor of enormous minimum wage hikes, declaring that it wouldn't increase unemployment.[24])

Now let's say you do find a job. The lower your pay, the more you have to work to achieve a given standard of living. But other regulations can make it harder for you to get the hours you want. Government-mandated overtime pay may make it too expensive for an employer to let you work more than a certain number of hours a week. And now Obamacare, by forcing certain employers to offer health insurance to employees who work more than 30 hours a week, has created an incentive for limiting hours even further.

Even if you manage to overcome these barriers, you face more obstacles, including a substantial tax burden. Low-income Americans don't generally pay income taxes, but they do pay sales taxes, gas taxes, and "sin taxes" on goods like cigarettes and alcohol. Most economists believe that the burden of corporate taxes falls on consumers in the form of higher prices, and on workers in the form of lower wages and fewer job opportunities. But the most significant taxes levied on those starting at the bottom are the payroll taxes that fund Social Security and Medicare. Payroll taxes alone amount to 15.3 percent of your income; money that is taken from you and handed out to the elderly. This means that you have to spend more than a month and a half each year working *without pay* in order to fund other people's retirement and medical care.

These aren't the only barriers to success. The government also makes it extraordinarily hard and expensive to enter many fields through occupational licensing laws, which prevent people from offering their services to willing customers. In his book on welfare reform, *American Dream,* *New York Times* journalist Jason DeParle describes how Jewel, a Milwaukee resident struggling to stay off welfare, ran into difficulties thanks to one such restriction: "She did know a lot about hair and nails, and her skills as a kitchen-table beautician kept her in demand. But absurdly, the state required a high school degree to work in a beauty shop."[25] Absurd, yes, but not unusual. Before the Institute for Justice helped change the laws, anyone who wanted to perform hairbraiding in Mississippi had to undergo 300 class hours in order to obtain a license—and anyone who wanted to *teach* hairbraiding had to spend *3,200* hours in cosmetology and cosmetology instructor programs, more than the state required to become a licensed paramedic.[26] Similar laws exist across the country in fields as varied as casket-making and animal massage. Today, roughly 30 percent of Americans need a professional license of one sort or another in order to work in their field.[27]

Some of the paths to entrepreneurship poor people have historically taken advantage of have been closed altogether. For example, in some places, sidewalk vendors are banned, either outright or through prohibitively expensive license fees. Perhaps the most egregious limits on entrepreneurship are Certificate of Need laws, which apply to various industries in more than thirty states. These laws don't require that businessmen go through training, get a degree, or pass a test in order to enter a field. Instead, Certificate of Need laws require would-be entrepreneurs to prove to the government that there is a "public need" for their business. "That's no easy task," notes Pacific Legal Foundational principal attorney Timothy

Sandefur, "given that most of these laws are written in such vague language that nobody knows what they mean. What is a 'public convenience and necessity'? Typically it's whatever the government says it is. And if officials decide new competition isn't necessary, they can deny a person the right to start a new business, no matter how skilled or qualified he may be." In practice, these laws amount to a "competitor's veto": they allow existing businesses to stop new entrants by complaining to government officials that the additional competition will threaten their revenues.[28]

Then there are unions. Unions, as we noted in chapter 2, have been given special powers by government that allow them to demand wages for union workers that are higher than those workers could earn on a free market. But these higher labor costs mean that employers will hire fewer workers, reducing employment and raising the costs of the goods they produce. Depending on how widespread unions are in the economy, even *unionized* employees can end up worse off. Their wages may be higher, but their standard of living will be lower since they are paying higher prices for all the other goods produced by other unionized workers.

And for someone who is ambitious and wants to rise through hard work, unions can be an enormous barrier, since they tend to reward *seniority* rather than *ability*. At a Giant Eagle grocery store in Edinboro, Pennsylvania, managers gave their highest-performing employees a raise. But the United Food and Commercial Workers Local 23 union took them to court to rescind the raises. "Why did Local 23 oppose higher pay for its members?" asks James Sherk, a scholar at the conservative think tank, the Heritage Foundation. "Because it upended their seniority system, allowing junior employees to make more [than] those with more seniority. Local 23 wanted uniform pay scales—even if that meant cutting some of its members' wages."[29]

Not only does the government make it harder for people to earn a living, but many of its restrictions on liberty work to dramatically raise the cost of living and so reduce the purchasing power of whatever money they do earn. We've already seen how the government raises labor costs in many ways, making virtually everything we buy more expensive. In the case of the minimum wage, for example, businesses may pass on their higher costs to customers. The chair of President Obama's Council of Economic Advisers, Christina Romer, has noted that often "the customers paying those prices—including some of the diners at McDonald's and the shoppers at Walmart—have very low family incomes. Thus this price effect may harm the very people whom a minimum wage is supposed to help."[30] And taxes, of course, drive up costs. But there is much more.

Take the cost of housing, which is often the greatest financial burden people face. Land-use laws, zoning restrictions, height restrictions, and minimum-lot-size requirements all constrain the supply of housing and help to raise prices in many areas.[31] Rent-control laws, among other evils, lead to poor quality of rent-controlled units and higher prices for non-rent-controlled units. So-called urban renewal projects have demolished much of the affordable housing once available to low-income Americans, largely in order to appease outsiders who had enough money to live elsewhere.[32] And the government's "affordable housing" crusade helped spur the housing bubble that drove up the cost of many houses, to the detriment of everyone who didn't yet own homes.

Then there are energy costs, which not only affect us directly through gas and electricity prices, but also indirectly, by adding to the production and transportation costs of all the others things we buy. Many of the EPA's regulations do nothing to make our environment safer, but they do hike up the price of energy. Renewable fuel standards, to take only one of countless examples, force refiners to blend corn-based ethanol into fuels, making fuel less efficient and achieving nothing except higher fuel and corn costs. Even Al Gore now opposes them. Then there are restrictions on petroleum drilling, "renewable energy" mandates and subsidies, the overregulation of nuclear power, and many other interventions that drive up the cost of energy.[33]

What it all adds up to is a burden so staggering that it's truly amazing so many Americans continue to rise out of poverty each year.

DENYING OPPORTUNITY TO INNOVATORS

Too often when people speak of opportunity their focus is solely on the ability of poor people to rise out of poverty. But opportunity is not about escaping poverty—it's about *everyone's* ability to rise from where they are today to greater and greater heights. A land of opportunity provides an unobstructed road to everyone committed to productive achievement, regardless of how much he's already achieved. Today, that road is littered with obstacles, and those obstacles hold back not only those striving to rise from the bottom, but the innovators who drive human progress.

Probably the freest industries in America today are found in the high-tech arena, epitomized by Silicon Valley, home to companies such as Hewlett Packard, Facebook, Google, Cisco, Oracle, and Intel. If you've visited the Valley and experienced its entrepreneurial culture, you'll be struck by how similar it is to the way America was described during the nineteenth and early twentieth centuries: the energy, the optimism, the fearless pursuit of success and achievement. In her book *Secrets of Silicon Valley,* author and entrepreneur Deborah Perry Piscione describes how, after living in the Valley for several months, she "started to appreciate how much people are in the driver's seat here. This culture of mavericks is more interested in moving the needle forward than following the path of tradition."[34]

Silicon Valley is in many ways a land of opportunity *within* the land of opportunity. Unsurprisingly, nearly 35 percent of Silicon Valley residents are immigrants (for the U.S. as a whole, it's only about 13 percent). Many of these immigrants notes Perry Piscione, "came with no English language skills, no family or friends, varying degrees of education, but a common drive to seek out better opportunities. If you are motivated in Silicon Valley, [then] you can make it, period."[35] What matters in the Valley is not where you were born or where (or even whether) you went to college. What matters is your ability. Talent is the currency of Silicon Valley, and individuals there use their talent to move us forward, pioneering revolutionary achievements in social media, big data, personalized health care, biotechnology, smartphones, mobile commerce, cloud technology, and 3D printing, to name just a few. Silicon Valley is the place creators like Elon Musk, Steve Jobs, and Peter Thiel go to make a fortune by inventing the future.

What made it all possible? No doubt there are many forces at work, but one enormous factor is the extent to which the government has kept its hands off the Valley. Perry Piscione points out the benefits of "the lack of heavy government regulation that would typically favor the interests of established banks, companies, and labor unions" over young upstarts.[36] People are free to act on their ideas and compete on ability, without having to wade through a minefield of government permissions before launching their ventures. It is, as Bill Gates once put it, business at the speed of thought.

But even Silicon Valley is not immune from the threat of government control, most notably from antitrust laws. Although these laws claim to protect competition, what they actually do is punish superlative competitors.[37] If you look at the tech companies targeted by antitrust, you'll find a who's who list of innovative producers, including Intel, Google, Apple, Adobe, and Microsoft. The case of Seattle-based Microsoft is especially tragic and illustrative of the profoundly destructive effects of these laws.

In the early 1990s, Bill Gates's Microsoft was one of the most innovative and successful companies of all time. But the company was dogged by antitrust authorities throughout that decade, and eventually, for the "crime" of giving away Internet Explorer for free, was forced to defend itself against a Justice Department antitrust suit. Initially Judge Thomas Penfield Jackson ordered that Gates's company be broken up, and while much of that decision would later be overturned, Microsoft was nevertheless saddled with direct government oversight for a decade. The experience scarred Gates and almost certainly contributed to his decision to step down as CEO in 2000. "The DOJ action took all the fun out of the job," technical analyst Rob Enderle of the Giga Information Group said after Gates announced he was retiring.[38]

With Gates out the door and antitrust monitors breathing down its neck, Microsoft became far less innovative and entrepreneurial over the next ten years. Under antitrust, producers have no way of knowing what they can and can't do. Take Microsoft's decision to give away Internet Explorer for free, for example. What if the company had charged for the product? Instead of being indicted for "predatory" activity it could have been charged with using its "monopoly power" to gouge customers. Antitrust regulations paralyze innovators: the only safe move is to stop innovating, stop competing, do nothing, and stagnate. "Since the antitrust suit, [Microsoft has] become much more cautious and much less aggressive," said MIT professor Michael Cusumano in 2011. "They're afraid, it seems. Whether it's antitrust in U.S. or in Europe, they seem to be slowly reacting to the world around them, rather than trying to get in there fast."[39] Antitrust regulation turned business at the speed of thought into business at the speed of the DMV. Microsoft may have been the first high-tech company crippled by antitrust, but it likely won't be the last. Today, Apple is facing the prospect of having its own antitrust overseer implanted in the company.

But if Silicon Valley's entrepreneurs aren't fully free to function, in other industries the situation is much worse. Just consider two fields that are vital to human progress and happiness, but that the government has made inhospitable to innovators: education and health care.

For well over a century, the government has basically monopolized the field of education. It is still legal to start private schools, of course (although there are enormous political barriers to doing so, especially at the high school level). The problem is that the market is limited because potential customers have to be able not only to afford a private school's tuition, but to continue to pay thousands of dollars a year to support the government schools. It's like telling consumers they are free to buy any car they want—as long as they also buy a Chrysler. This colossal financial burden means that there are precious few alternatives to government schools, and those that exist are usually geared toward a wealthier customer base. Even relatively affluent parents often choose simply to move to districts with somewhat better government schools, rather than pay double for their children's education. For poorer Americans, of course, this alternative is usually out of reach. They are stuck with whatever the government gives them.

Even in countries whose educational systems are comparatively successful (when judged by test scores, anyway), such as Finland or Japan, turning schools into state monopolies has rendered the entire field of education disturbingly stagnant. Nowhere do we see the diversity, choice, and innovation that define the high-tech industry. In the U.S., however, things are much worse. By almost every measure we are falling behind the rest of the world, yet because there is no competition or profit motive to punish poor performers and reward great achievers, there is no reason to expect things will get better any time soon. There are few innovators devoting their efforts to creating the educational equivalent of an Apple or a Google, and the innovators who do try to change the field are highly constrained by the government. Even a private school isn't fully free to set its own rules and standards—it has to answer to the state.

This is perhaps the worst effect of government control in the field of education: not how bad U.S. schools are compared to world leaders, but how much better all these systems could be if they were free. Set aside the countless innovations we can't even imagine. Just consider a few of the obvious choices that would exist absent a government monopoly on education: different schools would take different approaches to the *goal* of education (e.g., to prepare children for the job market, to make them good citizens, to develop their ability to think and value); they would adopt different *theories* of how children best learn (e.g., Progressive, Montessori); they would structure their curriculum in vastly different ways (e.g., Common Core, classical education); to say nothing of a million other choices relating to cost, class size, the role of technology, school hours, teacher training, approaches to discipline, and on and on. And every school would have to *compete* for customers, with the best schools thriving and the worst schools failing.

The government's monopoly on education represents an enormous abridgement of opportunity: the opportunity of entrepreneurs and educational innovators to profit by applying their creativity to the field, the opportunity of parents to choose a school that caters to their unique values and needs, and the opportunity of the poorest students to get even a halfway decent education.

One of the main arguments for government control over education is that it is necessary to ensure that children who wouldn't be able to afford an education in a free market can get one. But this is precisely one of the challenges that innovators could solve. There are huge profits to be made by discovering ways to educate children at a substantially lower cost. Some charter schools have already found ways to use computers to dramatically reduce the number of teachers needed to teach a given class size, while actually *improving* educational outcomes.[40] Even in the poorest parts of the world, as education scholar James Tooley has cataloged, there is a burgeoning private school system providing education to children of parents who earn only a few dollars a day—and who have the option of sending their children to free government schools.[41] That's to say nothing of the charitable resources, scholarships, and non-profit schools that would undoubtedly be available to help poorer children.

Finally, let's look briefly at health care. The American health care system is freer and more innovative than virtually every other health care system in the world.[42] But it nevertheless has more in common with our stagnant education system than with Silicon Valley. Although there are some areas in which entrepreneurs and visionaries have the opportunity to change and improve things, overall the story is one of bureaucracy and roadblocks.

The U.S. health care system is usually characterized as a free-market system (and all of its problems are inevitably *blamed* on this freedom), but the truth is that it is dominated by government. Even before Obamacare, about half of U.S. health care spending was government spending.[43] Starting with Medicare and Medicaid in 1965, the government has sought to guarantee us health care regardless of our ability to pay. But it turns out that allowing people to consume health care that they don't have to pay for (or don't have to pay full price for) is incredibly expensive, and shortly after the launch of these medical welfare state programs, the government started imposing rigid controls on doctors, hospitals, and insurers to keep expenses down. These and other controls—Medicare alone involves 132,000 pages of complex laws, rules, and regulations—have dramatically curtailed the freedom of health care providers and have actually driven *up* costs. It takes a typical hospital 38,400 man-hours each year just to meet Medicare's billing requirements, and hospital staff spend on average 30 minutes doing paperwork for each hour spent caring for a Medicare patient.[44] The costs of compliance, in terms of time and money, are so burdensome that it's hardly any wonder that, as physician Sandeep Jauhar notes:

> In surveys, a majority of doctors express diminished enthusiasm for medicine and say they would discourage a friend or family member from entering the profession. In a 2008 survey of twelve thousand physicians, only 6 percent described their morale as positive. Eighty-four percent said their incomes were constant or decreasing. The majority said they did not have enough time to spend with patients because of paperwork, and nearly half said they planned to reduce the number of patients they would see in the next three years or stop practicing altogether.[45]

Forcing doctors to spend large chunks of their days filling out forms instead of treating patients is bad enough. But even when they do treat patients, their medical judgment is often constrained by regulatory dictates. Jauhar describes a case in which one of his patients had been given antibiotics to treat pneumonia, even though the evidence he had pneumonia was slim. Jauhar stopped the treatment, but not soon enough: his patient contracted *C. difficile* colitis, an illness often brought on by the use of antibiotics. As Jauhar notes, "The complication stemmed from the requirement from Medicare that antibiotics be administered to a pneumonia patient within six hours of arriving at the hospital." The problem is that diagnosing pneumonia often takes longer than that and so "there is pressure to treat even when the diagnosis isn't firm, as was the case with this gentleman." Jauhar goes on to describe a conversation with a senior health care quality consultant, who worried that these sorts of Medicare guidelines, which pay doctors for treating patients in the ways regulators deem proper, could have "a chilling effect" on medical innovation. "What about hospitals that stray from the guidelines in an effort to do even better?" the consultant wondered. "Should they be punished for trying to innovate? Will they have to take a hit financially until performance measures catch up with current research?"[46]

Given how important health care is to our lives, it is shameful that we have entangled the men and women we entrust our lives to in this sort of bureaucratic web. We've said, in effect, that our "right" to have other people pay for our health care trumps the rights of doctors to practice medicine on their own terms. We will generously allow them to save our lives, but only if they surrender more of their autonomy to the government than the average car mechanic.

And doctors aren't the only ones with their hands tied. Medical device makers, for instance, have to go through an excruciating and expensive FDA approval process that takes on average 54 months before a new product is approved—nearly five times as long as approvals take in Europe, even though there is no evidence this lengthier process makes us safer.[47] Imagine if every Apple product had to go through four and a half years of government approvals. We would still be using our iPhone 3Gs. To make matters worse, Obamacare has hit device makers with a 2.3 percent excise tax on their *revenues* (not just their profits), which in many cases comes out of their R&D budgets. According to AdvaMed CEO Stephen Ubl, "The reduction in R&D is especially troubling as investments in research today are the cures and treatments of tomorrow. The effects of this tax could have a damaging ripple effect for decades to come if left unaddressed. This tax is not just a tax on medical technology companies. It's a tax on medical progress."[48]

And then there's the issue of health care costs. In freer industries, one of the main avenues for innovation is in cost reduction. By discovering ways to bring down costs, entrepreneurs can make their products more attractive to price-conscious buyers, much like Dell was able to lower its costs and rise to prominence by slashing the price of computers. But in the health care sector, there is disturbingly little innovation aimed at cutting costs. Why not? In large part because, thanks to government intervention in medicine, we *aren't* very price conscious. Welfare programs like Medicare and Medicaid, and tax incentives that encourage us to pay for even routine care with insurance, have created a "third-party payer" system: for every dollar of care a patient receives, on average he only has to pay fourteen cents out of pocket. It doesn't do doctors, hospitals, drug companies, or other potential health care innovators any good to search for ways to cut costs when the people making the buying decisions don't care about those costs.

One area in which we are cost-conscious is health insurance. But here, too, the government has closed the door to innovation. Health insurers are hamstrung by federal, state, and local regulations that effectively *force* them to offer costly plans. As the Cato Institute notes in its *Handbook for Policymakers:*

> Those regulations include restrictions on insurance pools' ability to limit or refuse coverage, to vary premiums according to risk, and to negotiate price discounts from providers. States also limit enrollees' freedom to purchase only the coverage they wish. Finally, states prohibit their residents from purchasing insurance from states with more consumer-friendly regulation.[49]

To appreciate the impact of these regulations on prices, consider each state's laundry list of insurance mandates. We aren't talking about

Obamacare's individual mandate, which forces us to buy insurance whether we want to or not. These state mandates dictate what coverage must be offered in the insurance packages citizens are permitted to buy. Rules vary from state to state, but here are some common mandates:

- Benefit mandates dictate what treatments, procedures, and diagnostic tests an insurance package has to cover. Even if you're young, don't want kids, and don't drink, these mandates can force you to pay top dollar for a package that covers everything from in vitro fertilization to liver transplants to alcohol rehab.
- Mandatory "guaranteed issue" forces insurance companies to insure anyone, regardless of personal or medical history.
- Guaranteed renewability requires insurers to renew policies, even for high-risk customers, as long as their premiums are paid.
- Guaranteed community rating forces insurance companies to insure everyone at the same rate, regardless of crucial differences in things like age, habits, or health. (In most cases, insurance companies today are subject to modified community rating standards, which allow some minor price differentiations.)[50]

Given these kinds of strictures, there is simply no way for health insurers to significantly reduce costs.

These and countless other interventions explain much of the rising cost of health care and its uneven quality. Freedom doesn't lead to mounting bureaucracy and skyrocketing prices—it leads to ever-improving customer satisfaction and steadily declining prices. That's what we see in the tech industry, in other parts of the insurance industry (life insurance, car insurance), and even in sectors of the medical industry that aren't dominated by government (LASIK eye surgery, cosmetic surgery).

The lack of freedom in the medical industry amounts to a declaration that, when it comes to health care, "Innovators Need Not Apply." When asked, "Can you imagine Google becoming a health company?" Google cofounder Sergey Brin replied, "Health is just so heavily regulated, it's just a painful business to be in. It's just not necessarily how I want to spend my time. . . . I think the regulatory burden in the U.S. is so high that I think it would dissuade a lot of entrepreneurs." Google's other cofounder, Larry

Page, went on to add that the health care industry is "so heavily regulated, it's a difficult area . . . I do worry, you know, we kind of regulate ourselves out of some really great possibilities."[51]

Whether you're an ambitious young worker just starting out or a successful creator who wants to find new ways to improve human life, your opportunity is becoming increasingly constrained by the state. Instead of protecting the freedom of individuals to rise by their own effort, we are making it harder to rise. And, at the same time, we're making it easier to live off the efforts of others.

THE WELFARE STATE VS. OPPORTUNITY

We're often told that the welfare state plays an important role in securing the American Dream, and that programs like Social Security, Medicare, and sundry "anti-poverty" schemes foster opportunity. But opportunity means you have access to an open road: it doesn't mean that other people have a duty to drive you down it.

The truth is that the welfare state is *part* of today's war on opportunity. Its basic principle represents a total inversion of the ideal of opportunity: whereas the American Dream linked rewards to achievement, the welfare state declares that if you achieve something, you have no right to your rewards, but if you fail to achieve something, you're entitled to the rewards of others. The effects of this inversion go far beyond stripping productive individuals of their wealth—although it's disturbing how little that counts for today. It also discourages many people from even attempting to become self-supporting and self-directing. Nowhere are the welfare state's corrosive effects on opportunity more clear than in its so-called War on Poverty.

The list of anti-poverty programs is long, amounting to 126 separate programs at the federal level alone, including the Earned Income Tax Credit, Supplemental Security Income, food stamps, housing subsidies, work-training programs, child care subsidies, Medicaid, and much more. Spending on these and state and local programs is enormous, amounting to nearly $1 trillion a year.[52]

The first thing to observe about these anti-poverty programs is that they haven't ended poverty—at least not poverty as the government defines it. (The *absolute* poverty we see in Haiti and Uganda was eliminated in the West long before the welfare state. When we speak about poverty in advanced countries we are talking about *relative* poverty.) The official poverty measure shows that the poverty rate remains about where it was when Lyndon B. Johnson launched his War on Poverty in the mid-1960s. That is somewhat misleading, however. Experts are in general agreement that the government's official poverty measure overstates poverty, and that better assessments suggest that poverty has been cut in half over the last fifty years.[53] What's more, most of the people the government classifies as "poor" live relatively comfortable lives. Despite the genuine hardships they face, today's poor typically enjoy an adequate diet, electricity, indoor plumbing, automobiles, and modern conveniences such as dishwashers, TVs, and DVD players. In fact, the average poor person in America lives in a home that is larger than what the average *non-poor* person in Europe lives in.[54]

But we can't celebrate just yet. Johnson claimed that the goal of the War on Poverty was to give poor Americans "opportunity not doles." The question is, have the welfare state's scores of anti-poverty measures succeeded in making poor people independent, or have they simply made it less unpleasant to be poor? The evidence is pretty clear. On the whole, what so-called anti-poverty programs have done is increase the ability of people to consume without producing. Judged from the perspective of creating opportunity, anti-poverty measures haven't just failed—they've made things worse.

Why do some people remain poor in the richest country on earth? One theory is that the welfare state is simply not "generous" enough to make it possible to rise out of poverty, although given the enormous sums spent on these programs—nearly $14,000 per poor person per year[55]—that is hard to justify. Hand that money directly to impoverished Americans and a family of four would receive $56,000 a year, more than the median household income. (Of course, that money doesn't get handed directly to poor people: much of it goes into the pockets of bureaucrats, social workers, poverty activists, outright hucksters, and who knows who else.)

A more plausible answer is that the jobs available to most poor people don't pay well enough to allow them to be self-supporting. But as political scientist Charles Murray notes, staying above the poverty line is relatively easy if you have a job: "As of 2010, a married man without children could have [stayed above the poverty level] if he worked 50.5 weeks at a minimum-wage job." This is all the more striking in light of the fact that 94 percent of hourly workers make more than the minimum wage.[56] In a similar vein, New York University professor Lawrence Mead observed that the poverty rate for adults who worked at all was only 7 percent in 2009, and only 3 percent for adults working full time throughout the year, while the poverty rate for people who didn't work was 23 percent that year.[57] Low wages, then, are usually not the explanation for poverty. If you're earning a wage, you're almost certainly not poor.

Overwhelmingly, the reason that most poor Americans are poor is because they aren't working. Mead points out that that the percentage of heads of poor families who work at least part of the year has declined from 68 percent in 1959 to 46 percent in 2009. The percentage who worked full time, all year, declined from 31 percent to 15 percent. (Some of this decline was due to the Great Recession, but this accounted for only a small part of the decline. In 1989, those percentages had already fallen to 48.9 and 16.2 percent, respectively.)[58]

Was this frightening decline due to a lack of low-skilled jobs? Surely that's part of the story, and here the job-killing minimum wage deserves its share of the blame. (According to journalist Jason Riley, "A 1995 study concluded that mothers in states that raised the minimum wage remained on public assistance an average of 44 percent longer than their peers in states where the minimum did not rise."[59]) But there are reasons—starting with the testimony of poor people themselves—to think a lack of jobs is not the major force driving this decline. NYU's Mead notes, "In 2009, only 12 percent of poor adults who did not work blamed this on their inability to find work. In 2007, before the recession, the figure was only 5 percent. In both years, this was the least common reason cited for not working. Much more often, respondents claimed illness, retirement, family responsibilities, or going to school as reasons."[60]

There are strong reasons to think that the decline in work among poor Americans has not happened *despite* the efforts of anti-poverty programs, but in significant part *because* of them. Anti-poverty programs haven't just been unsuccessful at leading more poor people to join the labor force—they've encouraged many to stay *out* of the labor force. We'll look at the data in a moment, but it's worth noting that this is a view shared by a lot of low-income workers.

In her study of Harlem's working poor, *No Shame in My Game*, Princeton sociologist Katherine S. Newman quotes several fast-food workers who believe that welfare undermines the work ethic. Here's one young worker, Ianna:

> I'm not knocking welfare, but I know people that are on it that can get up and work. There's nothing wrong with them. And they just choose not to. . . . They don't really need to be on [welfare]. They just want it because they can get away with it. I don't think it's right, because that's my tax dollars going for somebody who is lazy, who don't wanna get up. I can see if a woman had three children, her husband left her, and she don't have no job 'cause she was a housewife. Okay. But after a while, you know, welfare will send you to school. Be a nurse assistant, a home attendant, something![61]

Later, Newman introduces us to Patty:

> [O]ne imagines Patty would be tolerant of [welfare] recipients. After all, she has been there. Not so. Having finally taken the hard road to a real job, she sees no reason why anyone else should have an easier ride. "There's so much in this city; it's always hiring. It may not be what you want. It may not be the pay you want. But you will always get a job. If I can work at Burger Barn all week and come home tired and then have to deal with the kids and all of that, and be happy with one twenty-five a week, so can you."[62]

In an earlier investigation, *New Yorker* columnist Ken Auletta encountered similar attitudes. He quotes one ghetto resident, Leon Harris: "A lot of those on welfare stay on welfare 'cause they say, 'Why work? Someone is going to take care of me. As long as Uncle Sam will do it, why not?' Then they instill it in their children: 'Why should I have to go out there and bust my behind and have them take it out of my taxes?'"[63]

Auletta quotes another resident as saying, "When I meet someone with a welfare mentality, I know how it came about. It causes people who always wanted the best for themselves to learn to settle for less. They no longer have a standard of living, just merely surviving. They later raise their children to enjoy welfare mentality and learn to think little. . . . Also, after a while they begin to relax into this nothingness, enjoying this crutch welfare has provided for them. This is welfare mentality. It can make us irresponsible, lazy and depending on the system we claim treats us so unfairly."[64]

The lesson here is not that everyone on welfare is lazy and irresponsible, even if it's important to acknowledge that anti-poverty programs subsidize such behavior at the expense of hardworking Americans. The more important lesson is that anti-poverty programs incentivize even good people to drop out of the labor force, and discourage them from taking the entry-level jobs that can become a platform to greater opportunities. *We are paying people not to pursue opportunities.*

In the late 1990s, Kathryn Edin, a sociologist at Rutgers University, and Laura Lein, an anthropologist at the University of Texas at Austin, interviewed low-income single mothers. Most said that they would need to make roughly double the minimum wage in order to make it worthwhile for them to leave welfare and join the labor force. Newman summarizes their findings:

> Leaving welfare and entering the working labor force means new health costs (since few low-wage employers provide medical plans, and when they do, deductibles and copayments still raise expenses), new transportation costs both for traveling to the workplace and for traveling to the day care provider (commuting to the suburbs is time-consuming and inconvenient—buying and maintaining a used car is a huge goal for many single mothers), and, sometimes, higher housing costs (subsidized housing costs increase when incomes rise) and clothing costs (depending on the job). . . . Single mothers on welfare know that leaving welfare for a low-skilled job will make them worse off than they were on welfare.[65]

In a more recent study from the Cato Institute, Michael Tanner and Charles Hughes reached similar results. "The current welfare system provides such a high level of benefits that it acts as a disincentive for work. Welfare currently pays more than a minimum-wage job in 35 states, even after accounting for the Earned Income Tax Credit, and in 13 states it pays more than $15 per hour."[66]

Paul Krugman is admirably forthright about the implications: "[O]ur patchwork, uncoordinated system of antipoverty programs does have the effect of penalizing efforts by lower-income households to improve their position: the more they earn, the fewer benefits they can collect. In effect, these households face very high marginal tax rates. A large fraction, in some cases 80 cents or more, of each additional dollar they earn is clawed back by the government."[67]

This is tragic, because by discouraging people from accepting low-paying jobs, anti-poverty measures ultimately keep them from getting higher-paying jobs, and from acquiring the satisfaction and self-respect that comes from being self-reliant. Worse, even good people can find their desire to *be* self-reliant corroded by the welfare state.

Don's friend Jeremiah worked while he was going to college, but because he grew up in foster homes, he also received a small stipend from the government. During his sophomore year, Jeremiah was involved in an auto collision that totaled his car and put him into physical therapy. Although it would have been difficult, he could have kept working, but knowing that he had that stipend to fall back on, he let the job go. "If I didn't have that check I would have had to say 'What am I going to do to get out of [this situation]?'" Instead, "[I felt that] I can afford to let that job go because I'm going to get this check. So the check allowed me to sit there and wallow in my own self-pity rather than figure out how I was going to get out of that [situation]."

And that, Jeremiah says, is the most damaging aspect of welfare: not simply that it allows people to get by without working, but that it insulates people from the consequences of thinking of themselves as helpless victims, and thereby *encourages* them to think of themselves as victims. "That's what happens when you're on welfare. You look at things, and some of them are not your fault legitimately and some things you're convincing yourself are not your fault, [but] success in life is not a matter of figuring out whose fault it is. It's a matter of figuring out how you're going to get something done." But the welfare state "bankrolls a bad philosophy [i.e., a philosophy of victimhood], because you can afford to have that philosophy when there's a check there. Like if there was no check I couldn't dwell on whose fault it was too long because I'm hungry. [The welfare state] gives you the means by which to hold on to bad philosophy, dwell on it, grow it, until it seems like it's going to crush you."[68]

One of the worst features of the so-called poverty debate is that we have ended up equating fighting poverty with wealth redistribution. But poverty is not a distribution problem—it's a production problem. People are poor, in the end, because they have not created enough wealth to make themselves prosperous. The only thing that has ever achieved substantial reductions in poverty is *freedom* and the economic progress it unleashes.

Thanks to economic progress, poverty had been declining rapidly for years before LBJ declared war on it, and it was only once the War on Poverty started spending trillions of dollars to end poverty that the official poverty rate *stopped* declining.[69] While it's wrong to attribute this stagnation solely to the welfare state, there is no question that redistributive policies whittle away at progress. Taxes discourage production and handouts discourage work. To make matters worse, transferring income from savers to spenders reduces the capital available to fund new jobs, new businesses, and the expansion of existing businesses. These are lost opportunities, and the fact that their absence is largely invisible doesn't make the costs of redistribution any less real.

So-called anti-poverty programs are nothing of the sort. They are handouts, bought and paid for by productive individuals. Most people believe these programs are necessary in order to help those genuinely unable to support themselves through no fault of their own. History shows otherwise. Private charity has always been abundant in America, and because it isn't bound by the bureaucratic, one-size-fits-all strictures that necessarily govern state-run programs, it is in a position to distinguish between those who are unable to work and those who are *unwilling* to work—and to help those who are willing and able to get back on their feet if they fall on tough times.[70] But even those who remain unconvinced that we could do without the welfare state altogether should never lose sight of the fact that it is an opportunity destroyer, not an opportunity creator.

CHAPTER SIX
THE MONEY-MAKERS AND THE MONEY-APPROPRIATORS

THE DESERVING RICH?

The American Dream is more than an aspirational story about striving and success. It is, in the best sense, a morality tale: it says that if you do the *right* things—if you think, learn, strive, work hard, act responsibly—you can achieve *great* things. In America, what matters is not *privilege* but *merit*. Success is to be admired because, setting aside the occasional fraud and huckster, it is earned.

This is what most of us have in mind when we talk about fairness in society. It's the idea that our choices will shape our destinies, for better or for worse. The inequality critics argue that this, if it was ever true of America, no longer is. They argue that "the rich" are getting richer, not through merit, but through rigging the game in their favor, and that, as a result, the rest of us are working harder and harder and getting nowhere.

The truth is that some people today *are* getting rich through political privilege, although that is by no means true of most successful Americans. If we value fairness, we need to learn to distinguish between earned fortunes and unearned fortunes—and then we need to put an end to people's ability to capture the unearned.

What does it mean to say that someone "earned" his income? In short, that he *produced* it. If Robinson Crusoe builds a spear and uses it to catch a fish, he earned that fish—he produced it, it belongs to him, and it would be wrong for Friday to come along and take it. By the same token, we can earn values *indirectly*, by trading what we produce for the things that others produce. If Crusoe chooses not to eat his fish, but exchanges it with Friday for a coconut Friday chopped down from a tree, then Crusoe earned that coconut by obtaining it through the voluntary consent of Friday in a value-for-value trade.

In a division of labor economy, the principle is the same, but its application is less obvious. We don't produce and trade concrete items like fish and coconuts, as people do in barter economies. Instead, we produce in exchange for money, and we exchange the money for the things that others produce. How much money we receive for our productive efforts, and what we are able to buy with that money, is determined by the voluntary consent of the people we exchange with. To earn something, in a division of labor context, is to acquire it through production and voluntary exchange. What we merit is the economic value we create, *as judged by the people who voluntarily transact with us.*

It's a mistake to view economic rewards as payment for merit as such. We do not get paid in proportion to the laudable qualities we display—virtues such as diligence, integrity, and effort. Bill Gates worked hard to build Microsoft, but he's not a billionaire because he worked 20,000 times harder than the average American. To be sure, when a person is enormously successful, this almost always indicates virtue on his part. But the essential issue is that what a person merits or earns or deserves, in an economic context, is whatever rewards he can achieve through productive effort and voluntary exchange.

In 1997, J. K. Rowling published the first book in her Harry Potter series. Over the course of the next decade, she published six more Harry Potter books. Millions of delighted readers willingly paid about $10 to $20 for each one, making Rowling a billionaire.

One of the highest-paid CEOs in the last decade was Steve Jobs, who took home several billion dollars (mostly in the form of stock options). But over the course of his tenure as CEO, Jobs not only saved Apple from bankruptcy, but helped grow it from $3 billion in market capitalization to $347 billion—all through creating products that improved the lives of millions of customers, who happily paid hundreds or thousands of dollars for their Macs, iPods, iPhones, and iPads.[1]

Warren Buffett is the wealthiest investor of all time, with a net worth of about $60 billion. That's a lot of money, but Buffett helped grow his company, Berkshire Hathaway, from $22.1 million in market capitalization in the late 1960s to more than $300 billion today. Put another way, a $20.50 investment with Berkshire Hathaway in 1967 would be worth more than *$200,000* today—a track record no one else even comes close to.[2] Buffett amassed his extraordinary net worth by using his genius to identify opportunities that no one else could see, putting resources into companies that created an enormous amount of value for their customers and shareholders, standing by those companies through thick and thin, and helping guide them so that they could prosper.

These men and women of extraordinary ability achieved their fortunes through merit. They *deserve* their riches. The hallmark of deserved rewards is that they don't come at other people's expense. Bill Gates's billions didn't make anyone else poorer. He *created* billions of dollars of value by producing products that fueled the prosperity of his customers, suppliers and software makers and that played a pivotal role in the Internet revolution. His $50 billion gain is puny in comparison. However great the fortunes earned by the most successful creators, they represent but a fraction of the total value they create.

This point is more fully apparent when you realize that every dollar earned by these billionaires came from the voluntary consent of other people. Why did so many people willingly hand over so much money? Because what they got in return was even *more* valuable. This is the key to understanding how inequality arises under freedom—and why it should.

In 1996, J. K. Rowling's net worth hovered somewhere in the neighborhood of nothing. She grew rich through a massive number of voluntary transactions. Because millions of individuals chose to pay $20 for a copy of one of her books, inequality increased: her income and wealth rose, her fans' incomes didn't budge and their wealth fell slightly. But the net result was that everyone involved in these transactions was *better off*. The readers valued the book more than the $20; Rowling (and her publisher) valued the $20 more than that copy of the book. They were win/win transactions, and the totality of those voluntary, win/win transactions meant that Rowling joined the ranks of the top 0.1 percent of earners. Inequality increased, and the world was a better place as a result.[3]

If the hallmark of deserved rewards is that they emerge from voluntary, win/win transactions, then the hallmark of undeserved gains is that the relationship is involuntary and win/lose. Someone gains at someone else's expense. There is no question that there are a lot of people who have achieved undeserved gains today. But how do we identify them, and what should we do about it? On these questions, we'll see that the inequality critics get it wrong. Much of what they regard as exploitation is in fact productive achievement—and their solutions are actually unfair.

MERIT VS. PRIVILEGE

The first steam ship to run through the New York harbor was launched by Robert Fulton in 1807. Fulton went on to secure a guarantee from the New York legislature that no one else would have the liberty to run steamboats through New York waters for thirty years.

But ten years later, Fulton's monopoly was challenged by twenty-three-year-old Cornelius Vanderbilt. Working for New Jersey steamboat man Thomas Gibbons, Vanderbilt began running passengers from Elizabeth, New Jersey, to New York City, his ship flying a flag declaring "New Jersey must be free." New York authorities tried to capture Vanderbilt, but he dodged their efforts for sixty days, to the widespread support of the passengers benefiting from Vanderbilt's lower fares. According to author Andrew Bernstein, Vanderbilt "hid near the gangplank, then scurried off when police officers boarded so their papers could not be served. He constructed a secret closet in which to hide, so when law officers boarded him in the bay they found only a young woman steering the boat, whom they questioned to the taunts and derision of other passengers."[4]

Ultimately, the case went to court, and in 1824's *Gibbons v. Ogden*, the U.S. Supreme Court struck down Fulton's monopoly. The results were tremendous. "On the Ohio River," writes historian Burton Folsom, "steamboat traffic doubled in the first year after *Gibbons v. Ogden* and quadrupled after the second year." Innovation in the shipping industry skyrocketed, as competing shippers started using new, lighter, and cheaper boilers, and less costly fuel. According to Folsom:

> The real value of removing the Fulton monopoly was that the cost of steamboating dropped. Passenger traffic, for example, from New York City to Albany immediately dropped from seven to three dollars after *Gibbons v. Ogden*. Fulton's group couldn't meet the new rates and soon went bankrupt. Gibbons and Vanderbilt, meanwhile, adopted the new technology, cut their costs, and earned $40,000 profit each year during the late 1820s.[5]

Vanderbilt and Fulton symbolize two different routes to wealth: merit and privilege.[6] In her 1963 article "The Money-Making Personality," Ayn Rand labels those who grow rich through merit "Money-Makers," and those who grow rich through privilege "Money-Appropriators."

> The Money-*Maker* is the discoverer who translates his discovery into material goods. In an industrial society with a complex division of labor, it may be one man or a partnership of two: the scientist who discovers new knowledge and the *entrepreneur*—the businessman— who discovers how to use that knowledge, how to organize material resources and human labor into an enterprise producing marketable goods.
>
> The Money-*Appropriator* is an entirely different type of man. He is essentially non-creative—and his basic goal is to acquire an unearned share of the wealth created by others. He seeks to get rich, not by conquering nature, but by manipulating men, not by intellectual effort, but by social maneuvering. He does not produce, he redistributes: he merely switches the wealth already in existence from the pockets of its owners to his own.
>
> The Money-Appropriator may become a politician—or a businessman who "cuts corners"—or that destructive product of a "mixed economy": the businessman who grows rich by means of government favors, such as special privileges, subsidies, franchises; that is, grows rich by means of *legalized force*.[7]

It is common nowadays to refer to anyone with wealth or opportunities as "privileged." Loving parents don't pass on opportunities to their children, they bestow privileges. A self-made businessman who rose from rags to riches isn't a model of achievement—he's privileged. Using "privilege" in this way means that we don't distinguish between children who work to make the most of the opportunities their parents give them and entitled brats who expect everything to be handed to them—and it means we don't distinguish between those who achieve something through productive merit and those who get rich through the use of *political power*. In an economic context, the concept of "privilege" should be reserved for those who line their pockets by taking advantage of special favors from the government—what is often called "cronyism."[8]

Today, the opportunities for growing rich through cronyism are legion: there are government-granted monopolies, bailouts, subsidies, loan guarantees, favorable tax treatment, tariffs, regulations that favor some companies or harm competitors, and much more.[9] All of these special favors are win/lose. Government-granted monopolies mean higher prices and fewer choices for buyers, and a lack of opportunity for competitors; bailouts mean that taxpayers are forced to save a company that is going under, and competitors are denied the opportunity to take advantage of that failure; subsidies mean that the government takes money from some people in order to give it away to favored businesses, putting competitors at an unfair disadvantage; and so on.

An example of this form of privilege, for instance, is found in the rise of the Fanjul Family, which built its sugarcane empire through special low-interest loans from the government, and protectionist tariffs that allow the Fanjuls and other U.S. sugar growers to charge twice the world price for sugar, at an annual cost to Americans of $1.9 billion.[10] Agriculture in general receives enormous support from the government, amounting to more than $20 billion a year in direct subsidies alone.[11] But agriculture is just one area in which the government undermines freedom by handing out taxpayer cash. Carmaker Tesla started its electric car business with a $465 million loan from the Energy Department.[12] "Green energy" company Solyndra famously received $535 million from the Energy Department before going bankrupt. Meanwhile, under the leadership of CEO Jeffrey Immelt, General Electric has made government favors the centerpiece of its business strategy. Author Hunter Lewis describes GE as having a "close and indeed symbiotic relationship with government in finance, defense, green energy, television, technology, and export" and notes it is a "primary beneficiary of the [Obama] administration's stimulus bill."[13]

It's important to be clear about what does and doesn't count as cronyism. Many of the things labeled "cronyism" by the inequality critics *aren't*. When businesses lobby the government to *protect* themselves from destructive regulations, for instance, that is not cronyism, any more than paying ransom to a kidnapper represents bribery. In today's world, in which the government holds enormous arbitrary power, businesses are virtually forced to play the lobbying game out of self-defense.

There's no better example of this than the story of Microsoft. In 1997, Microsoft spent just $2 million on lobbying. As former Microsoft employee (and left-leaning journalist) Michael Kinsley reported, "Bill Gates resisted the notion that a software company needed to hire a lot of lobbyists and lawyers. He didn't want anything special from the government, except the freedom to build and sell software. If the government would leave him alone, he would leave the government alone."[14]

But that attitude didn't go over well in Washington, where Microsoft was warned that their "leave us alone" attitude would come back to haunt them.[15] And it did. For the alleged crime of giving away Internet Explorer for free, Gates faced the Justice Department antitrust suit we described in the last chapter, as well as a public scolding by the Senate Judiciary Committee, led by Republican Senator Orrin Hatch, who reportedly complained that "I have given [Microsoft] advice, and they don't pay any attention to it."[16] Gates suddenly faced the possibility that the company he had spent his life building would be taken away from him by the government.

The results? Microsoft increased its Political Action Committee (PAC) spending by a factor of five, contributing $2.3 million to House and Senate candidates in the 2010 elections, and even giving the maximum amount allowable at the time—$10,000—to Orrin Hatch's 2006 and 2012 campaigns. Overall, the company has spent more than $100 million on lobbying efforts since the Hatch hearings.[17] Kinsley sums up the takeaway:

> As the Microsoft example suggests, the Washington culture of influence peddling is not entirely or even primarily the fault of the corporations

that hire the lobbyists and pay the bills. It's a vast protection racket, practiced by politicians and political operatives of both parties. Nice little software company you've got here. Too bad if we have to regulate it, or if big government programs force us to raise its taxes. Your arch-rival just wrote a big check to the Washington Bureaucrats Benevolent Society. Are you sure you wouldn't like to do the same?[18]

One of the evils of today's system is that, in forcing businessmen to lobby in self-protection, it encourages lobbying for special favors and special treatment. As Timothy Carney observes, "[W]hile companies may first come to Washington to play defense, they soon learn how to profit off big government. Today, Microsoft isn't asking to be left alone. The company supported Obama's stimulus, which subsidized computers and also 'net neutrality' regulations, which would protect their current profit model."[19] In many cases, it is hard for a company to know whether it is playing defense or offense. The line is often fuzzy, and if there is a widespread problem of corruption in today's political system, this is perhaps the worst: Money-Makers are led to act as Money-Appropriators without necessarily even realizing it. Microsoft, however, cannot claim that excuse: in 2011, the software giant fully embraced the political game, bringing its *own* antitrust complaint against Google.[20]

The key issue in distinguishing money-making from money-appropriating is this: did a business gain wealth through voluntary exchange, or through the initiation of force? Did it use the power of the government to extract benefits that it could not have achieved on a free market, or is it lobbying the government so that it is free to compete on a free market?

As widespread as cronyism is, we've seen no evidence that it is the dominant cause of rising economic inequality. And even if it were the dominant factor driving up the incomes of "the 1 percent," that fact would not create any justification for further regulating or taxing top earners. The solution to widespread cronyism is to stop cronyism—not to loot every successful person regardless of how he achieved his success. That would be as unfair as responding to Lance Armstrong's doping by confiscating the prize money of every Tour de France winner.

There *is* an inequality problem involved in cronyism, however: cronyism is an example of *political inequality*. It allows a privileged group of people to rob and shackle others using the power of the government. When the critics of inequality object to cronyism, their complaint isn't that people are gaining special favors and unearned payments from the government, but that the *wrong people* are getting the special favors and unearned payments: "the 1 percent" rather than "the 99 percent." That is why, for instance, they object to bank bailouts but not auto bailouts. They don't want to eliminate political privilege—they want to change who gets what privileges.

THE COMPLICATED CASE OF FINANCE

In a public debate with Yaron, economist James Galbraith placed the blame for rising inequality squarely at the feet of the financial industry. "The major driver of increasing income inequality in the U.S., shown in tax records, is the financial sector, or was the financial sector up through the debacle in 2008. That's very clear in the data." (That wasn't clear to inequality hero Thomas Piketty, who claims that "80 percent of the top income groups are not in finance, and the increase in the proportion of high-earning Americans is explained primarily by the skyrocketing pay packages of top managers of large firms in the nonfinancial as well as financial sectors."[21])

Galbraith added that rising fortunes in finance were not the result of rising productivity, but of greed-induced fraud that was allowed to run wild thanks to government neglect. "What happened in the financial sector was a sequence of deregulation in the 1990s under the Democrats, desupervision in the 2000s under the Republicans in which the investigators into financial fraud were systematically withdrawn from the beat and the industry was given very clear signals that loan underwriting would not be supervised or enforced. Fraud became utterly rampant."[22]

Galbraith's views are widely shared. The financial industry is viewed as a place where the rich are getting obscenely richer, not through productive achievement, but through paper-shuffling, fraud, exploitation, and cronyism. This has a small element of truth: because government exercises so much control over the financial industry, there are a lot of opportunities for cronyism and misconduct—and because much of what the industry does is complex and opaque to outsiders, distinguishing between money-making and money-appropriating is hard. But three things are clear: (1) the financial industry is enormously productive and the fortunes earned by genuinely productive financiers are well-deserved; (2) in cases where financiers enrich themselves as the result of government control over the industry, the blame rests mainly on the government, and the solution is to make the industry more free; and (3) to the extent there is actual criminal behavior going on, such as fraud or embezzlement, the solution is not to pile more regulatory burdens on the innocent, but to root out and punish the guilty.

Finance is not merely productive—its contribution is the backbone of economic progress. Try to imagine a world without a financial industry. In such a world, some people would produce more than they consumed in a given period, but they could do nothing with their savings. They would literally have to stuff it under a mattress or lock it in a vault where it would sit idle until they decided to spend it. No financiers, no returns on savings. Say good-bye to your retirement fund.

Now say you wanted to buy a car in such a world. There would be no loans available. Nor could you use a credit card—that is a form of borrowing. You could only buy whatever you could afford to pay cash for. Not to worry though: there wouldn't be any cars to buy. Without the financial industry supplying the enormous amounts of capital required to manufacture automobiles, and the various loans needed to start and run a dealership, there could be no auto industry.

What if you wanted to start a restaurant? Or build an amusement park? Or search for a cure for cancer? Or launch a startup in Silicon Valley? Almost every business depends on access to capital and credit. Even home businesses that people start on the cheap usually depend on outsourcing things such as web-hosting and manufacturing to businesses that depend on the financial industry.

Finance is an enormously complex field, but all of its activities really boil down to three essential functions—lending, investing, and risk mitigation—that are all responsible for directing capital to its most productive uses.

Lending comes in many forms, from bank loans to corporate bonds to commercial paper. Basically it allows people with savings to make loans to people who need money, leaving both parties better off: the people who need extra money are able to get it, and when they pay back the loan with interest, the people who have extra money to lend are able to see their wealth grow.

Investment consists of providing capital in exchange for an ownership stake in productive enterprises, a function carried out by venture capitalists, private equity firms, hedge funds, investment banks, and stockholders, among others. A good idea in the head of an entrepreneur is worthless unless he can marshal the people and resources needed to bring the idea into reality. That's not cheap. Everything that makes up our amazingly high standard of living depends on the men and women who, in the words of economist Luigi Zingales, "match talent with money," putting resources into the hands of the Steve Jobses and Jeff Bezoses of the world.[23] By directing savings to their most valuable uses, financiers provide the capital that makes possible the dizzying array of goods and services that make all of us better off: from computers to cell phones to hotels to airlines. The reason we can hail an Uber from our iPhone in virtually any American city is because venture capitalists have poured hundreds of millions of dollars into the company, allowing it to grow at lightning speed. Investments like these are also win/win transactions. An investment doesn't always pay off, but it's undertaken because both parties believe they'll be better off. Take the stock market, for example. When a company goes public, it allows many individuals to buy ownership shares in the belief that they'll receive returns (through dividends and/or through selling the shares at a higher price in the future), and it allows companies to raise enormous amounts of capital to fund growth, and hopefully earn more money than they would if they remained privately owned.

Risk mitigation involves tools like derivatives, futures contracts, credit default swaps, and any number of other instruments that allow people to guard against unpredictable hazards. The most common form of risk mitigation is insurance. Absent financiers, we would all have to be self-insured, covering unexpected costs using our own savings. Insurance allows us to pay a fixed cost up front in order to shield ourselves from unknown and potentially catastrophic costs in the future. The insurer, meanwhile, is betting on its ability to assess risk accurately enough so that it takes in more money from fees (and from investment returns on those fees) than it pays out in claims. Both sides gain.

All of these transactions involve *judgment* and *risk*. Although inequality critics such as Piketty often imply that the rich automatically become richer whenever they invest their money, this simply is not true. The reason why successful financiers earn so much is because the value they generate is enormous, and because there are very few people with the skills to generate that value over any significant span of time.

None of this is to deny that there are plenty of examples of unproductive, bad, or even criminal behavior in the financial world. By itself, that is not proof the industry is corrupt. The fact that an industry is fundamentally moral and productive does not mean that everyone in the industry is moral and productive.

But the financial industry is dominated by government, and this makes things much, much worse. In a free market, in which everyone's rights are protected, the fact that economic relationships are voluntary means it is impossible to profit without creating value for other people, especially over the long run. If you're not creating value, or you're creating less value than your income warrants, or you're acting recklessly, the people you're dealing with have an incentive to discover and correct that fact. (If you're engaged in outright fraud, embezzlement, or some other crime, it's the government's job to stop and punish you.) But government intervention interferes with this process in countless ways, and so today there is a real question as to the extent we can say financiers deserve their incomes.

Take just one of many examples of government interference: cronyism in the finance industry. When the government creates regulations and makes decisions that help some people and hurt others, it's inevitable that people are going to try to influence the government—some in self-protection, some in the desire for the unearned, some from mixed motives. When it comes to the financial industry, that scramble for influence is magnified, both because government is *so* involved and because the stakes are *so* high. It is hardly surprising that the most regulated industry in America also spends the most on lobbying.[24]

Perhaps the most blatant form of cronyism over the last few decades is the government's semi-official policy that certain financial institutions are "too big to fail," which played a central role in the Great Recession. Economists continue to debate exactly what went wrong with the housing boom and bust. But one thing that is very clear is that many people in the financial industry engaged in incredibly risky behavior—risks that allowed them to make huge profits on the upside, but the downside of which harmed the rest of us to a far greater degree than it did them. What's crucial to understand is that this was a situation created by government intervention.

In a free market, risk carries both a potential upside (greater returns) and a potential downside (greater losses). Debt holders are quick to put on the brakes when a company starts taking on unmanageable risk. But many financial institutions in the lead-up to 2008 were leveraged at 30:1 or more—ratios that were far beyond what we see in other industries. What happened? A large part of the answer is that the government had spent two decades protecting large financial institutions from failure, repeatedly bailing out companies and protecting creditors from losses. The message was clear: "Don't worry about lending to highly leveraged banks—we won't let them fail." This situation effectively created a huge subsidy for the finance sector, enabling it to assume risks far beyond what would have been possible without the government's implicit guarantee.[25] As economist Russ Roberts notes, "Capitalism is a profit and loss system. The profits encourage risk taking. The losses encourage prudence. When taxpayers absorb the losses, the distorted result is reckless and imprudent risk taking."[26]

The bottom line is that the large sums earned by financiers *in a free market* are totally deserved. They are the insignia of enormous productivity. But that is not fully true today. Given government's influence, it is impossible to fully distinguish between productive actions and profits earned through government distortions. It is wrong to give a blanket condemnation of the industry *or* a blanket dispensation. What we can say is that, despite all the burdens, the finance industry is overall incredibly productive: from the venture capitalists who keep spurring the growth of new tech startups to the hedge funds who help their clients grow their wealth in uncertain times to the speculators who allow farmers and other businessmen to protect themselves from volatile prices, the extent to which our economy remains dynamic is in significant part the finance industry's achievement. And if we want the industry's income to reflect its productive contribution, and *only* its productive contribution, then we need to *roll back* government's distortionary influence. Not wage war on inequality.

THE TRUTH ABOUT CEO PAY

CEOs matter. The wrong CEO can sink a company, the right CEO can raise a company to great heights, and even the marginal difference made by the typical CEO can be more than enough to justify an extraordinary pay package. In a column for the *Atlantic*, Manhattan Institute senior fellow James Manzi illustrates this with a look at Smith International, the 250th company on the 2009 Fortune 500 list. Manzi notes that given Smith International's $1.6 billion in operating income, even a small shift can have a large impact: a "1% swing in $1.6 billion is $16 million." Observing that the median Fortune 500 CEO in 2009 received about $6 million in total annual compensation, Manzi goes on to conclude that

> . . . as a shareholder of Smith International going into the market to hire a CEO, the question I would ask myself if presented with the choice of paying $6 million per year or, say, doubling this to $12 million per year, is not "Will the CEO I get for $12 million fundamentally transform my business?" or whatever; instead, I'd rationally ask myself, "Can the $12 million dollar CEO drive about 0.6% more operating profit than the person I would hire at $6 million?"[27]

CEO pay is, on average, far higher than it was forty years ago (although it is lower today than it was a decade ago).[28] But is this increase in pay deserved? Is it a product of rising productivity among top business executives? Not according to the critics of inequality. Not only do they argue that executive compensation is unjustifiably high—they often claim that undeserved pay for top executives is the basic *driver* of rising inequality since the 1980s. As Thomas Piketty argues, "[T]he vast majority . . . of the top 0.1 percent of the income hierarchy in 2000–2010 consists of top managers. . . . [T]he increase in the proportion of high-earning Americans is explained primarily by the skyrocketing pay packages of top managers of large firms . . ."[29]

The main question we have to ask ourselves when thinking about CEO pay is: "Who has the right to decide what constitutes fair pay in this matter?" And the only defensible answer is: the people cutting the check, i.e., the company's owners. Any shareholder who judges a CEO's pay is too high is free to sell his share of the company's stock, or to try to influence the board's compensation decisions. Anyone who is *not* an owner is free to use his right to free speech to denounce a company's compensation decisions, or to use his freedom of contract to boycott the company.

What the inequality critics want to do is *impose* their own views of what constitutes fair pay on the owners and executives by physical compulsion. They—not a shareholder acting with his own money—are the ones who should have the ability and the right to decide what pay is fair. "It turns out that these shareholders, who are wonderfully thoughtful and collectively incisive, become quite stupid when it comes to paying the boss, the guy who works for them," then congressman Barney Frank said in 2007.[30]

Such condescending remarks ignore that crafting a compensation package that will attract, retain, and motivate the best CEO is complicated. Companies have to weigh thousands of facts and make many subtle judgments in order to assess what a CEO is worth. What should be the mix between base salary and incentive pay? What kind of incentives should be offered—stock options, restricted stock options, stock appreciation rights? How should those incentives be structured—over what time frame and using which metrics? And what about a severance plan? What kind of plan will be necessary to attract the best candidate? And on and on. The fact that there are people who make their living as executive-pay consultants illustrates how challenging the task can be.

Even pay packages that *seem* self-evidently misguided to outsiders can make sense given a richer understanding of the context. As Paul Krugman acknowledges, "[N]either the quality of executives nor the extent to which that quality matters are hard numbers. Assessing the productivity of corporate leaders isn't like measuring how many bricks a worker can lay in an hour. You can't even reliably evaluate managers by looking at the profitability of the companies they run, because profits depend on a lot of factors outside the chief executive's control."[31] Take the case of a CEO who gets a bonus when his company loses money. As Krugman concedes, the profitability of a company is not fully within the control of the CEO, and his bonus could reflect the judgment of the company's owners that, absent the CEO's actions, the company would have lost even more money. The same holds true for so-called golden parachutes. Although outsiders are often outraged when they hear that an ousted CEO has received a large payout, shareholders can justifiably view these contractual commitments to pay an outgoing CEO as cost-*saving* measures: paying to make a bad CEO go away quickly and quietly can protect a business from further costly decisions and from costly litigation.

Inequality critics like Frank cavalierly dismiss these complexities and declare that they can somehow divine that lower pay for executives will not hinder a company, and go on to argue that the only reason CEO pay is so high is because it *doesn't* reflect the judgment of a company's owners about the productive contribution of the CEO. Instead, they claim, CEOs exercise undue influence over boards of directors to the detriment of shareholders. "Who determines how good a CEO is, and how much he has to be paid to keep another company from poaching his entrepreneurial know-how?" asks Krugman. "The answer, of course, is the corporate boards, largely selected by the CEO, hire compensation experts, almost always chosen by the CEO, to determine how much the CEO is worth. It is, shall we say, a situation conducive to overstatement both of the executive's personal qualities and of how much those supposed personal qualities matter for the company's bottom line."[32] Piketty concurs, adding, "It may be excessive to accuse senior executives of having their 'hands in the till,' but the metaphor is probably more apt than Adam Smith's metaphor of the market's 'invisible hand.'"[33]

But the case for these claims is embarrassingly weak. For starters, research by University of Chicago professor Steven N. Kaplan and Stanford University professor Joshua Rauh suggests that the rise in CEO pay is in line with the rise in pay for superstar performers generally: top financiers, lawyers, and professional athletes have all seen their incomes rise more or less in tandem with top executives, which, as Kaplan and Rauh explain, "is less consistent with an argument that the gains to the top 1 percent are rooted in greater managerial power or changes in social norms about what managers should earn.[34]

Another study by Kaplan is equally enlightening. Kaplan finds that, since 2000, both average and median CEO pay for S&P 500 CEOs has declined—hardly what you would expect if CEOs were strong-arming boards without restraint. Perhaps most revealing is the fact that, according to Kaplan, CEOs of privately held companies are generally paid even *more* than execs at publicly held companies. This is a huge deal. The boards of directors at public companies typically own a nominal amount of stock, and are often appointed by the CEOs, which means that it's easier for the interests of owners and managers to diverge. But shares of private companies are generally held by a small group of hands-on owners who have a lot at stake and a lot of influence. No one denies that they have the incentive and the ability not to overpay executives. "[I]f one uses evidence of higher public company executive pay as inherent evidence of capture or managerial power," concludes Kaplan, "one has to explain why private company executives and the other professional groups have had a similar or higher growth in pay where managerial power concerns are largely absent."[35]

But the most compelling fact turns out to be that when offered the chance to vote on CEO pay—so-called say-on-pay provisions that give shareholders a non-binding vote on CEO compensation—shareholders have almost always rejected such measures. (When say on pay was mandated at certain companies by the 2011 Dodd-Frank Act, shareholders endorsed their companies' executive pay policies in over 98 percent of cases.[36]) If shareholders feel powerless, they have a funny way of showing it.

So what has driven pay up for CEOs and other superstar performers? There are a lot of different theories, and while there is strong evidence for some of them, none has been proved definitively (nor are they necessarily mutually exclusive). One theory posits that as firms become larger, the relative value of a CEO who is even a little bit better than his competitors is magnified. Another focuses on the way that globalization has expanded the market for superstar performers: the best performers are providing value to the entire world, not just a specific region or sector.[37]

According to Piketty, any account of CEO pay that appeals to such market forces cannot explain why "the explosion of compensation . . . has affected some countries while sparing others (Japan and continental Europe are thus far much less affected than the United States)."[38] But of course changing market conditions aren't the *only* thing relevant to CEO pay. One crucial factor is how much competition there is for CEO talent. As inequality critics Robert Frank and Philip Cook acknowledge, although "there has been a dramatic increase in the extent to which American firms compete with one another for the services of top executive talent," the situation is different in places like Germany and Japan, "where CEOs are still promoted almost exclusively from within [a given company]." This means that there is "no reason to pay the most talented senior officers what they [are] worth, because they . . . have no place else to go."[39] In other words, Frank and Cook are arguing that there *is* a cultural element to CEO pay, but it's actually the reverse of what critics like Krugman and Piketty claim: the U.S. doesn't pay CEOs *more* than they are worth—other countries pay them *less* than they would be worth if there was competition for their talents.

Whatever the truth, there is simply no credible evidence for the thesis that CEO pay has risen because of corporate governance failures (which is not to say that such failures never happen). And it turns out, the inequality critics never really try to offer evidence for this thesis. Instead, they claim that the academic literature can't fully explain CEO pay trends in terms of market forces and then go on to treat the corporate governance hypothesis as the *default* explanation for this gap. Piketty, for instance, argues that:

> The most convincing proof of the failure of corporate governance and of the absence of a rational productivity justification for extremely high executive pay is that when we collect data about individual firms . . . it is very difficult to explain the observed variations in terms of firm performance. If we look at various performance indicators, such as sales growth, profits, and so on, we can break down the observed variance as a sum of other variances: variance due to causes external to the firm (such as the general state of the economy, raw material price shocks, variations in the exchange rate, average performance of other firms in the same sector, etc.) plus other "nonexternal" variances. Only the latter can be significantly affected by the decisions of the firm's managers. If executive pay were determined by marginal productivity, one would expect its variance to have little to do with external variances and to depend solely or primarily on nonexternal variances. In fact, we observe just the opposite: it is when sales and profits increase for external reasons that executive pay rises most rapidly.[40]

Some of the problems with Piketty's claims are fairly technical. But the most glaring error is treating the fact that "it is very difficult to explain the observed variations in terms of firm performance" as evidence for "the failure of corporate governance." There are countless other explanations, which Piketty doesn't even acknowledge. It could be that Piketty's study was simply poorly designed. (In our view, trying to tease out "marginal productivity" from messy empirical data is a dubious exercise.) It could be that Piketty's interpretation is not the only one consistent with the data. As Jim Manzi points out, "it may be that when times are booming in an industry, it's worth more to keep the CEO on board. In fact, there [are] multiple papers that provide evidence for exactly this effect" that are "as strong (or really, as weak) as Piketty's."[41] It could be that *government intervention* has partially severed the link between CEO pay and performance. To take just one example, laws and regulations that make hostile corporate takeovers more difficult insulate CEOs from the competitive forces that tend to align pay and marginal productivity.[42] It could be a lot of things, but what's for sure is that Piketty never presents evidence *for* his preferred explanation. He presumes the onus is on others to prove an alternative account.

None of this is to deny that some CEOs get paid more than they're worth. Again, determining what a CEO is worth to a company is really, really hard, and it's always possible to make mistakes. A company can hire an incompetent CEO, or structure a pay package that rewards executives for short-term profits at the expense of the company's long-term welfare. But a company suffers from such mistakes: shareholders earn less, managers need to be fired, and competitors gain market share. In a free society, the right to make decisions about pay rests with the owners—owners who bear the consequences of those decisions and therefore have every incentive to make good decisions. Even if it were true that top incomes were being increased beyond an amount that was justified by executive productivity as the result of corporate governance failures, this would be a problem a free market could and (eventually) would solve.

But the inequality critics have absolutely no basis for their confident assertions that rising pay at the top *is* being fueled by CEOs finding a way to get paid more than they're worth. The critics have not been convinced by the evidence. Rather, they show a clear track record of cherry-picking studies that are consistent with their view that high CEO pay is inherently bad because it promotes inequality.

What the inequality critics object to is not that CEOs are getting paid more than they're worth—what they object to is high pay as such. Barney

Frank admitted as much when he threatened to "do something more" if say-on-pay legislation didn't sufficiently reduce CEO compensation.[43] In a discussion of the pay package received by Home Depot CEO Robert Nardelli, another critic of high CEO pay confessed that "it's hard to believe that those leading the charge against his pay package . . . weren't upset mainly by the fact that Nardelli had a $200 million pay package in the first place—no matter how he had performed."[44] And in his first presidential campaign, Barack Obama declared, "We have a [moral] deficit when CEOs are making more in ten minutes than some workers make in ten months."[45] But if CEOs are *producing* more wealth in ten minutes than some workers produce in ten months, how is that a moral problem?

Ultimately, the critics cannot accept that a CEO could be worth so much money—they simply do not believe that some people *do* produce more in ten minutes than others produce in ten months. "[L]et me tell you," writes journalist Geoffrey James, "your average CEO is of, well . . . average intelligence. At best. And that's OK because, frankly, the job just ain't all that difficult."[46] Left-wing radio host Thom Hartmann wonders, "[W]hat part of being a CEO could be so difficult—so impossible for mere mortals—that there are only a few hundred individuals in the United States capable of performing it?"[47]

One answer to that question comes from none other than leading inequality critic Robert Reich. In a 2007 *Wall Street Journal* column, Reich admitted that, "There's an economic case for the stratospheric level of CEO pay," namely the fact that "CEO pay has risen astronomically over [the last 40 years], but so have investor returns."

As Reich explains, the job of modern CEOs is infinitely more competitive and demanding than that of past executives. Only a handful of executives have been able to rise to the challenge, and those who have are getting paid accordingly. "The proof is in the numbers. Between 1980 and 2003, the average CEO pay in America's 500 largest companies rose sixfold, adjusted for inflation." Meanwhile, he notes, "The average value of those 500 companies also rose by a factor of six, adjusted for inflation."

But, Reich adds, "This economic explanation for sky-high CEO pay does not justify it socially or morally. It only means that investors think CEOs are worth it."[48] Of course it doesn't justify it—not if you equate justice with economic equality.

THE QUESTION OF INHERITANCE

In recent years, discussions of economic inequality have focused mainly on *income* inequality. But that's started to change with Thomas Piketty's *Capital in the Twenty-First Century*, which argues that *wealth* inequality is our biggest long-term problem. In Piketty's view, there are certain inherent laws of capitalism that cause wealth to accumulate in the hands of unproductive heirs rather than value-creating entrepreneurs—unless, that is, we adopt his program of "confiscatory tax rates" and a global wealth tax.

Piketty's basic argument, he tells us, comes down to a simple equation: $r > g$, where r stands for the rate of return on capital and g stands for the growth of the economy. If, argues Piketty, "the rate of return on capital remains significantly above the growth rate for an extended period of time (which is more likely when the growth rate is low, though not automatic), then the risk of divergence in the distribution of wealth is very high." He goes on to elaborate on the implications:

> [I]t logically follows that inherited wealth grows faster than output and income. People with inherited wealth need save only a portion of their income from capital to see that capital grow more quickly than the economy as a whole. Under such conditions, it is almost inevitable that inherited wealth will dominate wealth amassed from a lifetime's labor by a wide margin, and the concentration of capital will attain extremely high levels—levels potentially incompatible with the meritocratic values and principles of social justice fundamental to modern democratic societies.[49]

Although most economists grant that if r remained greater than g "for an extended period of time," inequality would grow—all else being equal—they also argue that there are very good reasons to doubt such a scenario, above all because other forces are likely to have a countervailing effect on inequality trends.

As economist Deirdre McCloskey explains, Piketty's argument "is conclusive, so long as its factual assumptions are true: namely, only rich people have capital; human capital doesn't exist; the rich reinvest their return; they never lose it to sloth or someone else's creative destruction;

[and] inheritance is the main mechanism, not a creativity that raises g for the rest of us just when it results in an r shared by us all."[50]

These and numerous other assumptions made by Piketty have been challenged by economists—including several critics of economic inequality. For example, Lawrence Summers, former director of the National Economic Council under President Obama, argues:

> This rather fatalistic and certainly dismal view of capitalism can be challenged on two levels. It presumes, first, that the return to capital diminishes slowly, if at all, as wealth is accumulated and, second, that the returns to wealth are all reinvested. Whatever may have been the case historically, neither of these premises is likely correct as a guide to thinking about the American economy today.[51]

Regarding the first problem, Summers points out, "Economists universally believe in the law of diminishing returns. As capital accumulates, the incremental return on an additional unit of capital declines." The question, Summers says, is how much the return to an additional unit of capital declines, relative to a unit of labor; all of the economic literature, he claims, suggests that the return to capital will decline by a larger amount than is necessary for Piketty's thesis to hold true.[52]

On the reinvestment point, Summers notes:

> A brief look at the *Forbes* 400 list also provides only limited support for Piketty's ideas that fortunes are patiently accumulated through reinvestment. When *Forbes* compared its list of the wealthiest Americans in 1982 and 2012, it found that less than one tenth of the 1982 list was still on the list in 2012, despite the fact that a significant majority of members of the 1982 list would have qualified for the 2012 list if they had accumulated wealth at a real rate of even 4 percent a year. They did not, given pressures to spend, donate, or misinvest their wealth. In a similar vein, the data also indicate, contra Piketty, that the share of the *Forbes* 400 who inherited their wealth is in sharp decline.[53]

Other scholars have observed that, although Piketty presents hundreds of pages of data, the actual evidence for his theory is strikingly thin. Daron Acemoglu, an economist at Massachusetts Institute of Technology, and

James A. Robinson, a professor of government at Harvard, point out that "Piketty does not engage in hypothesis testing, statistical analysis of causation or even correlation. Even when there are arguments about inequality increasing because r exceeds g, this is not supported by standard econometric or even correlational work. In fact . . . the evidence that inequality is strongly linked to r—g does not seem to jump out from the data—to say the least."[54] (And as we noted in chapter 2, the data themselves should not be treated as gospel.)

Piketty's prediction is not based on any "laws" of capitalism or economics—it is pure speculation.[55] But even assuming his prediction comes true, what's the problem? On this point, Piketty is vague, but basically he says that economic inequality can only be tolerated when there is a strong "social justification" for it, and while he grants that there might be a good reason for society to "allow" an entrepreneur to make a fortune (so long as the government taxes most of it away), he can see no social justification for allowing an entrepreneur's children to inherit a fortune, and worries that these "undeserving" heirs will somehow corrupt the political system. A clearer statement of this view comes from economist James Galbraith, in his debate over inequality with Yaron.

> There are social benefits to having small numbers of big prizes and to having many more people think they have a shot at them than is actually the case. That is a formula that we have used very successfully in this country to promote technological change. Where does the problem come in? The problem plainly comes in with inheritance, with the next generation, with dynasty, with plutocracy, with oligarchy, the curse of the favored sons. I don't object to having Mitt Romney but five more Romney's coming down the pike, that's to me a little bit too much. What is the cure? The cure is an established institution in these United States. It's the estate tax which has and could still incentivize the transfer of wealth from the living, well, for example, to this university creating much greater equality than existed before. It's, to my mind, a great solution. It's the American way.[56]

Notice that both Piketty and Galbraith are invoking a collectivist framework that assumes that wealth belongs to society, and that individuals must prove, not that they gained their wealth honestly, but that their having it provides "social benefits." But even those who agree with the individualist premise that wealth is created by individuals and rightfully belongs to those individuals are often suspicious of inherited wealth. It seems unfair for people to benefit from a fortune they haven't earned.

But the earned doesn't exhaust what a person has a right to. If a person enters a sweepstakes and wins a car, he hasn't earned it in the sense that he earns his paycheck. But he gained it through a perfectly fair process, and it would be just as wrong for a thief to steal his car as it would be to steal yours. The salient point is that the car offered in the sweepstakes *was earned*—it was earned by whoever is giving the prize. They have every right to dispose of their property as they see fit. The same goes double for inheritances. It is the parents who earned the wealth, and to prevent them from turning it over to an heir is a monstrous violation of their rights. If parents judge that their child merits inheriting their money after their death, denying them the freedom to pass on their wealth is no different from denying them the freedom to pay for their child's education while they're alive.

And when it comes to the heir, there is an important sense in which his bequest *does* have to be earned. Given the dynamism of a free society, an heir who inherits a business empire will have to be able to improve upon it and outcompete innovative rivals, or else risk going broke. Even an heir who decides to live off of investments has to exercise judgment about how to invest his money. That, too, is a productive achievement, which helps launch new ventures, expand old ones, create new jobs, and fund new research. An inherited fortune, as much as one created from scratch, provides the fuel for economic progress.

Inheritance taxes, on the other hand, undermine investment and production. They are a tax on savings. To the entrepreneur who earns a fortune they are like a giant sign that says, "Don't save. Spend, spend, spend!" There is nothing wrong with enjoying the fruits of your labor, but by depriving successful individuals of the freedom to pass on their wealth to their heirs, it encourages them to consume their fortune even though they might prefer to invest it. If inheritance taxes are high, it leads people to ask: "Why shouldn't I buy that extra yacht or that private plane or that extra vacation home? After all, I can't take my money with me, and I can't pass it on to the people I love." Much of what isn't spent ultimately goes, not into the savings of their heirs, but into the coffers of the government, to be doled out in foreign aid, welfare handouts, sugar subsidies, congressional salaries, and bridges to nowhere. Less savings, less investment, less economic progress. As economist Steven Landsburg concludes, "[Y]ou don't need rich parents to be a victim of the death tax. You don't need to own a family business or family farm. You only need to be someone who works in a factory or shops in a grocery store or gets sick and goes to the hospital."[57]

For those who do own a business, especially a small, family-owned business, it's worse. As Timothy Carney explains:

> [C]onsider your favorite local restaurant for a moment. Perhaps the owner opened it 40 years ago and bought the building after 10 years, renting out the other units to other businesses. Now, his mortgage is completely paid off. The building's value (surely appreciated) plus the value of his equipment could add up to $2 million. When he dies, his son, who has been running the business for the past five years might owe $500,000 in estate taxes. But the business may not generate anything close to that much profit per year. The son will have no choice but to sell his inheritance—the business, the building, or both—in order to pay the taxes for receiving it.[58]

That is what inequality critics like Galbraith consider "the American way."

PUTTING THE PIECES TOGETHER

In this chapter, we've tried to lay out the principles for distinguishing between deserved and undeserved fortunes, and to highlight how hard it is to distinguish them in a mixed economy. It is only to the extent that the government protects rights, and ensures that economic relationships are voluntary, that we see an alignment of merit and money.

Although the inequality critics often claim to object only to *undeserved* success, it is revealing that their solutions don't distinguish between deserved and undeserved incomes. While complaining of cronyism, they advocate raising taxes on every high earner. While complaining of CEOs getting paid more than their performance warrants, they say that *no* company's CEO should be paid more than twenty or fifty times what its lowest-paid workers make. While complaining of unworthy heirs, they want to limit inheritances for worthy heirs. This apparent inconsistency is the result of a class warfare perspective, in which "the rich" are seen as a monolithic group of powerful exploiters who inevitably rig the system at the expense of the powerless and oppressed "non-rich." On this approach, there's no need to inquire too closely into how a person got his money. The fact that he *has* money tells the inequality critics all they need to know. To the extent they bother to highlight specific crimes (real or alleged), their purpose is not to spot bad apples, but to validate their belief that the whole lot is rancid.

But the class warfare framework is wrong. And it is *obviously* wrong. Although wealthy individuals sometimes get special favors from the government, so does everyone else. What we see today is not a system rigged for the benefit of "the rich," but a mixed economy ruled by pressure group warfare. The sugar industry lobbies for tariffs; the green movement lobbies for subsidies for wind and solar, and to shut down the coal industry; the agriculture industry lobbies for aid to farmers; the beer industry lobbies for regulations that stifle microbrewers; the auto industry lobbies for bailouts; the unions lobby for power over the auto industry; the elderly lobby for ever-larger Social Security and Medicare handouts; left-wing groups lobby for ever-larger handouts for the poor; conservative groups lobby for ever-greater restrictions on abortion and immigration; religious groups lobby to get prayer into schools and Darwin out of schools; and on and on it goes.

One thing we don't see in all of this mess is what the inequality critics tell us we *should* see. They say the system is rigged in favor of the interests of "the rich," and that these interests consist of *less* government regulation and *less* welfare state spending. But as we've seen, the regulatory-welfare state has only grown over the last forty years.

Or consider the issue of taxes. The critics tell us that the primary interest of "the rich" is to keep their tax bills as low as possible. Now, it's true that top marginal rates are lower than they were forty or fifty years ago, but that's far from the whole story. Wealthy Americans bear the vast, vast majority of the income tax burden. In 2012, the top 1 percent of earners paid 38.1 percent of federal income taxes—even though they earned only 21.9 percent of total income. As we see in Figure 6.1, their contribution alone amounted to

3.32 percent more in federal income taxes than the entire bottom 90 percent combined—a proportion that has been growing over the very time that their incomes (and supposedly their political influence) have been rising.[59] Meanwhile, the overall effective income tax rate of the 1 percent was 23 percent—for the bottom half of income earners, the effective tax rate was only 3 percent.[60] (Factoring in payroll taxes, as well as state and local taxes, makes this picture less dramatic, but does not change the bottom line.)

What about the claims of people like Warren Buffett, who say that the very rich pay less in taxes than middle-class Americans? According to economist Stephen Moore, "Many very rich people get their income from capital gains and dividends, which are taxed at a lower rate—because the money is already taxed at the corporate level at 35 percent. The real capital gains tax when taking into account corporate taxes, is closer to 44 percent. Mr. Buffett ignores the corporate tax when he says he pays less than his secretary."[61] America's corporate income tax, by the way, is among the highest in the world (the highest if you include state corporate income taxes). America's federal corporate income tax is 35 percent, compared to 34.4 percent in France, 26.1 percent in Canada, and 22 percent in Sweden.[62]

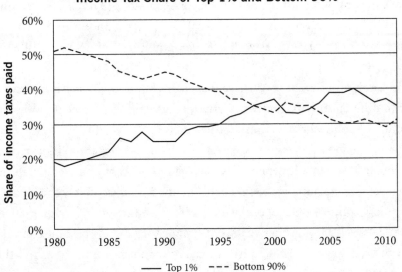

Figure 6.1
Income Tax Share of Top 1% and Bottom 90%

——— Top 1%   – – – Bottom 90%

Of course, even if the wealthy were paying low taxes, that would not amount to a special favor from government. But the fact that they *aren't* paying low taxes, but are carrying the vast bulk of the tax burden, has to make you wonder: if rich Americans wield so much power and aren't afraid to use it to their advantage, then why are they doing such a lousy job of it?

What's happening in America today is simply not consistent with the narrative that the 1 percent are holding down the 99 percent—but it *is* consistent with our story, that the government is using its arbitrary coercive power to benefit any pressure group that presents itself as the face of "the public good," and to punish any group that can't.

The deeper problem with the class warfare perspective is that its basic assumption is wrong: "the rich" do not exist. Obviously there are people who are rich. But the concept of "*the* rich" means something more than that. Terms such as "the rich" and "the 1 percent" are not neutral descriptions of an individual's income or wealth. They assume that there are such things as economic classes, which are made up of essentially similar people with a coherent set of interests—interests that clash with those of other economic classes.

But what did a visionary CEO like Steve Jobs have in common with a con man like Bernie Madoff besides the fact that both had a lot of money? What do the right-leaning Koch brothers have in common with the left-leaning George Soros? What does an innovator like Amazon's Jeff Bezos have in common with the political favor-seeking CEO of GE, Jeffrey Immelt? How do the interests of a young, ambitious, and poor Sam Walton clash with the interests of an older, ambitious, and successful Sam Walton?

The highest-earning Americans are a diverse group of men and women with different beliefs, motives, virtues, faults, and achievements. When it comes to political convictions, for instance, a 2011 Gallup poll found that among the top 1 percent of income earners, only 33 percent self-identify as Republicans, while Independents make up 41 percent and Democrats 26 percent. (These numbers were roughly in line with the country as a whole.) Similarly, only 39 percent of the top 1 percent self-identify as conservative, while 41 percent consider themselves moderate, and 20 percent consider themselves liberal. (These too were basically in sync with the rest of the country.)[63]

If we examine spending on elections, we find even less support for the notion that "the rich" have a shared agenda. Looking at PAC spending, Republicans generally have a slight advantage: in the 2014 election, $245.4 million went to Republicans and $193.9 million to Democrats. However, in the previous non-presidential election cycle, Democrats dominated, receiving $245.3 million from PACs as opposed to Republicans, who received only $185.1 million.[64] The same trend holds for Super PAC spending. In the 2014 election, the top ten Super PACs were about evenly split: five supported Democrats, four supported Republicans, and one (the National Association of Realtors) supported both (with about twice as much money going toward Republican candidates).[65] In total, conservative Super PACs spent $152.9 million in 2014, while liberal Super PACs spent $176.8 million.[66]

None of this should come as a shock. Wealthy Americans—like all Americans—not only support political policies for any number of reasons besides economic self-interest, such as moral and political conviction, but they also do not always agree on what their economic interests are. The free market appeals to innovators, creators, and entrepreneurs who want to match their best against the best that their competitors have to offer, and win or lose according to the free, voluntary decisions of buyers. But some businessmen fear competition, and are eager to use the government to protect themselves from newcomers. Established businesses regularly support increased taxes and regulations, which they can afford, but which smaller rivals often cannot. And, of course, not every wealthy person is a businessman. Some are artists, doctors, or lawyers. Others are unproductive heirs, university administrators, or *New York Times* columnists. Many of these people see the free market as a threat to their position (and their values).

For these reasons, we reject the very concept of "the rich" (and "the poor," for that matter). That label is worse than useless because it leads us to think of wealthy people, not as individuals, but as interchangeable members of a "class," when in fact they have nothing in common other than a sizeable bank balance. Above all, it prevents us from distinguishing those who earn what they get from those who take what others earn. If we care about fairness, no distinction could be more important.

Yes, there is a threat to the American Dream today. But it's not that "the rich" are rigging the system. The threat is that we've forgotten—or have never fully learned—what the American Dream is and what it depends on.

What's great—*uniquely* great—about America is its founding ideal: that no matter where we start out, each of us is free to decide what we want out of life, to move toward that vision without interference from other people, and to rise as high as our ability and ambition will take us. Some of us will create new technologies, some of us will create new industries, some of us will make world-changing discoveries—and some of us will find something we're passionate about and be the best we can be, however modest our achievements. All the while, we will each benefit from living in a society where human ability is unrestricted—and where, as a result, human progress is unlimited.

That is the American Dream. *That* is what made America the land of opportunity. But, on the whole, we've been moving further and further away from that ideal for decades. The game is becoming rigged—not because of economic inequality, but because of political inequality: our equal rights are no longer being equally protected. Regulators, politicians, and their cronies have the power to use government to impose their will on others, to put up roadblocks to success, and to line their pockets with other people's money.

The economic inequality critics have crafted a narrative that completely reverses this story. In their telling, opportunity doesn't require reviving freedom, but dramatically increasing government control over our wealth and our lives. It doesn't consist of the liberty to make a go at success, but of the "security" of guaranteed handouts. It doesn't mean the fairness of getting what you deserve according to what you earn, but of having your needs satisfied regardless of what you earn (and of not being free to earn too much more than others). What made America great, in their view—to the extent they grant that it ever was great—was not freedom, but the post–New Deal regulatory-welfare state. The danger they see today is the alleged breakdown of that regulatory-welfare state in the name of laissez-faire capitalism. The key to saving the American Dream, they conclude, is to move rapidly in the direction of a European social welfare state.

We have seen that every element of this narrative is false—in many cases it is wildly false, based on inexcusable errors, fallacies, and even deceptions. The inequality critics attempt to prove we are stagnating—by playing statistical games that evade the fact that as inequality has increased, so has our standard of living. They have told us that prosperity is possible—not by liberating production but by intensifying redistribution. They have told us that opportunity is a myth—because we are too free. They have told us that we're being exploited by the economic power of "the rich"—and that the solution is to give more arbitrary political power to the state. They have told us that they want to help "the poor"—by teaching them to think of themselves as helpless victims, robbing them of the chance to work, and lulling them into dependency through handouts. They have blamed inequality for everything, and credited freedom and human ability with nothing—except for all of the evils and ills supposedly unleashed by inequality.

The inequality alarmists, as we might call them, are not some fringe group. They include many of our leading politicians, journalists, and intellectuals. How could they have gotten things so wrong? If we want to revive the American Dream, it is crucial that we answer that question—and confront the possibility that reviving the American Dream is not, in fact, their goal.

CHAPTER SEVEN

UNDERSTANDING THE CAMPAIGN AGAINST INEQUALITY

POWER

A few years back, Don met and got to know two brothers, Jack and Gus (not their real names). They're close in age and grew up under the same roof, in a rural midwestern town. But that's about where the similarities end.

Early on, Jack decided that he was unhappy living in a small town and wanted something better for his life: to make a lot of money, do work that he enjoyed, and be able to live wherever he wanted to live. Although he was no stranger to a good party, he took his schoolwork seriously and graduated with solid grades. His parents couldn't afford to send him to college, so he spent a few years in community college, and then went on to a prominent university to finish his degree at his own expense. After school, and after a long and difficult job search, he devoted himself almost totally to his work, putting in long hours, exceeding his employer's expectations, expanding his capabilities, and saving and investing a sizeable part of the money he earned. Today, he's far from a millionaire, but by any standard he is incredibly successful.

Gus was intelligent, and got decent grades in high school, but he wasn't very motivated and never made a plan for his life. He went to college for a few years, then dropped out and went to work in the fast-food industry. He daydreamed of success, and would devour books on how to get rich fast, but he didn't want to work for it. He wanted easy money. Any money he did get his hands on didn't last long, though, and he eventually ended up buried in credit card debt.

So here's the question: what would it take to equalize Jack and Gus? You might, for instance, seize some of Jack's money and give it to Gus. You might make Jack pay for Gus to go to college (assuming Gus would bother to finish). You might cap Jack's pay, or make Jack hire Gus as a paid consultant, or simply bash Jack over the head so that he could no longer work. In one way or another, you'd have to prop up Gus with unearned gifts and impose burdens and punishments on Jack by *force*.

Economic inequality, as we've seen, is an inevitable by-product of freedom. When people are free to make their own decisions and chart their own course, some people do well, some people do incredibly well, and others fail miserably. If economic inequality emerges from the free, voluntary choices of individuals, then the only way to fight economic inequality is to use force to override the free, voluntary choices of individuals.

Consider some of the proposals the inequality alarmists offer to fight economic inequality. Minimum wage hikes? This means *forcing* employers to pay wages higher than they would if left free (and forcibly preventing people from working if no one will pay them the minimum wage). A maximum wage for CEOs? This means *forcing* a company's owners to offer an executive less than they think he's worth. Free college? This means *forcing* some people to finance other people's education, instead of using the money they earned to pursue their own goals and aspirations. "Universal health care"? This means *forcing* some people to finance other people's medical care, *forcing* doctors and hospitals into a socialized health care scheme, and *rationing* care to patients. A larger welfare state? This means *forcing* some people to produce without compensation so that others can consume without producing.

Under political equality, no person has a right to rule over another, or to step in and prevent people from dealing with each other on mutually agreeable terms. Fighting economic inequality requires us to jettison political equality, and install a politically privileged class of "elites" who have the power to dispose of other people's time, effort, and wealth by force. To understand the campaign against inequality, the first thing to understand is that the inequality alarmists want to be those privileged elites.

The inequality alarmists are authoritarians, and, like all authoritarians, they desire the power to dictate how other people live. They see themselves as a uniquely compassionate and intellectually gifted elite, entitled to control the rest of society for the alleged good of society. Far from wanting to end political privilege in order to create a society of merit, they believe that their superiority merits bestowing them with unlimited political privilege.

The litmus test of authoritarianism is that it does not seek to *persuade* people, but to override their independent judgment. Authoritarians do not seek to convince you to act as they want: they want your obedience, not your understanding. Typically, authoritarians do not simply come out and say this—not in America, anyway. They do not say that what they want is to be given arbitrary power to control people's choices. Instead, they argue that certain choices are right, appealing to "science" and "experts" and "studies"—but this is not an honest appeal to people's rational judgment. The authoritarian's conclusion is not that you should *choose* to change your ideas or behavior in light of such evidence—it's that the government should *impose* these things by force, regardless of whether you are convinced.

Economist Robert Frank, for example, argues that beyond a certain point, most of our spending is on goods that do not make us healthier or happier. We buy a bigger home, not because we really desire a bigger home, but because we are driven to "keep up with the Joneses." Inequality makes us unhappy because it means we have to work harder and harder to keep up with the Joneses. If those damn Joneses didn't have such a big home, we would be just as happy with a smaller, more affordable one. We wouldn't have to engage in so much wasteful spending. And this means that the government can fight inequality and make everyone happier in the process by bringing the Joneses down.

So, what does Frank conclude? Is he trying to *persuade* us that a lot of our spending is wasteful, and that we would be just as happy if we stopped comparing ourselves to our neighbors and consumed less? No. He concludes that, based on his argument—all of it backed by "science" and "data" and "studies," of course—the government should *force* us to consume less through steeply progressive consumption taxes. What if we disagree with his claims? How can you disagree with Science?[1]

This is what authoritarianism, as practiced by the alarmists, looks like: it *seems* to appeal to persuasion, but its bottom line is that your judgment is irrelevant. The argument amounts to the claim, "We're going to impose our views on individuals regardless of their own conclusions, but don't worry—we're experts and we know what we're doing."

Take another example. Many inequality alarmists claim that employers can increase how much they pay their employees and actually *increase* their profits. They point, for instance, to a successful company like Costco, which pays its workers a rate nearly double that of other big box retailers, and confidently predict that every retailer would prosper if it followed suit. If an increase in worker pay automatically led to greater profits, you would expect to see companies leaping at the chance to improve their bottom line. But rather than allowing companies to be persuaded by their allegedly compelling logic and profit by voluntarily raising wages, the inequality alarmists conclude that their "evidence" justifies imposing an unprecedented 100 percent hike in the minimum wage.[2]

Here's another example. The inequality alarmists claim that they can scientifically prove that CEOs aren't being paid for performance, which means that a company's owners would be better off if they paid CEOs less. So, do they attempt to *persuade* companies to pay their CEOs less? Not a chance. Instead, they assert that it's inherently wrong for a CEO to make 200 times more than the lowest-paid worker at his company. What is the right ratio? That's for *them* to decide.

Or, finally, take Obamacare. Not only does the president's program force individuals to buy health insurance whether they want it or not, it dictates what *kind* of coverage an individual has to buy—as hundreds of thousands of Americans found out when, despite Obama's assurance that "If you like your health-care plan, you'll be able to keep your health-care plan," their plans were canceled because regulators deemed them "inadequate."

All of this reflects a collectivist worldview that holds that individuals are incompetent to support their own lives and make their own decisions, and that their interests—or what they take to be their interests—have to be subordinated to "the common good." Given such a worldview, a privileged elite empowered to override people's independent choices is not simply permissible—it's mandatory.

The biggest obstacle authoritarians face is the independence of the people they want to rule. And this helps us understand why a core part of their platform is to take away that independence by making everyone dependent on the government—especially the middle class. (Obama calls this "middle-class economics.")

In countries that are very poor, it is relatively easy for authoritarians to rise to power, promising gifts to the have-nots in exchange for unquestioning obedience. In affluent societies, where the vast majority are able to live self-supporting lives, it is much harder to tell people what to do. You don't have a lot to offer them that they can't get for themselves. But what if they depend on you for their health care? Or their retirement? Or their children's education? Well, that's exactly what the regulatory-welfare state advocated by the alarmists achieves—and is *intended* to achieve: to make everyone dependent on the government and on the experts who *control* the government. As an example of how this works, consider the case of retirement.

One of the most powerful tools for independence in old age today are 401(k) accounts, in which Americans can set aside part of their pre-tax income, invest it in mutual funds, and reap the rewards of compound interest. If someone sets aside as little as $200 a month for forty years, he can easily end up with half a million dollars or more, securing for himself a standard of living in old age far beyond that offered by Social Security. Are there risks? Sure. But, with prudence, they are negligible over the long run. The biggest risk is that an individual might choose *not* to save and invest his income, something which is entirely in his own control.

What is the attitude of the inequality alarmists to 401(k) accounts? In his book on inequality, journalist Hedrick Smith denounces 401(k)s, bemoaning the fact that their creation meant it was "up to employees to provide for their own retirement savings and to manage their money for long-term security, a task beyond the capability of millions . . ."[3] What is so impossibly hard about saving for one's own retirement? Smith quotes retirement specialist Alicia Munell, who explains that the problem is it requires people to think.

The individual has to make a choice every step along the way. . . . The individual has to decide whether or not to join the plan, how much to contribute, how to allocate those contributions, how to change those allocations over time, decide what to do when they move from one job to another, think what to do about company stock. And then the hardest thing is, what are they going to do when they get to retirement and somebody hands them a check? How do you figure out how to use that money over the span of your retirement?[4]

In order to cure us of this bothersome need to think and choose how to manage our own financial affairs, Smith suggests we might be better off forcing everyone into "one big new U.S. retirement fund run by America's best professional money managers" who would "be picked and overseen by a new Federal Retirement Board."[5] Other alarmists, such as Senator Elizabeth Warren, prefer to solve the "problem" of individual choice by increasing Social Security payments, even though Social Security is already on an unsustainable course, so that we don't have to bother to save so much.[6] Since history shows that, left free, the vast majority of people can and do plan rationally for old age, what could all of this mean except that they want us to be *more* dependent on the government so the government will have *more* control over our lives?[7]

Today, as American Enterprise Institute scholar Nicholas Eberstadt points out, we are witnessing a disturbing trend: in the richest nation in history, nearly half of the population lives in a household that receives at least one government "entitlement," a figure that is growing rapidly thanks mainly to the unprecedented expansion of means-tested welfare programs (Table 7.1).[8] What's critical to understand is that the inequality alarmists do not view this as a *failure* but as an *achievement*. And from their perspective, it is. As collectivists, they believe that we should all "be in it together." Well, when our standard of living is dependent on government rather than our own achievements, we are.

The inequality alarmists would deny that they are authoritarians. They are, they would say, proponents of democracy. But this is a smoke screen. What they mean by democracy is not a constitutional republic in which we elect representatives whose responsibility it is to protect our equal rights. Nor do they even mean democracy in the original, literal sense of unlimited

TABLE 7.1
ENTITLEMENT DEPENDENCE IN AMERICA
1983 VS. 2012

Recipiency Status & Program	3rd Quarter, 1983*	3rd Quarter, 2012*	Difference*
All People	224.3	308.9	84.6
	(100.0)	(100.0)	(–)
Received benefits from at least			
1 program	66.5	152.9	86.4
	(29.6)	(49.5)	(19.9)
Social Security	31.7	51.5	19.8
	(14.1)	(16.7)	(2.6)
Medicare	26.7	48.2	21.5
	(11.9)	(15.6)	(3.7)
Received benefits from at least			
1 means-tested program	42.1	109.3	67.2
	(18.8)	(35.4)	(16.6)
Federal SSI	3.2	20.4	17.2
	(1.4)	(6.6)	(5.2)
Food Stamps	18.7	50.8	32.1
	(8.3)	(16.5)	(8.2)
AFDC	9.3	5.4	–3.9
	(4.2)	(1.8)	(–2.4)
Women, Infants, & Children	2.4	22.7	20.3
	(1.1)	(7.3)	(6.2)
Medicaid	17.5	83.1	65.6
	(7.8)	(26.9)	(19.1)

*The first line of each entry is the number in millions. The second line (in parentheses) is the percentage.

majority rule. What they advocate is a peculiar notion of democracy, which they call "deliberative democracy."

If we want to picture what the alarmists have in mind when they refer to democratic deliberation, we might start by thinking of a giant assembly room. According to the alarmists, if we all enter that room as equal and informed citizens, if we are each given the same amount of time to speak, if we all are committed to arguing in terms of what policies will be for the good of the entire group rather than our own good, and if at the end of that process of deliberation we each get one vote to decide the outcome, the result will be governance aimed at "the common good." According to President Obama's former regulatory czar, Cass Sunstein:

In such a system, politics is not supposed merely to protect preexisting private rights or to reflect the outcomes of interest-group pressures. It is not intended to aggregate existing private preferences, or to produce compromises among various affected groups with self-interested stakes in the outcome. Instead it is designed to have an important deliberative feature, in which new information and perspectives influence social judgments about possible courses of action. Through exposure to such information and perspectives, both collective and individual decisions can be shaped and improved.[9]

Sunstein goes on to add, "[W]e might even define political truth as the outcome of this deliberative process . . ."[10]

Given this setup, imagine some of the ways in which deliberative democracy might break down. What if, for instance, some members get more time to speak than other members? Or they get more votes than other members? Or some wealthy members spend the evening before this assembly wining and dining other members? Suddenly, the results become distorted: they will no longer be aimed at "the common good" but at the private welfare of the rich and powerful few.

Deliberative democracy depends on no one having too much power and influence: a bigger wallet, better connections, a larger platform for speaking to audiences (e.g., a talk radio show). Inequality distorts this kind of democracy by allowing some people (especially "the rich") to pervert the democratic process so that the government works for their "special interests" rather than "the general interest." And so, say the alarmists, it follows that in order to protect democracy, we have to limit (and ideally eliminate) inequality on all fronts.

This is why we say that the alarmists' claim to be in favor of democracy is a smoke screen. Although they tell us that "political truth" is the "outcome of this deliberative process," they are actually stacking the deck: the one issue we can't deliberate over is whether the government should wage war on inequality. The need to fight economic inequality is an unquestionable axiom, and anyone who supports people's freedom to earn and spend a lot of wealth is anti-democratic: he's trying to "rig the game" in favor of "the rich."

The inequality alarmists are not champions of democracy, let alone of a limited government that protects the equal rights of its citizens. They have an agenda, and they intend to force it on us whether we like it or not. What is that agenda, and how do they justify it?

SOCIAL JUSTICE

Way back in chapter 2 we encountered Paul Krugman's claim that "middle-class America didn't emerge by accident. It was created by what has been called the Great Compression of incomes that took place during World War II."[11] We've already seen that the economic progress unleashed by freedom lifted millions of Americans into the ranks of the middle class long before World War II, and that Krugman himself acknowledges this fact.

What Krugman means when he refers to the "middle-class America" made possible by "the Great Compression of incomes" is not the fact that more and more Americans were able to participate in economic progress. Instead he is celebrating the fact that society was more *equal* because *wealthier Americans were worse off.*

Support for this interpretation can be found throughout his book *The Conscience of a Liberal.* "Middle-class societies don't emerge automatically as an economy matures, they have to be *created* through political action. Nothing in the data we have for the early twentieth suggests that America was evolving spontaneously into the relatively equal society I grew up in."[12] (No, America was evolving into a prosperous, though unequal, society.) A few paragraphs later, Krugman discusses the creation of this more equal society, writing approvingly, "It was only with the New Deal that the billionaires more or less vanished from the scene, dropping in number to sixteen [from thirty-two] in 1957 and thirteen in 1968."[13] Later he celebrates "the great narrowing of income differentials that took place between the twenties and the fifties [which] involved leveling downward: the rich were significantly poorer in the fifties than they had been in the twenties. And I literally mean poorer: We're not just talking about relative impoverishment, a failure to keep up with income growth further down the scale, but about a large absolute decline in purchasing power."[14] How did America achieve such a glorious result? "Basically the New Deal taxed away much, perhaps most of their income."[15] For Krugman the only mystery is "the absence of effective demands that the government do more to soak the rich" before the New Deal.[16]

When inequality alarmists like Krugman hold up the post-war era as a model, they are not doing so in the name of prosperity, or even "shared prosperity," but economic *equality*—equality as an end in itself.

Most Americans believe that vast inequalities of wealth and income are just as long as they are earned justly, i.e., via production and voluntary trade, rather than through fraud, force, or expropriation (including government favors and government handouts). We've argued that today's inequalities result from both justly earned fortunes and (to a far lesser extent) unjustly acquired fortunes that owe their existence to government intervention.

Although the inequality alarmists argue that most of today's inequality is the result of exploitation and expropriation, and although they will *say* (when it is politically convenient) that they do not oppose honestly earned fortunes, the truth is they are skeptical (at best) that substantial economic inequality can ever be just. Why? Because they have a distinctive conception of justice—a concept that, if defined explicitly and openly, we believe most Americans would reject.

Thomas Piketty opens his book *Capital in the Twenty-First Century* with an epigram from the French Declaration of the Rights of Man and the Citizen, which says, "Social distinctions can be based only on common utility." Whatever the original meaning of that statement, Piketty's own view is that economic inequalities must be justified by reference to some higher "public good."[17] Later in the book he writes, "One reasonable interpretation [of the phrase "based on common utility"] is that social inequalities are acceptable only if they are in the interest of all and in particular of the most disadvantaged social groups. . . . The 'difference principle' introduced by the U.S. philosopher John Rawls in his *Theory of Justice* is similar in intent."[18]

This means, for instance, that if you earn a million dollars when most people make less than $100,000, you have to prove not only that your fortune was honestly earned, but that it benefits society (or the least well-off in society) to let you keep it. It's hard to see how this view has any more foundation than the idea that you have to justify living longer than the average person by reference to "the public good." If you acquire a fortune without violating anyone else's rights, then doesn't that fortune belong to you? Don't you have a right to dedicate your efforts to making yourself as rich and successful as possible—regardless of how much inequality this leads to? The answer we get from the alarmists is a resounding "no." Why not? For that, we need to turn to the philosopher Piketty cites in support of his theory: the late Harvard philosopher John Rawls.

Most inequality critics today are economists, journalists, politicians, policy wonks, or political commentators. But most of their ideas are derived from *egalitarian philosophers:* Rousseau, Marx, and their modern heirs—people like Nagel, Dworkin, Singer, Cohen, and above all Rawls. Whatever their differences, these thinkers have a distinctive view of justice and of its implications for political and economic issues, one that shapes the thinking of the inequality alarmists at the deepest levels.

Justice, *properly* understood, is first and foremost a virtue to be practiced by individuals. It is the commitment to judging other people objectively, granting to each what he or she deserves. Above all, justice guides us in making *moral* assessments of people. Are we dealing with a good person who therefore deserves praise and rewards, or a bad person who deserves condemnation and punishment?[19]

But while justice primarily has to do with specific individuals assessing what they owe to other specific individuals, we can also evaluate whether a *social system* is just. A social system, in Ayn Rand's definition, is "a set of moral-political-economic principles embodied in a society's laws, institutions, and government, which determine the relationships, the terms of association, among the men living in a given geographical area."[20] To determine whether a social system is just, we need to look at its laws, institutions, and government and assess whether they treat individuals as they deserve to be treated.

We have argued that a just social system is a *free* system—one that respects individual dignity by protecting each person's equal rights to life, liberty, and the pursuit of happiness. The egalitarians, on the other hand, have a very different view of what constitutes a just social system, which they call "social justice." For the egalitarians, the central requirement for social justice is *equality*. What do they mean by equality? Here there is disagreement, but on one point they're united: they *don't* mean equality of rights—at least not in the economic realm. Here's how Rawls sums up his view: "All social values—liberty and opportunity, income and wealth, and the bases of self-respect—are to be distributed equally"—and here Rawls adds a famous caveat—"unless an unequal distribution of any, or all, of these values is to everyone's advantage."[21] How does one determine whether a given level of inequality is "to everyone's advantage," according to Rawls? By asking whether it benefits *the least well-off in society.*

Rawls calls this caveat the difference principle. We presume, in other words, that "social values" should be equal, but we will allow them to be unequal if trying to reduce the inequality would harm the worst-off members of society. In the ideal world envisioned by egalitarians, the government would confiscate everyone's property and dole it out equally, so that a drug-addicted slacker would enjoy the same opportunities, income, and wealth as a talented inventor. Rawls's innovation is to say that because that would harm the poor by reducing economic growth, social justice is consistent with allowing individuals who have earned a fortune to, in the words of Elizabeth Warren, "keep a hunk of it." "Injustice, then," Rawls concludes, "is simply inequalities that are not to the benefit of all."[22] We can allow the inventor to prosper to the degree it enriches the slacker—but only to that degree.

It's worth noting that some egalitarians think Rawls doesn't go far enough. In Rawls's conception, allowing Steve Jobs to earn billions is okay if it incentivizes him to do things that are good for the least well-off. Leading egalitarian philosopher G. A. Cohen demurs. "The worst off benefit from incentive inequality in particular only because the better off would, in effect, go on strike if unequaling incentives were withdrawn."[23] But talented people, such as Jobs,

> . . . could not claim, *in self-justification,* at the bar of the difference principle, that their high rewards are necessary to enhance the position of the worst off, since, in the standard case it is they themselves who *make* those rewards necessary, through their own unwillingness to work for ordinary rewards as productively as they do for exceptionally high ones, an unwillingness which ensures that the untalented get less than they otherwise would. Those rewards are, therefore, necessary

only because the choices of talented people are not appropriately informed by the difference principle.[24]

In other words, according to Cohen, it's not that Steve Jobs *can't* create Apple unless he's able to earn a fortune—it's that the greedy SOB *won't*. In Cohen's view, that's immoral. The difference principle only sanctions inequalities that are *necessary* for advancing the interests of "the untalented." If Jobs refuses to work unless he is paid more than janitors and dishwashers, then he isn't living up to the difference principle. Jobs *owes* "the untalented" the benefits of his talent and effort, and if he insists on being rewarded for creating Apple then, in Cohen's view, he "must be thought of as outside the community."[25] Consequently, although Rawls's difference principle seems to allow for a substantial amount of inequality, Cohen concludes: "I want to record here my doubt that the difference principle justifies *any* significant inequality."[26]

Cohen aside, Rawls draws out some of the political implications of his view of social justice. He ends up endorsing two forms of government that are potentially consistent with social justice: (1) a socialist state, in which the government owns the means of production, or (2) a regulatory-welfare state similar to that seen in the United States and especially in Europe, but one which much more aggressively pursues economic equality as a goal. According to Rawls, there should even be a "distribution branch" of government:

> Its task is to preserve an approximate justice in distributive shares by means of taxation and the necessary adjustments in the rights of property. . . . [For example], it imposes a number of inheritance and gift taxes, and sets restrictions on the rights of bequest. The purpose of these levies and regulations is not to raise revenue (release resources to government) but gradually and continually to correct the distribution of wealth and to prevent concentrations of power . . .[27]

That, at the broadest level, is how egalitarians approach the concept of justice. And it explains what the inequality alarmists have in mind when they speak of social justice: not respecting people's equal rights, but coercively equalizing income, wealth, and opportunity.[28]

On the face of it, such equality is manifestly unjust. If your parents worked and saved in order to send you to a better school than your neighbors, why is it fair to force you to attend a worse school? If you create a billion dollars in wealth, and come away with a $100 million fortune, why is it fair to seize your fortune and give it to people who created nothing? Why are "the least well-off" entitled to our first consideration, and the geniuses on whom the human race depends entitled to no consideration?

In order to defend economic equality as a moral ideal, the critics engage in an intellectual pincer attack aimed at discrediting the principle that a person deserves what he earns. First, they challenge the idea that what a person acquires through production and trade on a free market *is* earned. Second, they say that it's unfair for you to keep what you haven't earned, and that society should take your unearned wealth and give it to people who need it more.

YOU DIDN'T BUILD THAT

Why is it just to deprive people of their opportunities and fortunes? Because, the egalitarians answer, they haven't earned them. Now, it's obviously true that not every rich person earned his fortune, particularly today when there are so many opportunities to get special privileges from the government. The question at issue is: if someone in a free society grows rich through productive work for which others voluntarily choose to pay him, hasn't he earned his riches? And it's here that the egalitarians say: absolutely not.

Why not? Because, the egalitarians argue, to earn something you have to be responsible for achieving it. And successful individuals can't claim to be responsible for achieving their fortunes because their success is the product, not of their choices, but of luck: the luck of being born intelligent, or wealthy, or to loving parents, or with the ability to run fast or jump high, etc. A just society shouldn't reward or punish people for luck: instead, it should seek to compensate people for bad luck by depriving other people of the results of good luck. This is the basic premise behind Rawls's difference principle. According to Rawls:

> The difference principle represents, in effect, an agreement to regard the distribution of natural talents as a common asset and to share in

the benefits of this distribution whatever it turns out to be. Those who have been favored by nature, whoever they are, may gain from their good fortune only on terms that improve the situation of those who have lost out. The naturally advantaged are not to gain merely because they are more gifted, but only to cover the costs of training and education for using their endowments in ways that help the less fortunate as well. No one deserves his greater natural capacity nor merits a more favorable starting place in society. But it does not follow that one should eliminate these distinctions. There is another way to deal with them. The basic structure can be arranged so that these contingencies work for the good of the least fortunate. Thus we are led to the difference principle if we wish to set up the social system so that no one gains or loses from her arbitrary place in the distribution of natural assets or his initial position in society without giving or receiving compensating advantages in return.[29]

Now, you might say that sure, luck plays some role in success, but most of what successful individuals achieve is the result of their choices: to think, to learn, to work really, really hard. Woz, after all, didn't trip, fall, and end up with the first personal computer. He spent countless hours dedicating himself to understanding computers and designing them. According to the egalitarians, this is a superficial way of looking at things. After all, if Woz had been born in 1800, or had an average IQ, or if his father hadn't been an engineer but a farmer, then obviously his achievements would have been impossible. Woz didn't choose when to be born, or how smart he would be, or who his parents were. Even his choice to work hard wasn't really a choice, but a product of his genes and upbringing. On these and many other points, Woz was lucky. As Rawls puts it:

Perhaps some will think that the person with greater natural endowments deserves those assets and the superior character that made their development possible. Because he is more worthy in this sense, he deserves the greater advantages that he could achieve with them. This view, however, is surely incorrect. It seems to be one of the fixed points of our considered judgments that no one deserves his place in the distribution of native endowments, any more than one deserves one's initial starting place in society. The assertion that a man deserves the superior character that enables him to make the effort to cultivate his abilities is equally problematic; for his character depends in large part upon fortunate family and social circumstances for which he can claim no credit. The notion of desert seems not to apply to these cases. Thus the more advantaged representative man cannot say that he deserves and therefore has a right to a scheme of cooperation in which he is permitted to acquire benefits in ways that do not contribute to the welfare of others. There is no basis for his making this claim.[30]

The same holds true, the egalitarians add, for those who end up poor for having made *bad* decisions. Had they been born smarter or richer or more athletic or with better parents or a better work ethic, they might not have ended up poor. And just as no one earns his good luck, so no one earns his bad luck.

This view—that success is fundamentally dependent on luck and that people therefore don't earn their success—is echoed relentlessly by the inequality critics. President Obama refers to successful Americans as "society's lottery winners."[31] Explicitly invoking Rawls, Piketty writes, "To the extent that inequality of conditions is due, at least in part, to factors beyond the control of individuals, such as the existence of unequal family endowments (in terms of inheritances, cultural capital, etc.) or good fortune (special talents, luck, etc.), it is just for government to seek to reduce these inequalities as much as possible."[32]

Law professor James Kwak is even more explicit about the implications of this principle. "Even if differences in outcomes were entirely due to differences in abilities and effort (which they're not)—would that make it OK? I think most people would say that it's fine for smart people to make more money than other people. But why? Why are smart people any more deserving than anyone else?" Although Kwak acknowledges that intelligence can make a person more productive, he goes on to say that just because "a capitalist economy functions this way doesn't make it morally right that the 'winners of the genetic lottery' . . . have better outcomes than the losers." What about people who simply choose to work really, really hard? Don't they, at least, deserve to prosper? "I'm not convinced of that, either. The ability to work hard is something that you either inherit from your parents or that you develop in your early childhood as a function of the environment around you. Either way, whether or not you have it is as much a matter of luck as is your IQ. . . . [F]airness dictates that policy should attempt to improve outcomes for the unlucky, even if that requires hurting outcomes for the lucky."[33]

Something is clearly wrong here. No honest person believes that Woz didn't earn the millions he made at Apple by pioneering the first personal computer, but instead just "got lucky" and "won the lottery." The key error in this argument is that it totally mischaracterizes what it means to earn something. For the egalitarians, the results of our actions don't merely have to be *under our control,* but *entirely of our own making.*[34] To earn something, it's not enough that Woz chose to apply his mind to the task of building a personal computer—Woz needed to be *fully* responsible for *everything* that led to the creation of the first personal computer, including his own genetic makeup. But there is nothing like that in reality, and so what the egalitarians are ultimately doing is wiping out the very possibility of earning something.

In reality, responsibility doesn't require omniscience or omnipotence. It requires only that our actions be voluntary and that we know what we are doing.[35] A restaurant owner whose business is failing because he sits on the sidelines drinking Jack Daniels while his kitchen staff turns out overcooked food and his waiters and waitresses bad-mouth the customers is *responsible* for his failing business, because it is within his power to choose to test the food before it goes out and to hire friendlier servers—and because he does (or should) *know* this. As a result, his failure is earned. By the same token, if he chooses to set down the whiskey glass and shape up his business, he has earned whatever success he goes on to achieve.

The same principle applies to someone like investing genius Warren Buffett, who has echoed Rawls's argument, claiming that his own success is owed to the luck of having been born in the right place, at the right time, with the right skill set. It's true that Buffett didn't "earn" his brain, or his parents, or being born in twentieth-century America, in the sense of having achieved those things through his own choices. Those aren't the sorts of things that *can* be earned. But that is irrelevant to whether he earned his fortune. Not everything non-earned is *unearned.* We need the concept of "earn," not to distinguish between people who earn their brains and parents and those who don't, but to distinguish those who use their abilities and resources to create something from those who don't. The fact is that Buffett *was* born in twentieth-century America, as were millions of other people, but *he* chose to make certain investment decisions and they *didn't*. Indeed, Buffett himself has, in other contexts, written eloquently *against* the notion that his investment results were mere good luck: instead, he argued, they were the product of a rational investment philosophy, intelligently applied.[36] That, in essence, is all that is required to say he earned his fortune.

What about people who make *good* choices yet suffer bad results? What about the woman who is born poor but works her way to a supervisor role at the local manufacturing plant, only to lose her job when the factory goes out of business, and is unable to find an equally well-paying position? Isn't she the victim of bad luck, and isn't it unfair that she should suffer for her luck while others get to reap the rewards of good luck? As egalitarian philosopher Larry Temkin puts it, "Egalitarians generally believe that it is bad for some to be worse off than others through no fault or choice of their own. This is because, typically, if one person is worse off than another through no fault or choice of her own, the situation seems comparatively unfair, and, hence, the inequality will be objectionable."[37] It is obviously unfortunate—even tragic—when bad things happen to good people. But that doesn't automatically make it unfair. Unfairness involves one person mistreating another. The out-of-work supervisor didn't lose her job *because* other people kept theirs, and their continued success doesn't come at her expense. To punish people because someone else suffered a misfortune they had no part in creating is what would be profoundly unfair.

But let us not grant too much to the egalitarians. Luck is seldom the decisive factor in life. It's not an accident that the Olympics are filled with people who spend years dedicating an enormous amount of time and energy to their sport. It's not an accident that Silicon Valley is filled with people who spent years learning to program. It's not an accident that those who have risen from rags to riches inevitably tell the same story: of working day and night, living on a shoestring, enduring failure after failure on the way to success. And it's not an accident that most unsuccessful people have not done these things.

In a fascinating study described in their book *Great by Choice,* Jim Collins and Morten T. Hansen assessed the role of luck in business success. They looked at seven industries, and for each industry chose two representative organizations: a moderately successful one and a "10X" company. 10X companies, they explain, "didn't merely get by or just become successful. They truly thrived. Every 10X case beat its industry by at least 10 *times*."[38] Then, for each company, they cataloged what they called "luck events," events in which "(1) some significant aspect of the event occurs largely or entirely independent of the actions of the key actors in the enterprise, (2) the event has a potentially significant consequence (good or bad), and (3) the event has some element of unpredictability."[39] Every company, they observed, had its share of good and bad luck. What they wanted to know was "does luck play a *differentiating* role, an explanatory role, a definitive role in creating 10X success?"[40]

What they found was striking. No matter how they looked at the data, there was no significant difference in luck between 10X companies and the comparison companies. In many cases, the comparison companies received either more good luck or less bad luck. "The real difference between the 10X and comparison cases," the authors concluded, "wasn't luck per se but what they *did* with the luck they got. . . . The critical question is not 'Are you lucky?' but 'Do you get a high *return on luck*?'"[41]

The concept of "return on luck" is profound. "[W]hen we look at the 10Xers, we see people like [Bill] Gates who recognize luck and seize it, leaders who grab luck events and make more of them than others do. It's the 10X ability to get a high return on luck at pivotal moments that distinguishes them and this has a huge multiplicative effect."[42] Whatever the merits and demerits of Collins and Hansen's study, *this* is the right way to think about luck.

Yes, accidents happen. Yes, luck plays a role in our lives. But if we really believe outside forces play a dominant role, then we wouldn't bother exerting effort, and we wouldn't teach our children to study, work hard, or make good decisions. Who needs all that stress when it won't matter anyway? Just wait for opportunity to knock. The most successful individuals are those who recognize that what counts in life is not the luck you get—but what you do with it.

To be in control of our lives does not require us to be omnipotent, able to determine our fate through a sheer act of will. To be in control of our lives requires us to be able to deal with the circumstances of our lives as we judge best, without having our choices thwarted by other people. Politically, then, the only role for the government is to protect our freedom and property. To grant the government the power to counteract the influence of luck by abridging our freedom is to put ourselves totally at the mercy of others. It is to hand a blank check to force-wielding politicians, allowing them to strip us of everything we have worked for and achieved. All they have to do is declare: *You say you earned that? I say you were lucky.*

There is a variant of the luck argument that has become popular in recent years. Instead of focusing on the general role of luck in making our achievements possible, this argument focuses on the role of one specific outside force: other people.

In 2011, then-senatorial candidate Elizabeth Warren went on a rant that found its way onto YouTube and made Warren the darling of the political left.

> There is nobody in this country who got rich on his own—nobody. You built a factory out there? Good for you. But I want to be clear. You moved your goods to market on the roads *the rest of us* paid for. You hired workers the rest of us paid to educate. You were safe in your factory because of police-forces and fire-forces that the rest of us paid for. You didn't have to worry that marauding bands would come and seize everything at your factory—and hire someone to protect against this—because of the work the rest of us did. Now look, you built a factory and it turned into something terrific, or a great idea. God bless— keep a big hunk of it. But part of the underlying social contract is, you take a hunk of that and pay forward for *the next kid* who comes along.[43]

Less than a year later, President Obama echoed these sentiments in his infamous "you didn't build that" comments.

> Look, if you've been successful, you didn't get there on your own. You didn't get there on your own. I'm always struck by people who think, well, it must be because I was just so smart. There are a lot of smart

people out there. It must be because I worked harder than everybody else. Let me tell you something—there are a whole bunch of hardworking people out there. If you were successful, somebody along the line gave you some help. There was a great teacher somewhere in your life. Somebody helped to create this unbelievable American system that we have that allowed you to thrive. Somebody invested in roads and bridges. If you've got a business—you didn't build that. Somebody else made that happen.[44]

As with the luck argument, the "you didn't build that" argument switches the standard of earning something from "under your control" to "entirely of your own making." To truly create something, it's not enough to *build* on the achievements of others. An achievement is only an individual achievement if others contributed to it in no way whatsoever. And since, in this sense, no one creates anything alone—even an author relies on his education and his editors—no individual can claim that he earned his wealth or success.

But that is the wrong way to think about achievement. Human achievement is primarily intellectual, and it consists, not of creation *ex nihilo*, but of building on the achievements of others and taking them further. What a person adds through his own thought and effort is *his* achievement. Here is how Howard Roark, the innovative architect in Ayn Rand's novel *The Fountainhead*, explains it:

From this simplest necessity to the highest religious abstraction, from the wheel to the skyscraper, everything we are and everything we have comes from a single attribute of man—the function of his reasoning mind.

But the mind is an attribute of the individual. There is no such thing as a collective brain. There is no such thing as a collective thought. An agreement reached by a group of men is only a compromise or an average drawn upon many individual thoughts. It is a secondary consequence. The primary act—the process of reason—must be performed by each man alone. . . .

We inherit the products of the thought of other men. We inherit the wheel. We make a cart. The cart becomes an automobile. The automobile becomes an airplane. But all through the process what we receive from others is only the end product of their thinking. The moving force is the creative faculty which takes this product as material, uses it and originates the next step. This creative faculty cannot be given or received, shared or borrowed. It belongs to single, individual men. That which it creates is the property of the creator.[45]

Contrary to the collectivist view, wealth is not a social product or a "social value," to use Rawls's terminology. It does not emerge as a single blob of "national income" that must be divided up by society. Wealth is created by, and morally belongs to, the individual creator. If Robinson Crusoe is tired of trying to scoop up fish with his hands and figures out how to turn a tree branch into a spear, increasing his daily catch tenfold, can Friday, who never thought to make a spear, properly complain that Crusoe has received an "unfair distribution" of fish?

Whatever the complications and intricacies involved, the basic issue is the same whether we're talking about a remote island or a complex division of labor economy like America's. An individual uses his mind, his effort, and his existing property (i.e., previously created wealth) to bring new wealth into existence.

Virgin Group's Richard Branson, for instance, got his start selling record albums out of the back of his car. The albums? They were his property. The money he made by selling them? His property. Branson used that money to implement his ideas for making records cheaper, phones more user-friendly, air travel more glamorous. He didn't grab a bigger piece of some socially produced pie any more than Crusoe did. He brought new wealth into existence.

Did Branson work with other people to create his products? Of course, but that doesn't change the essential issue. Branson used his property, i.e., his capital, to hire help in his productive ventures. Each Virgin employee brought wealth into existence as an individual—and was paid accordingly. The profits that Branson (and his fellow shareholders) received already reflected the contribution of Virgin's employees: those profits are what he achieved *after* they were paid for their work.

What about the countless others who contributed *indirectly* to Branson's achievements? What about his parents? His teachers? Or the inventor of the airplane? The inventors of language? The "you didn't build that" view amounts to the claim that because these people don't receive financial remuneration for their contribution to Branson's achievements, Branson is profiting off their backs, and the government is there to make up for that sin with high taxes. Of course, most of these people *were* paid for their services when they performed them, monetarily or otherwise. It's not as if Branson's teachers were working for free, waiting for the day he would grow up, become a billionaire, and send them a check. And it's not as if taxing Branson will do anything to repay the individuals who helped him.

In fact, the only people who don't get paid anything close to their actual contribution to human well-being are the men and women of extraordinary ability whose *ideas* contributed to Branson's achievements. The geniuses who pioneered air travel, and cell phones, and music players— and before that language, and logic, and science—did indeed give Branson and all of us far more than they received in return for their achievements. As Rand notes, "*this* is the creative over-abundance of the genius . . . (What does the genius want for this? Just 'Thank you.')"[46] What we owe people who give us benefits over and above what we have to pay for is recognition and *gratitude*. Yet that is exactly what the "you didn't build that" argument denies them. Instead of recognizing that the men and women of extraordinary ability *contribute* the most to human progress, the argument claims that they *benefit* the most from "society," and that they therefore *owe* the most to the government. If you earned a fortune, you didn't build anything—you took something, and now you must "give something back."

The fact is that if a person chooses to act productively, develops valuable skills, and thereby creates a vast amount of wealth, he has *earned* his fortune. It is totally irrelevant whether other factors outside his control played a role in his success—other factors *always* play a role. To treat either omnipotence or self-sufficiency as the standard for earning something means that none of us earns anything—and that the government can therefore deprive us of everything.

SACRIFICE

The key to making sense of the egalitarians' admittedly bizarre arguments is to keep in mind that they are thorough collectivists—collectivists in the full, philosophic sense. "[C]ollectivists," Rand explains, "see society as a super-organism, as some supernatural entity apart from and superior to the sum of its individual members."[47] Traditional religion sees the source of our innate characteristics as caused by God, and demands that individuals use their God-given gifts to serve Him. Collectivists, in effect, replace God with society, and demand that individuals use their "gifts" to serve *it*. Since these "gifts"—intelligence, beauty, ambition, moral character, etc.—aren't earned by the individual, the individual doesn't deserve to profit from them. He isn't to use his talents to better his own life—he is to use his talents to benefit society.

Since there is no such entity as "society," only particular individuals, what this means in practice is that some individuals must serve others. What determines who are the servants and who are the served? *Need.* The duty of the "haves" is to sacrifice themselves for the "have-nots." A person doesn't deserve what he has earned. (No one, in the egalitarian view, earns anything.) What a person deserves is to have his needs fulfilled by others. "Need," in this context, doesn't refer merely to the biological requirements of remaining above ground. It refers to anything one person lacks that other people have. (This is why the inequality alarmists can say that today's poor *need* air-conditioning, automobiles, and expensive new drugs, even though the richest Americans didn't have these things a century ago.)

What about the liberty of those forced to foot the bill? What about their hopes and dreams? To collectivists, sacrificing the rights and aspirations of the "haves" is a small price to pay. In their view, forcing people who are relatively well-off financially to give up some less important opportunities (say, the ability to buy a bigger house) in order to provide those who aren't well-off financially with more important opportunities (say, the ability to buy health insurance) makes society as a whole better off.

But you can't compare the values of different people in this way. Contra collectivism, there is no super-organism—"the public"—that can benefit from such a tradeoff. There are only individuals, each of whom is properly concerned primarily with his own life and happiness. Although—for a given individual—health insurance may be more valuable than the chance to buy a larger home, *other people's* health insurance is not more valuable to him than the chance to buy a new house. Sacrificing his wants doesn't achieve some higher social good—it just allows other people to gain at his expense.

The notion that a person is entitled to have his needs fulfilled by others is generally treated as non-controversial. But, taken seriously, it has disturbing implications, and some egalitarians have drawn out those implications. Peter Singer, one of the most widely respected and influential egalitarian philosophers, argues that if we really believe that we have a moral obligation to fulfill the more important needs of others before we tend to our own, less important needs, then this means radically curtailing our own standard of living.

> [W]hile the cost of saving one child's life by a donation to an aid organization may not be great, after you have donated that sum, there remain more children in need of saving, each one of whom can be saved at a relatively small additional cost. Suppose you have just sent $200 to an agency that can, for that amount, save the life of a child in a developing country who would otherwise have died. You've done something really good, and all it has cost you is the price of some new clothes you didn't really need anyway. Congratulations! But don't celebrate your good deed by opening a bottle of champagne, or even going to a movie. The cost of that bottle or movie, added to what you could save by cutting down on a few other extravagances, would save the life of another child. After you forego those items, and give another $200, though, is everything else you are spending on as important, or nearly important, as the life of a child? Not likely! So you must keep cutting back on unnecessary spending, and donating what you save, until you have reduced yourself to the point where if you give any more, you will be sacrificing something nearly as important as a child's life—like giving so much that you can no longer afford to give your children an adequate education.

He concludes, "[I]f the basic argument presented above is right, then what many of us consider acceptable behavior must be viewed in a new, more ominous light. When we spend our surplus on concerts or fashionable shoes, on fine dining and good wines, or on holidays in faraway lands, we are doing something wrong."[48]

This is what Ayn Rand refers to as treating human beings as sacrificial animals, morally bound to surrender their hopes and dreams as long as there is anyone, anywhere else on the globe, who has less.[49]

But why should we view things this way? Why should we think that everyone should be held down to the lowest common denominator? Why not instead say that each person has a right to make the most of his own life, and take responsibility for improving it? Of course, we *can* help out other people if we choose. That's part of how we pursue our happiness—by supporting the people and causes we care about. But to view everyone else's needs as a *debt* we have to repay before we focus on our own aspirations? What could justify that? According to the egalitarians, *this* is what it means to treat people with dignity.

THE ATTACK ON DIGNITY

To respect human dignity, writes Rawls, is "to recognize that [other individuals] possess an inviolability founded on justice that even the welfare of society as a whole cannot override. It is to affirm that the loss of freedom for some is not made right by a greater welfare enjoyed by others."[50] On this we agree. Where we disagree with Rawls *profoundly* is on *what* this inviolability consists of.

We are individualists, and in our view, to treat people with dignity means to treat them as *individuals*—as people who have the right to exist for their own sake, not as servants of the group, forced to justify their existence by the service they render to other people. They have a right to pursue their own happiness by exercising their independent judgment, which no appeal to "the welfare of society" can override.

As a result, what justice demands in a social context is first and foremost that we respect others' freedom—including economic freedom and property rights. As Rand explains, "Man has to work and produce in order to support his life. He has to support his life by his own effort and by the guidance of his own mind. If he cannot dispose of the product of his effort, he cannot dispose of his effort; if he cannot dispose of his effort, he cannot dispose of his life. Without property rights, no other rights can be practiced."[51] Our right to our property doesn't come from the fact that we need that property more than others, but the fact that we earned it, and have the right to use it to achieve our aspirations. To treat individuals with dignity means recognizing that their right to improve their own lives does not have a contingency clause—"unless they achieve more than other people, at which time it's other people's lives that count."

In a free society, you cannot earn a fortune without creating tremendous values that, by necessity, improve the lives of countless other people. But a person's right to better his life is not some favor that we extend people in exchange for their service, as if their lives were public property—they are born with that right, and we have a sacred obligation to respect it.

That's what the American Dream is all about. It means that you have the moral and political right to treat your life as your supreme value: there is no justification for treating your goals as less important than those of someone who has yet to succeed, no matter how rich and successful you've become. Just as you don't have fewer rights because you are poor, neither do you have fewer rights because you are rich. We are politically equal. As long as you improve your life by creating and trading values rather than plundering them from others, your freedom and property should be regarded as sacrosanct.

In an admirably accurate summary of the individualist view, egalitarians Liam Murphy and Thomas Nagel write:

> Each person, on this view, is in certain respects inviolable. . . . Our original sovereignty over ourselves—a moral given, not created by the state—leaves us free to employ our capacities and implies that others have no right to interfere with that freedom, unless in using it we transgress the rights of others.
>
> The state cannot change this. It is not a collective arrangement whereby we all own shares in each other, which we can exploit for the common good. Rather, each of us has the right to decide what to do with our own capacities, and how to dispose of the product of any enterprise, individual or cooperative, that we have voluntarily undertaken. The state has no more right to demand a cut of the profits for redistribution in exchange for maintenance of the peaceful conditions of cooperation than it would have to demand adherence to a particular religion for the same reason. To champion other liberal rights while belittling economic freedom is morally inconsistent.[52]

However, Murphy and Nagel add, this is a view they are "out of sympathy with."[53] Egalitarians *do* believe that the state is "a collective arrangement whereby we all own shares in each other, which we can exploit for the common good." In what respects, then, *do* they view the individual as inviolable? They will typically list things like freedom of speech and freedom of religion. But when it comes to economic freedom and property rights, it's deuces wild: here "we can exploit" the individual "for the common good." In contrast to individualists, Murphy and Nagel write in their aptly titled *The Myth of Ownership*, "[e]galitarian liberals simply see no moral similarity between the right to speak one's mind, to practice one's religion, or to act on one's sexual inclinations, and the right to enter into a labor contract or a sale of property unencumbered by a tax bite." They do generously allow for "[s]ome forms of personal discretion—including the basic . . . right to hold personal property" but "unimpeded economic freedom is not one of them."[54]

How is ordering people around and draining them of their achievements consistent with treating them with dignity? Egalitarians hold that, in the economic realm, dignity does not consist of being treated as rational beings with equal rights to the product of our own labor, but of having the same amount of *stuff* as other people. They believe that a person's dignity suffers to the extent he lacks as much wealth as his neighbors, since it undercuts his self-respect. According to Rawls, "A person's lesser position as measured by the index of objective primary goods [in other words, having less opportunity and wealth than his neighbors] may be so great as to wound his self-respect. . . . [S]ociety may permit such large disparities in these goods that under existing social conditions these differences cannot help but cause a loss of self-esteem."[55]

For a rational person, self-esteem is rooted in his own choices: Has he done his best to make something of himself? Has he been honest, just, productive? Has he lived with integrity? For egalitarians, self-esteem is *comparative:* Is he better or worse than others? More talented or less? Richer or poorer? Thus, one person's dignity can suffer as the result of another person's achievements. If an individual achieves too much, if he is too good or too rich, he will deprive other people of their dignity. The respect in which the egalitarians regard the individual as inviolable in the economic realm, then, is his *envy*—envy for any value that others have earned, but he hasn't. We can strip people of the wealth they've achieved and of the opportunities they've created, forcing them to forego everything but their most important needs, as Singer demands—but if we value human dignity, the one thing we dare not do is upset someone's desire for the unearned.

By defining dignity in terms of material equality, the egalitarians call on us to view the achievements of others, not as a source of inspiration, but as an affront to our self-worth, which we are to bolster by *punishing the successful for being successful*. It's hardly an exaggeration to say that the egalitarian conception of dignity is *degrading*.

And it is destructive. If we want to live in a society that is hospitable to ability and achievement, then our first concern should be to respect the right of each individual to use (and develop) his natural capacities to achieve values, and to enjoy the values he does achieve. We should celebrate, encourage, and reward success. This is the precondition of human progress. The egalitarian conception of justice amounts to a perverse inversion. Instead of rewarding people for their achievements, it rewards people for *not* achieving anything. Instead of teaching us to celebrate success, it teaches us to condemn the successful for making society more unequal and for stirring up resentment in the unsuccessful. It teaches us that the only way to show compassion toward others is to grind everyone down to the lowest common denominator.

A rational concept of fairness is grounded, not in equality, but in treating people as they deserve. There is a sense in which this requires equality. It is, as Aristotle said, just to treat equal things equally. But for the same reason, he added, we must treat unequal things unequally. Achievement is unequal, and so equal is unfair.

This is the key thing to realize about the inequality alarmists. They regard economic inequality as inherently unfair. Whatever concessions they make, however much they argue that the inequalities we see today are the result of exploitation and cronyism rather than merit, in the end, they are skeptical of the propriety of *any* inequality. Piketty, for instance, notes that, historically, "Inequalities with respect to labor [income, as opposed to wealth] usually seem mild, moderate, and almost reasonable"—but hastens to add, "to the extent that inequality can be reasonable—this point should not be overstated."[56] In the alarmists' ideal world, no one should be able to achieve anything that others have not achieved or enjoy any values that others cannot enjoy. But as Rand observes:

> If there were such a thing as a passion for equality (not equality *de jure*, but *de facto*), it would be obvious to its exponents that there are only two ways to achieve it: either by raising all men to the mountaintop— or by razing the mountains. The first method is impossible because it is the faculty of volition that determines a man's stature and actions; but the nearest approach to it was demonstrated by the United States and capitalism, which protected the freedom, the rewards and the incentives for every individual's achievement, each to the extent of his ability and ambition, thus raising the intellectual, moral and economic state of the whole society. The second method is impossible because, if mankind were leveled down to the common denominator of its least competent members, it would not be able to survive (and its best would not choose to survive on such terms). Yet it is the second method that [the egalitarians] are pursuing.[57]

The essence of the egalitarian project is to *level down,* i.e., to destroy values as an end in itself. And every once in a while, egalitarians will admit this. As egalitarian philosopher Christopher Ake puts it:

> What about the case of someone who suddenly comes into good fortune, perhaps entirely by his or her own efforts? Should additional burdens . . . be imposed on that person in order to restore equality and safeguard justice? . . . Why wouldn't it be just to impose any kind of additional burden whatsoever on him in order to restore equality? The answer is that, strictly speaking, it would be.[58]

His fellow egalitarian Larry Temkin makes the point even more vividly: "I, for one, believe that inequality is bad. But do I *really* think that there is some respect in which a world where only some are blind is worse than one where all are? Yes. Does this mean I think it would be better if we blinded everyone? No. Equality is not all that matters."[59]

That is chilling enough. But what happens when people decide that equality *is* all that matters?

AN EGALITARIAN NIGHTMARE

Egalitarianism presents us with an ideal—a conception of what we should aim toward and aspire to. To evaluate any alleged ideal, it's important to ask what it would mean if implemented consistently. This is not to suggest that its advocates necessarily *support* the consistent application of the ideal. That's a separate question, which we'll come back to. The question at this point is simply: what would this ideal mean in practice, if we took it seriously?

No society has fully implemented the egalitarian doctrine, but one came as close as any society can come: Cambodia's Khmer Rouge. The Khmer Rouge were Cambodian communists who came to power in 1975. (A Khmer is a native Cambodian, and Rouge means "red," i.e., communist.) Most of their leadership, including their general secretary, Pol Pot, were educated in France. Studying with French intellectuals, and coming under the influence of Rousseau, Marx, and other collectivist intellectuals, the Cambodians adopted a radical egalitarian ideology. Here's how the Khmer Rouge's head of state, Khieu Samphân, would later summarize the cabal's philosophy:

How do we make a communist revolution? The first thing you have to do is to destroy private property. But private property exists on both the material and the mental plane. . . . To destroy material private property, the appropriate method was the evacuation of the towns. . . . But spiritual private property is more dangerous, it comprises everything that you think is "yours," everything that you think exists in relation to yourself—your parents, your family, your wife. Everything of which you say, "It's mine" . . . is spiritual private property. Thinking in terms of "me" and "my" is forbidden. If you say, "my wife," that's wrong. You should say, "our family." The Cambodian nation is our big family. . . . That's why you have been separated: the men with the men, the women with women, the children with children. All of you are under the protection of Angkar [i.e., the Khmer Rouge]. Each of us, man, woman and child, is an element of the nation. . . . We are the child of Angkar, the man of Angkar, the woman of Angkar. The knowledge you have in your head, your ideas, are mental private property, too. To become a true revolutionary, you must . . . wash your mind clean. That knowledge comes from the teaching of the colonialists and imperialists . . . and it has to be destroyed. . . . If we can destroy all material and mental private property . . . people will be equal. The moment you allow private property, one person will have a little more, another a little less, and then they are no longer equal. But if you have nothing—zero for him and zero for you—that is true equality. . . . If you permit even the smallest part of private property, you are no longer as one, and it isn't communism.[60]

Once in power, the Khmer Rouge would put this philosophy into practice with brutal consistency. They began their reign of terror by driving people from the nation's capital, Phnom Penh, in a trail of tears that left 20,000 dead. Virtually the entire country was forced onto collective farms. They abolished private property, private exchange, and even money. As Pol Pot explained:

Up to now, the fact we do not use money has greatly reduced private property and thus has promoted the overall trend towards the collective. If we start using money again, it will bring back sentiments of private property and drive the individual away from the collective. Money is an instrument which creates privilege and power. Those who possess it can use it to bribe cadres . . . [and] to undermine our system. If we allow sentiments of private property to develop, little by little people's thoughts will turn only to ways of amassing private property. . . . If we take that route, then in one year, or 10 or 20 years, what will become of our Cambodian society which up to now is so clean?[61]

The result was that production ground to a halt—there was, after all, no incentive to do anything more than the minimum necessary to avoid punishment. Food, such as there was, was rationed, and had to be eaten communally. Foraging for lizards, crabs, and spiders became common but was soon banned, since it meant that some people would have more to eat than others. As British journalist Philip Short explains in his definitive biography of Pol Pot, "When the choice was between allowing starving people to feed themselves, and observing absolute egalitarianism (in the process letting food go to waste), the regime chose egalitarianism."[62]

Any hint of individualism was ruthlessly stomped out. The Khmer Rouge was particularly harsh toward any sign of intelligence—people were sometimes murdered merely for wearing eye glasses. According to Short, "Individual rights were not curtailed in favour of the collective, but extinguished altogether. Individual creativity, initiative, originality were condemned per se. Individual consciousness was systematically demolished."[63]

Economic inequality emerges from the free choices of individuals, and so it was inevitable that to achieve economic equality, the Khmer Rouge had to resort to brutality and violence. The death penalty was its punishment of choice. The final tally, according to Short?

> Over . . . three years, one and a half million people, out of a population of seven million, would be sacrificed to the working out of [Pol Pot's] ideas. A sizeable minority was executed; the rest died of illness, overwork or starvation. No other country has ever lost so great a proportion of its nationals in a single, politically inspired hecatomb, brought about by its own leaders.[64]

This is pure evil, and our point in recounting these horrors is not that all egalitarians want to bring the Khmer Rouge's bloodshed to America. Most don't. They are compromisers who concede that, beyond a certain point, equality must give way to other concerns. But what they are doing is advocating an ideal that, taken seriously, *has* to lead to brutality, and which, in *any* dose, can only be realized through the initiation of physical force, i.e., by barring people from achieving more than others or by confiscating the rewards their achievements have made possible. Egalitarianism is evil, not because it puts us on a slippery slope toward the Khmer Rouge—it is evil because, in any dose, it amounts to waging war on human values: achievement, virtue, independence, intelligence, wealth, opportunity, *everything* that makes human life and happiness possible. The fact that egalitarianism *does* put us on a slippery slope toward mass carnage only makes matters worse.

It is common today to hear that any ideal taken to an extreme is disastrous, and that the lesson we should draw from a case such as the Khmer Rouge is the need for moderation. But the question is, if this is what the so-called ideal of economic equality means when taken seriously, who would want any part of it?

"ONE DAY I'M GONNA GET THAT BASTARD"

America became the land of opportunity because it celebrated and protected ambition and achievement. And even today, we are unique in the extent to which we regard success as something to be admired and emulated. We look up to the star athlete and even the billionaire businessman (so long as we believe he really earned his success) and draw inspiration from their achievements.

This isn't true of every society. U2 front man Bono, who is originally from Ireland, summed up the distinctive American outlook when he told Oprah:

> [I]n Ireland, people . . . have an interesting attitude to success. They look down on it. . . . [I]n America, you look up at the house on the hill, the mansion on the hill and say, "One day . . . that could be me." In Ireland, they look up at the mansion hill and go, "One day I'm gonna get that bastard."[65]

Without a doubt, one of the most troubling features of the campaign against inequality is that the alarmists almost never speak of intelligence, ability, or achievement except to mock, condemn, or discredit those values. Beneath their comments, you can't help but sense a seething resentment of "millionaires and billionaires," a phrase that political leaders such as Barack Obama and Elizabeth Warren invoke frequently and with derision.

The alarmists tell us that we must not think of successful Americans as creators who make our lives better through their achievements. To do so would be to buy into what Paul Krugman calls "the myth of the deserving rich" and to violate Hillary Clinton's dictum: "Don't let anybody tell you that, you know, it's corporations and businesses that create jobs."[66] As Richard Wilkinson and Kate Pickett counsel in their popular book *The Spirit Level,* "Rather than adopting an attitude of gratitude towards the rich, we need to recognize what a damaging effect they have on the social fabric."[67]

Radio host Thom Hartmann, after reflecting on why there are so few people capable of running America's most successful companies, concluded that only sociopaths are capable of being CEOs.[68] In fact, the latest fad in academia is to publish studies that allegedly show that people with more money are sociopaths who lack empathy, and have no qualms about lying, cheating, and stealing. Citing some of these studies, Demos writer and research associate Sean McElwee concludes, "Rather than being better than the rest of us, in many ways the rich are worse."[69]

Journalist Rob Kall tells us: "Nature doesn't approve of really big. Matter of fact, it kills or severely handicaps biological anomalies and freaks that become really big. I'm suggesting that we do such a 'natural' thing with billionaires—eliminate their existence and prevent them from developing."[70] Another columnist summed things up this way: "[W]hen it comes down to it, rich people, whoever you are, fuck you guys."[71]

Anyone who objects to this disturbing invective is summarily dismissed. "The Internet is replete with apologias for the rich," writes McElwee. "They are thinly sourced and even less well thought. The goal is simple: to justify the unjustifiable chasm between the rich and poor, globally and within our nation."[72] When successful Americans themselves object to being demonized, they are castigated for complaining. Best-selling author Barbara Ehrenreich explains, "To the extent that any demonization is going on, one can't help thinking that the rich have been, perhaps inadvertently, asking for it." (How have they been "asking for it"? Like a good Rawlsian, Ehrenreich complains that they've used their money to buy things that make other people jealous.)[73]

In light of these comments, consider some of the solutions to inequality offered by the alarmists. When it comes to propping up the "have-nots," their proposals are almost never focused on making the unsuccessful more productive or self-reliant. Instead they involve *demanding* more from the successful: via the welfare state, via unions, via regulations such as the minimum wage. More troubling, many of their proposals don't pretend to help the poor and middle class at all, but instead call on us to throttle and confiscate the wealth of successful Americans as an end in itself.

Vox.com founder Matthew Yglesias has come out with a proposal to set a *maximum* wage.[74] *Gawker*'s Hamilton Noah wrote an earlier piece with the same proposal, in which he declared that $1.25 million is "far more than anyone should be earning," but munificently offered to cap pay at $5 million a year. "A $5 million per year ceiling is, if anything, too generous. But we can always crank it down later." "This," he adds, "is a baby step. . . ."[75] Hartmann offered a similar proposal directed at wealth, rather than income: "I say it's time we outlaw billionaires by placing a 100% tax on any wealth over $999,999,999. Trust me, we'll all be much better off in a nation free of billionaires."[76]

Or consider Thomas Piketty's solutions to the problem of rising inequality. Piketty's chief proposals for fighting inequality are an annual global wealth tax of up to 10 percent a year, inheritance taxes in the neighborhood of 70 to 80 percent, and self-described "confiscatory" top marginal income tax rates as high as 80 percent.[77] Are these taxes to be used to help lift up those below the top? Not according to Piketty. In every case, Piketty acknowledges that "these very high brackets never yield much" in the way of tax revenues. That is not the point. The point, he says, is "to put an end to such incomes and large estates."[78]

The most consistent alarmists—those who value equality above all else—openly admit that they do not care about freedom and progress. Best-selling author Naomi Klein argues that to truly deal with the problem of inequality, we must reject capitalism altogether, give up on the idea of economic progress, and embrace a decentralized agrarian form of socialism.[79] In *The Spirit Level*, Wilkinson and Pickett reach a similar conclusion, telling us that "we need to limit economic growth severely in rich countries." Would this mean greater human suffering? Absolutely not, they say. "Once we have enough of the necessities of life, it is the relativities which matter."[80] Besides, they go on to explain, we have a real-life example which proves that stagnation need not mean misery. What country are they talking about? Who is it America should aspire to emulate? Communist Cuba.[81] (The *New York Times*, meanwhile, recently condemned rising prosperity in Cuba, made possible by loosened controls at home and loosened trade restrictions with the U.S., for increasing Cuban inequality.[82])

It's important to understand that the inequality alarmists' ire is not directed only at "the rich," but at something much broader: at anyone who desires to become rich and at the political-economic system that liberates people to pursue riches. This is what explains the fact that they not only support policies that harm the ambitious poor—they do so *in the full knowledge* that they are handicapping those who desire a better life. The clearest example here is their obsession with increasing the minimum wage, despite the fact that it prevents many poor people from taking the first step on the ladder of success. Recall the disturbing statement from McElwee, which we saw in chapter 5, that even if "unemployment rose and prices increased, a higher minimum wage could still be an acceptable policy. We must ask ourselves whether we want to live in a society when the poorest working people cannot afford to purchase basic necessities."[83] For the inequality alarmists, compassion consists of sentencing millions of poor people to the welfare rolls, so that they are barred from achieving the opportunity and self-respect that come with holding even a low-paying job.

The inequality alarmists are working to turn America into a land *inhospitable* to opportunity. You want to make something of your life? The message is: don't bother, mobility is a myth. You have made something of your life? The message is: you didn't build that—you got lucky. You struggled, worked, took risks, gave up time with your friends and family, and made something great? The government will take 80 percent off the top, 5 or 10 percent of what's left every year after that, and then 80 percent of what you want to pass on to your kids. All the while, you'll be told that you're a greedy, sociopathic exploiter and that the country would be better off without you.

No one is so foolish as to think that *this* is the path to reviving the American spirit and saving the American Dream. That is not the goal of the inequality alarmists. What is their goal?

CHOPPING DOWN THE TALL POPPIES

The Australians call it "Tall Poppy Syndrome." When a poppy dares to grow taller than the others, you cut it down to size. It's a metaphor for an attitude toward success that is certainly not confined to any one country. A healthy attitude toward the sight of other people's success is goodwill, admiration, and emulation. It can even include a healthy sense of competition: the desire to match your best against the best that others have to offer, not in a war where the loser suffers, but in a mutually respectful campaign where the only question is who will rise the highest. It is totally natural to look at others' achievements and think, "I want that—I want *more* than that—so I'm going to work harder and be better." For some people, however, the sight of ambition and achievement evokes different feelings: hostility, resentment, and envy.

Don't confuse this with run-of-the-mill jealousy. Many a corporate executive or Ivy League academic has quietly, or not-so-quietly, fumed over his colleague's bigger paycheck or bigger office. Those feelings can have many sources. Sometimes it's the rational conviction that the recipient isn't truly deserving, which isn't even jealousy, but a sense of justice. Other times it's similar to a thief's desire for the values others have earned. But Tall Poppy Syndrome is different. It is not a desire for personal success, but the desire to tear down the successful. Not the longing to have what others have, but the longing for them to *lose* what they have. Not the wish to compete with others, but the wish to see them destroyed.

It's so hard for most of us to comprehend such a desire that many people question whether it really exists. But the evidence is all around us. We see it in the school bully who beats up the straight-A student, even though this will not make the bully any smarter. We see it in the attacks on Google and other companies who provide free bus service to their Silicon Valley employees, even though banning those buses won't provide the attackers with additional transportation. We see it in the well-known phenomenon of *Schadenfreude*, taking pleasure in other people's misfortunes. We saw it, tragically, in the "crab-pot" attacks on ambitious young people struggling to escape the ghetto. We saw it in the horrors of twentieth-century totalitarianism, where people were starved, enslaved, and murdered, not for any "practical" purpose, but as an end in itself.

When some people see intelligence, ability, ambition, or achievement, their reaction amounts to the feeling that "You're showing me up." They do not want to struggle, to work, to learn, to grow—and since this is what success requires, their goal becomes the destruction of success, as if by tearing down the achievements of others, no one can expect any achievements of them.

Nowhere is this attitude more pronounced in our own time than in the envy some politicians and intellectuals have of businessmen. Successful businessmen don't simply earn enormous amounts of money, they also display a self-confidence and independence that comes from the knowledge that they can solve problems and build things: they are powerful and efficacious in a way that the envious politicians and intellectuals are not. Nothing is more alarming to the enviers than the keen sense that *they* need businessmen—and that businessmen have no need for them. The politician knows (and resents) that he needs businessmen to fund his campaigns (and his welfare-state giveaways). The intellectual knows (and resents) that he needs businessmen to fund his university so he can spend his time churning out papers attacking business and capitalism. What they resent most of all is that they depend on businessmen and other creators for their very *survival*—for their phones, their cars, their food, their fuel. To prove their superiority, the enviers seek to assert their power: not the power to create, but the power to destroy creators.

Envy is so ugly a motive that we are compelled to keep it hidden, not just from others, but from ourselves. It has to be justified, or more accurately, rationalized. "Rationalization," Rand explains, "is a cover-up, a process of providing one's emotions with a false identity, of giving them spurious explanations and justifications—in order to hide one's motives, not just from others, but primarily from oneself. . . . Rationalization is a process not of perceiving reality, but of attempting to make reality fit one's emotions."[84]

To justify their hatred of creators, enviers seize on any number of rationalizations. "They're not that smart—anyone could do what they do." "They didn't earn their wealth—they're society's lottery winners." "They're greedy." "They're selfish." "They exploit the poor." These catchphrases don't come out of nowhere: they are the product of the more ambitious enviers, who spin out entire *systems of thought* that seek to justify tearing down the successful.[85]

Take communism, for example. As author Joseph Epstein argues:

> The doctrine of Marxism is many things, but one among them is a plan
> of revenge for the envious. How else can one view Karl Marx's central
> idea, the perpetual class struggle, ending in the defeat and eradication

of the aristocracy, the rentier class, the bourgeois, everyone, really, but the working class, which will arise at last in the form of the glorious dictatorship of the proletariat? "It is only in Marxism, the abstract and glorified concept of the proletariat, the disinherited, and exploited," writes Helmut Schoeck, "that a position of implacable envy is fully legitimized." In certain minds, Marxism can be seen as less a body of economic theory than as an act of collective vengeance: soak the rich, is its rally cry, in their own blood, is implied.[86]

This analysis is confirmed by British historian Alan Bullock, who observes, "The Russian revolutionary tradition made a virtue of a complete indifference toward human life in the pursuit of a more just and equal society." The collectivist ideal gave a moral sanction to terrorizing, imprisoning, and executing individuals in the name of this "higher purpose," so that "[i]f any lingering inhibitions were left in [the communist's] mind they would have been exorcised by that sense of mission that provided an automatic justification [i.e., rationalization], and armored him against any feelings of compassion or guilt for the millions of lives he destroyed as the agent of historical necessity."[87]

Egalitarianism, as a modern philosophic movement, in many ways arose as a response to the failure of communism (and every other form of socialism) during the twentieth century. For a long time, collectivist intellectuals argued that capitalism was immoral because it impoverished the masses, and that socialism of one form or another would raise everyone's standard of living and, as Khrushchev had assured the world, bury the capitalist West. But it was becoming increasingly clear that it was socialism that impoverished the masses and capitalism that generated undreamed-of levels of prosperity. This created a crisis for the intellectuals who remained committed to socialism as a moral ideal. Instead of embracing capitalist prosperity, many of them simply redefined the goal: not economic prosperity but *economic equality*.

Economic equality is not a new ideal. It goes back at least to Rousseau; the Marxists, socialists, and American Progressives had all long complained about economic inequality under capitalism. But the modern egalitarians define equality as good in and of itself, not as a means to progress and prosperity. Despite the fact that free and economically unequal societies have been eliminating poverty from the globe, the egalitarians insist that we have a moral obligation to fight inequality by restricting freedom. Their goal and motive is to tear down the successful. This is not an incidental by-product of their doctrine—it is the whole point.

Take the most influential egalitarian moral premise, Rawls's difference principle, which alarmists such as Krugman and Piketty invoke in their work. The difference principle, recall, says that economic inequalities should be tolerated only to the extent that they work to the advantage of the worst off. This principle is actually the *most* permissive of inequalities among those advocated by egalitarians. Yet what this means is that, in the words of philosopher David E. Cooper, "where the choice is between a situation in which the advantages of some do not benefit the rest and a situation in which there are no advantages to be enjoyed [by anyone], the egalitarian must prefer the latter." If everyone can't attend prestigious private schools, for example, and if those schools don't work to the advantage of the least well-off, then according to the difference principle, we should want to see them abolished. "But," Cooper goes on to ask, "is not this preference . . . precisely the mark of envy? After all, the 'have-nots' do not gain by abolishing the advantages; it's just that the 'haves' lose them."[88] The difference principle is not motivated by compassion toward the least well-off, but hatred of ability and achievement.

Leading egalitarian philosopher Thomas Nagel is even more explicit, declaring that "a person does not deserve his intelligence, and I have maintained that he does not deserve the rewards that superior intelligence can provide." In Nagel's view, "When racial and sexual injustice have been reduced, we shall still be left with the great injustice of the smart and the dumb, who are so differently rewarded for comparable effort." But wouldn't remedying this "injustice" mean that "the interests of some are being sacrificed to further the interests of others"? Of course, but that's okay because "it is the better placed who are being sacrificed . . ."[89]

Egalitarianism is the ultimate rationalization for hatred of ambition, ability, and success. Whereas the older doctrines had to argue that wealthy individuals were exploiters, despite the fact that the people they were supposedly exploiting were living better and better lives, egalitarianism views tearing down the successful as an end in itself as an act of justice.

Egalitarianism has never appealed to Americans, and so today's inequality alarmists are back to playing the same game as earlier collectivists by appealing to people's desire for progress, prosperity, and opportunity, and telling them that the way to realize the American Dream is to fight economic inequality. But this appeal to the American Dream is a façade. Their goal is not to save the American Dream—not as Americans have long understood it—but to redefine it. The American Dream is no longer to be thought of in the way that James Truslow Adams did when he coined the phrase, as "that dream of a land in which life should be better and richer and fuller for everyone, with opportunity for each according to ability or achievement"—it's to be thought of as the dream of a land in which there is no opportunity for ability and achievement to create inequality.[90] In seeking to redefine the American Dream, the inequality alarmists are, in reality, seeking to destroy it.

If we want to save the American Dream and create a more just, more prosperous society, it's clear what's required of us: we must reject the collectivist-egalitarian doctrine advanced by the inequality alarmists, and instead champion an individualist ideal that celebrates human achievement and liberates human ability.

CONCLUSION

HOW TO SAVE THE AMERICAN DREAM

WHY THE AMERICAN DREAM MATTERS

As we were wrapping up work on this project, Don became a father for the second time, welcoming his son Landon into the world. Part of what makes the experience of having children so incredible is the sense of infinite possibilities. There's no limit to who our kids can become and what they can achieve.

Today's debate over inequality is not fundamentally about tax rates or government spending or which political party will win the next election. It's really a debate about whether individual lives matter and whether individual happiness matters. To the inequality alarmists, Landon's life *doesn't* matter. Because his father is white, educated, and relatively affluent, the moral thing to do, on the collectivist-egalitarian premise, is to hold him back, deprive him of opportunities, and, if he does make something of his life, use him as fodder in the campaign against success. To whatever extent the inequality alarmists succeed at influencing the way we think or the political policies we endorse, it will come at the expense of every individual who values his own happiness and the happiness of the people he loves.

We cannot take the American Dream for granted. In the United States, Don can expect Landon to live a long and healthy life, to always have enough to eat, to have educational and job opportunities that will allow him to make of his life whatever he chooses. That is not something that has been true for most parents throughout history—or for many parents in many places in the world today. We should never forget that in places like Cuba, desperate parents continue to risk their lives and their children's lives just for the chance of opportunity. There but for the grace (and courage) of the Founding Fathers go we.

But freedom, prosperity, and opportunity, once established, aren't guaranteed for all time. They are things we need to continually work for and fight for. That starts with striving to make something of our own lives. We need to make ourselves into self-supporting, self-directing individuals, eager to chart our own course and pay our own way. If we find that there is part of us that desires the unearned, that thinks of ourselves as helpless victims, that doesn't want to take responsibility for our own choices, or that resents other people's opportunities and success, then we should work to change that and to nurture the best in ourselves: our rationality, our independence, our commitment to justice, our desire for joy. And we should also fight for a better culture—one that regards the pursuit of success and happiness as sacrosanct, and that views the achievement of success and happiness as something to be celebrated. This will require opposing the philosophy that denounces ability, achievement, freedom, and personal happiness—the collectivist-egalitarian philosophy of the inequality alarmists.

HOW TO OPPOSE THE CAMPAIGN AGAINST INEQUALITY

The key to opposing the inequality campaign is not only to counter its specific claims, but to challenge its entire framework. The inequality alarmists, in Piketty's words, put "the distributional question . . . at the heart of economic analysis."[1] We must insist on putting *production* at the heart of economic analysis.

The inequality alarmists take the existence of progress and prosperity for granted. For them, the goods are here, and the only question is who should get them. How did they get here? That's irrelevant.[2]

But we can't take progress and prosperity for granted. They aren't like the air we breathe, which is as plentiful in North Korea as it is in North America. They depend on the achievements of individuals, and it is immoral and self-destructive to ignore the preconditions of those achievements.

We need to start by asking one very simple question: where does wealth come from? The answer, as we've seen, is that it is *created,* and so one man's fortune does not come at anyone else's expense. How is wealth created? By individual thought and effort. Morally, what an individual creates through his own thought and effort belongs to him. Politically, an individual can only exercise thought and effort if he is free. This is the individualist framework that's required to defeat the campaign against economic inequality.

Maintaining a consistent individualist framework cannot be reduced to a sound bite. But there are a few key points that we need to keep at the forefront of any discussion of inequality, in order to cut the alarmists off at the knees.

Name your standard. The inequality debate is ultimately a debate about right and wrong. Is it right that some people make a lot more money than other people? Or is that an injustice that we need to fight? But how we answer questions about right and wrong depends on our standard. A standard of value is an abstract principle that allows us to evaluate things as right or wrong, moral or immoral, just or unjust.

For the inequality alarmists, their standard of value is the collectivist notion of "the good of society." According to this view, the fact that you worked and earned something that will help you live a richer, fuller life doesn't mean you're entitled to it—not if some people have less and therefore "need it" more than you do. Justice, in the collectivist view, is not about individuals getting what they deserve according to what they earn—it's about members of society getting what they need regardless of what they earn.

On the individualist standard of value, each individual is an end in himself, not a means to the ends of others. An individual's pursuit of happiness is not something that has to be justified by reference to the good of society—a society is good to the extent that it leaves individuals free to pursue their own happiness. Each of us has the right to seek out happiness and success, and we deserve whatever we earn in that pursuit. No one is entitled to take away the values we have achieved, and by the same token, we are not entitled to the values achieved by others. Our life is our responsibility, and if we want something from other people, justice requires that we earn it through voluntary exchange. The bare fact that we want or need something from other people doesn't give us a right to it. Other people are not our servants, and their job isn't to spend their days and hours working for our benefit rather than their own.

In any discussion, we have to be clear about our standard. If the inequality critics say that it's wrong for CEOs to get paid so much, what's their standard? Is it wrong because a given CEO didn't earn his pay? Or is it wrong because, irrespective of whether he earned it, he makes so much more than other people? If they say it's wrong for people to make only the minimum wage, what's their standard? Are they arguing that some people are being paid less than their productive contribution warrants? Or are they arguing that people deserve a "living wage," regardless of what their productive contribution warrants? If they say that it's unfair for Wall Street bankers to get bailouts, what's their standard? Is it unfair because the government shouldn't have the power to force some people to subsidize others? Or is it unfair because "the rich" should subsidize the non-rich, and not the other way around?

Distinguish between the non-problem of inequality and any legitimate issues. Inequality refers simply to the fact that people differ in their incomes or wealth. On the individualist standard of value, there is absolutely nothing wrong or even suspicious about that. But the inequality alarmists invariably package the issue of inequality with things that someone using an individualist standard of value could legitimately oppose: stagnating wages, skyrocketing health care costs, declining mobility, high unemployment, the failure of government to educate children. Those are all issues worthy of discussion and debate. But they shouldn't be treated as problems of inequality: we would be concerned about stagnating wages even if everyone's wages were stagnating equally, or about a failing education system even if children were equally ignorant.

Reject collectivist terminology. Taken straight, the collectivist worldview is highly implausible. It describes a world in which society as a whole creates an anonymous blob of wealth, which government has to divide up and distribute "fairly." But rarely is an explicit argument made in favor of the collectivist worldview. Instead, it is assumed via collectivist terminology. We speak of "society's wealth," and "the distribution of income." We speak of "the public interest" and "the common welfare," which assumes that the standard of value is not the individual but the group. We speak of "the rich" and "the poor" and "the middle class," which assumes that there are such things as economic classes with clashing interests. We need to reject philosophically loaded terms, and be scrupulous in how we conceptualize economic phenomena.

Don't equate opportunity with the ability of poor people to escape poverty. What we should be concerned with is not "the poor" or "the middle class" or "the 99 percent," but the individual. And that means *each* individual. Opportunity is not only about escaping poverty: it's about each individual's freedom to think, to work, and to make his life as happy and successful as he can, regardless of how much he has already achieved. Being poor doesn't entitle a person to special consideration by the state. It is true that we should cheer people trying to make something of their lives, and we naturally feel compassion toward those who struggle to do so in the face of huge challenges. And while there is nothing wrong with helping them *privately* and *voluntarily*, we should always keep in mind that no matter what help we privately give them in the short term, the best thing we can do for them in the long haul is to speak out for their (and our own) freedom: when political privilege trumps merit, it is the people of merit, especially at the bottom, who are the biggest victims.

Make the inequality alarmists justify their proposed solutions. You will no doubt encounter many claims that you can't easily evaluate: academic studies that say inequality undermines mobility or economic progress, claims about "the bulk of the gains" going to "the rich" rather than the middle class, stories about injustices supposedly committed by "the 1 percent" against "the 99 percent." In these cases the question to ask is: "Assuming this is a problem, what is your solution?" Inevitably, the inequality critics' answer will be that some form of force must be used to tear down the top by depriving them of the earned, and to prop up the bottom by giving them the unearned. But nothing can justify an injustice, nor can any statistical model erase the fact that all of the values human life requires are a product of the human mind, and that the human mind cannot function without freedom.

Don't concede that the inequality alarmists value equality. The egalitarians pose as defenders of equality. But there is no such thing as being for equality across the board: different types of equality conflict. Namely, economic equality (including equality of opportunity) is incompatible with political equality. We must choose between political equality and economic equality. It's one or the other. It is the defenders of freedom and individual rights who are the true champions of political equality.

HOW TO LIBERATE ABILITY

We do face problems today, but they aren't economic inequality problems—they are political inequality problems. Our equal rights as human beings aren't being protected. If we want to save the American Dream, we need a program to secure those rights and thereby liberate human ability. In our first book, *Free Market Revolution,* we laid out a full program for establishing laissez-faire capitalism in America. Here are five steps that, while not erasing all of the government's barriers to success, would go a long way toward restoring opportunity to America.

1. **Abolish all forms of corporate welfare so that no business can gain unfair advantages.** This includes bailouts, subsidies, tariffs, government-granted monopolies, and the like. Businesses should have to compete for customers on a free market. They should not be able to line their pockets by striking deals with politicians, or to slow down and stop innovators from challenging convention and improving how we live.

2. **Abolish government barriers to work so that every individual can enjoy the dignity of earned success.** Opportunity depends in part on being able to find a job, any job, and work your way up. We should end all laws and regulations that prevent people from finding jobs. Above all, we should abolish the minimum wage, pro-union laws, and occupational licensing requirements that act as barriers of entry for would-be workers and entrepreneurs.

3. **Phase out the welfare state so that America can once again become the land of self-reliance.** The welfare state represents the total inversion of the ideal of opportunity: instead of liberating us to live self-supporting, self-directing lives, the welfare state

prevents us from living self-supporting, self-directing lives. Social Security and Medicare alone force younger people to work more than a month and a half each year without pay in order to supply elderly Americans with handouts. But it's not just about the money we lose. These paternalistic programs take away our freedom to plan our lives as we judge best, telling us how to prepare for retirement or how to fulfill our health care needs. The welfare state is unnecessary, destructive, and immoral. The vast majority of Americans are capable of being self-supporting throughout their lives, and would be in a far better position to be self-supporting if so much of what they earned didn't go into other people's pockets. (For more on what's wrong with the welfare state and how to phase it out, see Don's book *RooseveltCare: How Social Security Is Sabotaging the Land of Self-Reliance.*)

4. **Unleash the power of innovation in education by ending the government monopoly on schooling.** The cruelest, most destructive aspect of what government does is deprive children of their potential through the government school system. At the same time that we hesitate to give government control over our health care decisions, we give the state total control over the ideas and values our children are taught. It is bad enough that today's schools are filled with propaganda—including attacks on capitalism, the Founding Fathers, and business—but much worse is the fact that children are not even taught how to think. We should start by giving parents tax credits if they decide to opt out of the government schools to search for better alternatives. But ultimately, if we value opportunity and our children's future, we should abolish the government schools and open the field to creators and innovators.

5. **Liberate innovators from the regulatory shackles that are strangling them.** Human progress depends on innovators being free to "think different" and challenge the status quo. Regulations are innovation killers because, unlike legitimate laws, which proscribe criminal behavior, regulations proscribe and prescribe

productive behavior. The worst villain here is antitrust, which punishes the most successful innovators for the very business activities that make them successful. Cutting prices equals "predatory pricing." Raising prices equals "price gouging." Keeping prices in line with competitors equals "collusion." Buying up businesses and expanding into new markets equal "intent to monopolize." A superlative product and a legion of passionate customers equal "barriers to entry." Profits amount to proof of "market failure" and "monopoly power." If we could do only one thing to encourage innovation and show that we value innovators, it should be to abolish antitrust, totally and immediately—and to apologize to its victims.

CREATING A CULTURE OF ACHIEVEMENT

In a 1995 interview, Steve Jobs said:

> When you grow up you, you tend to get told that the world is the way it is and your life is just to live your life inside the world, try not to bash into the walls too much, try to have a nice family life, have fun, save a little money. That's a very limited life. Life can be much broader, once you discover one simple fact, and that is [that] everything around you that you call life was made up by people that were no smarter than you. And you can change it, you can influence it, you can build your own things that other people can use. . . . That's maybe the most important thing. It's to shake off this erroneous notion that life is there and you're just gonna live in it, versus embrace it, change it, improve it, make your mark upon it.[3]

A few years back, Yaron visited Cambodia. He saw villages with no electricity, in which the few appliances available had to be run using car batteries. No matter how hot or rainy it was outside, farmers spent all day in the fields just to subsist. Others resorted to selling anything they could get their hands on—including garbage—to tourists just so they could eat.

The distance between that world and ours was created by those who, like Jobs, made their mark upon the world: the thinkers, the producers, the creators who turned steam into power, steel into tractors and train tracks, sand into silicon, petroleum into pharmaceuticals. We owe them recognition. We owe them gratitude. We owe them freedom.

Yet that is exactly what the campaign against economic inequality denies them. By refusing to ask the question—*where does wealth come from?*—by taking the modern world for granted, by attributing success to luck, and by condemning achievement for creating inequality, the alarmists are attempting to perpetrate an obscene injustice: to redistribute the achievements of the men and women of extraordinary ability, all the while branding those men and women as immoral.

This is nothing new. It's the same attack that's been going on since the start of the Industrial Revolution. In Ayn Rand's hymn to human ability, the 1957 novel *Atlas Shrugged,* copper magnate Francisco d'Anconia speaks to his friend, the great industrialist Hank Rearden, about how Rearden has been treated by the world:

"All your life, you have heard yourself denounced, not for your faults, but for your greatest virtues. You have been hated, not for your mistakes, but for your achievements. You have been scorned for all those qualities of character which are your highest pride. You have been called selfish for the courage of acting on your own judgment and bearing sole responsibility for your own life. You have been called arrogant for your independent mind. You have been called cruel for your unyielding integrity. You have been called antisocial for the vision that made you venture upon undiscovered roads. You have been called ruthless for the strength and self-discipline of your drive to your purpose. You have been called greedy for the magnificence of your power to create wealth. You, who've expanded an inconceivable flow of energy, have been called a parasite. You, who've created abundance where there had been nothing but wastelands and helpless, starving men before you, have been called a robber. You, who've kept them all alive, have been called an exploiter."[4]

Isn't that what we hear, day in and day out, from the inequality alarmists? How long can we expect to live in a land of prosperity when this is how we treat those who prosper? How can we say that we value the opportunity to succeed when this is how we treat those who turn opportunities into success? What will become of the next Steve Jobs or Thomas Edison or John Rockefeller, if this is what he or she has to look forward to?

Creating a culture that is hospitable toward success is not something that happens easily or automatically. It requires us to do the opposite of what was done to Rearden and *celebrate* success. We can't all be Hank Reardens or Steve Jobses or Thomas Edisons, but we can strive to live up to their example on whatever scale we can—and to practice what our colleague Onkar Ghate has called "the virtue of admiration."

> To practice the virtue of admiration *does* demand much of a man. He must respect and nurture the best within himself and within any man: his ability to produce and create on whatever scale he is capable of. His God must be man's competence. He must be willing to look up and to exert the effort to learn from those of superior knowledge and ability. He must be willing to acknowledge the intellectual gifts that he receives from those more productive than him, which he can become worthy of in part by showing his gratitude. He must judge the world scrupulously, deciding for himself what deserves his "Yes" and his "No." And then he must further and fight for that which he sees to be good, for that to which he has granted his "Yes." To practice the virtue of admiration is to stand, head lifted, and give thanks for the greatness of another man and all that it, and its sight, will make possible in one's own life. It is to be *motivated* by the best possible to oneself and to man.[5]

Creating a culture hospitable to success will require us to nurture certain ideas: that individuals are fundamentally in control of their own lives; that they are responsible for their own failure or success; that success is something good, desirable, and admirable, not something that has to be atoned for by "giving something back." And it will require us to fight—self-confidently and unapologetically—for political policies that protect our *freedom* to pursue and enjoy success. That's a fight worth fighting—and it's a fight that can be won.

THE LAST WORD

We want to end on a personal note. To those who have created the modern world, who have struggled, fought, and succeeded, we want to say *thank you*. To those who are just starting out in life, who are dreaming big dreams, and hoping to make their mark on the world, we want to say: best wishes. Success is possible and the struggle is worth it.

ACKNOWLEDGMENTS

A great many people contributed to this book, in large and in small ways. In particular, we want to thank Steve Simpson, Rob Tarr, Adam Edmonsond, Chad Morris, Manjari Narayan, Carl Svanberg, Lin Zinser, Angela Dietrich, Jeremiah Cobra, Eric Dennis, Peter Schwartz, Kyle Steele, and Jason Crawford for their input and assistance at various stages of this project. We also wish to thank Donna Montrezza and Rachel Knapp for proofreading the manuscript, and Patrick Ryan for supplying the graphs and charts.

Our greatest debt of gratitude goes to Alex Epstein, Gregory Salmieri, and, above all, Onkar Ghate, whose editorial feedback were indispensable in the writing of this book.

Finally, we would like to thank the Ayn Rand Institute and its supporters for helping to make this project—and all of our work—possible.

NOTES

CHAPTER 1

1. Yaron Brook, Republican Party of Virginia 2009 State Convention, May 30, 2009.
2. William A. Galston, "America's Challenge: Growth That Works for All," *Wall Street Journal*, September 9, 2014, http://online.wsj.com/articles/william-galston-americas-challenge-growth-that-works-for-all-1410304351 (accessed April 12, 2015); *Gallup*, "Most Important Problem," http://www.gallup.com/poll/1675/most-important-problem.aspx (accessed April 12, 2015); Bruce Stokes, "The U.S.'s High Income Gap Is Met with Relatively Low Public Concern," *Pew Research Center*, December 6, 2013, http://www.pewresearch.org/fact-tank/2013/12/06/the-u-s-s-high-income-gap-is-met-with-relatively-low-public-concern/ (accessed April 12, 2015).
3. Barack Obama, "Remarks by the President on Economic Mobility," *The White House*, December 4, 2013, http://www.whitehouse.gov/the-press-office/2013/12/04/remarks-president-economic-mobility (accessed April 12, 2015).
4. Joseph E. Stiglitz, *The Price of Inequality* (New York: Norton, 2013), p. 2.
5. Timothy Noah, *The Great Divergence: America's Growing Inequality Crisis and What We Can Do About It* (New York: Bloomsbury Press, 2013), chapter 1.
6. Thomas Piketty, *Capital in the Twenty-First Century* (Cambridge, MA: Belknap, 2014), pp. 1, 514.
7. Obama, "Remarks by the President on Economic Mobility."
8. James Truslow Adams, *The Epic of America* (Garden City, NY: Garden City Books, 1933), p. 317.
9. Obama, "Remarks by the President on Economic Mobility."
10. Joseph E. Stiglitz, "Conclusion: Slow Growth and Inequality Are Political Choices. We Can Choose Otherwise," *Washington Monthly*, November/December 2014, http://www.washingtonmonthly.com/magazine/novemberdecember_2014/features/conclusion_slow_growth_and_ine052716.php (accessed April 12, 2015).
11. Obama, "Remarks by the President on Economic Mobility."
12. Piketty, *Capital in the Twenty-First Century*, pp. 513, 517.
13. Richard Wilkinson and Kate Pickett, *The Spirit Level* (New York: Bloomsbury Press, 2009), pp. 225–26.
14. Naomi Klein, *This Changes Everything: Capitalism vs. the Climate* (New York: Simon & Schuster, 2014).
15. Thom Hartmann, "The No Billionaires Campaign," *OpEdNews*, July 18, 2012, http://www.opednews.com/populum/printer_friendly.php?content=a&id=153218 (accessed April 12, 2015).
16. Stiglitz, *The Price of Inequality*, p. 8.
17. Obama, "Remarks by the President on Economic Mobility."
18. Robert H. Frank and Philip J. Cook, *The Winner-Take-All Society* (New York: Free Press, 1995), p. vii.

19. Piketty, *Capital in the Twenty-First Century*, p. 19.

20. See, for instance, Daniel T. Rodgers, *The Work Ethic in Industrial America 1850–1920* (Chicago: University of Chicago Press, 1979), pp. 1–4.

21. Gordon S. Wood, *The Radicalism of the American Revolution* (New York: Vintage, 1992), p. 139.

22. J. Hector St. John de Crèvecœur, "Letters from an American Farmer: Letter III—What Is an American," http://avalon.law.yale.edu/18th_century/letter_03.asp (accessed April 23, 2015).

23. Rodgers, *The Work Ethic*, p. 5.

24. Daniel Yergin, *The Prize* (New York: Free Press, 2008), p. 15.

25. Francis J. Grund, *The Americans in Their Moral, Social, and Political Relations*, 2 vols. (London: Longman, Rees, Orme, Brown, Green and Longman, 1837), pp. 1–2, 5. Quoted in Rodgers, *The Work Ethic*, pp. 5–6.

26. John Locke, *The Second Treatise of Government*, V, 34.

27. Quoted in Jon Ward, "Paul Ryan Reads from 1850 Irish Government Poster to Make Case for Immigration Reform," *Huffington Post*, June 12, 2013, http://www.huffingtonpost.com/2013/06/12/paul-ryan-poster-irish-im_n_3428852.html (accessed April 23, 2015).

28. Robert Rector and Rachel Sheffield, "Understanding Poverty in the United States: Surprising Facts about America's Poor," *Heritage Foundation*, September 13, 2011, http://www.heritage.org/research/reports/2011/09/understanding-poverty-in-the-united-states-surprising-facts-about-americas-poor (accessed April 12, 2015).

CHAPTER 2

1. Robert B. Reich, *Beyond Outrage* (New York: Vintage, 2012), pp. 6–7.

2. Joseph E. Stiglitz, "Equal Opportunity, Our National Myth," *New York Times*, February 2013, http://opinionator.blogs.nytimes.com/2013/02/16/equal-opportunity-our-national-myth/ (accessed April 12, 2015).

3. Thomas Piketty, "Capital in the Twenty-First Century," March 2014, http://piketty.pse.ens.fr/en/capital21c2 (accessed April 12, 2015).

4. On some of the problems with Piketty's data on wealth inequality, see Phillip W. Magness and Robert P. Murphy, "Challenging the Empirical Contribution of Thomas Piketty's *Capital in the Twenty-First Century*," *Journal of Private Enterprise*, Spring 2015, http://papers.ssrn.com/sol3/papers.cfm?abstract_id=2543012 (accessed April 12, 2015); Malin Sahlén and Salim Furth, "Piketty Is Misleading about the Swedish Case," *Timbro*, November 7, 2014, http://timbro.se/en/samhallsekonomi/articles/piketty-is-misleading-about-the-swedish-case (accessed April 12, 2015); Phillip W. Magness, "5 Remaining Problems for Thomas Piketty in the Wake of the FT Controversy," *Atlas Network*, June 16, 2014, http://www.atlasnetwork.org/news/article/5-remaining-problems-for-thomas-piketty-in-the-wake-of-the-ft-controversy (accessed April 12, 2015); and Alan J. Auerbach and Kevin Hassett, "Capital Taxation in the Twenty-First Century," *American Economic Association*, January 3, 2015, https://www.aeaweb.org/aea/2015conference/program/retrieve.php?pdfid=421 (accessed April 12, 2015). On problems with Piketty's data on income inequality, see Phil Gramm and Michael Solon, "How to Distort Income Inequality," *Wall Street Journal*, November 11, 2014, http://www.wsj.com/articles/phil-gramm-and-michael-solon-how-to-distort-income-inequality-1415749856 (accessed April 12, 2015); and Alan Cole, "Income Data Is a Poor Measure of Inequality," *Tax Foundation*, August 13, 2014, http://taxfoundation.org/article/income-data-poor-measure-inequality (accessed April 12, 2015).

5. See, for instance, David A. Henderson, "Economic Inequality: Facts, Theory and Significance," *National Center for Policy Analysis*, June 2008, http://www.ncpa.org/pdfs/st312.pdf (accessed May 20, 2015).

6. Phillip Magness, "Picking Piketty Apart," *Freeman*, March 31, 2015, http://fee.org/freeman/detail/picking-piketty-apart (accessed May 20, 2015).

7. Paul Krugman, "Losing Our Country," *New York Times*, June 10, 2005, http://www.nytimes.com/2005/06/10/opinion/10krugman.html (accessed April 13, 2015).

8. Robert A. Margo, "Wages and Wage Inequality" in chapter Ba of *Historical Statistics of the United States, Earliest Times to the Present: Millennial Edition*, edited by Susan B. Carter,

Scott Sigmund Gartner, Michael R. Haines, Alan L. Olmstead, Richard Sutch, and Gavin Wright (New York: Cambridge University Press, 2006), http://dx.doi.org/10.1017/ISBN -9780511132971.Ba.ESS.04 (accessed May 20, 2015).

9. Michael R. Haines, "Expectation of Life at Birth, by Sex and Race: 1850–1998." Table Ab644-655 in *Historical Statistics of the United States, Earliest Times to the Present: Millennial Edition*, edited by Susan B. Carter, Scott Sigmund Gartner, Michael R. Haines, Alan L. Olmstead, Richard Sutch, and Gavin Wright (New York: Cambridge University Press, 2006), http:// dx.doi.org/10.1017/ISBN-9780511132971.Ab644-911 (accessed May 20, 2015).

10. W. Michael Cox and Richard Alm, *Myths of Rich & Poor* (New York: Basic Books, 1999), p. 55.

11. Kathryn M. Neckerman, "The Emergence of 'Underclass' Family Patterns, 1900–1940," in Michael B. Katz, ed., *The "Underclass" Debate* (Princeton: Princeton University Press, 1993), p. 206.

12. Quoted in Edward Chase Kirkland, *Industry Comes of Age* (Chicago: Quadrangle, 1967), p. 405.

13. J. Bradford DeLong, "Cornucopia: The Pace of Economic Growth in the Twentieth Century," NBER Working Paper No. 7602, March 2000, http://www.nber.org/papers/w7602.pdf (accessed April 13, 2015).

14. Paul Krugman, *The Conscience of a Liberal* (New York: W. W. Norton & Company, 2009), p. 19.

15. William H. Branson, Herbert Giersch, and Peter G. Peterson, "Trends in United States International Trade and Investment Since World War II," in Martin Feldstein, ed., *The American Economy in Transition* (Chicago: University of Chicago Press, 1980), http://www.nber.org /chapters/c11297.pdf (accessed April 13, 2015).

16. See, for instance, Diana Furchtgott-Roth, "Does Immigration Increase Economic Growth?" *e21 Issue Brief No. 2*, December 2014, http://www.manhattan-institute.org/pdf/e21_02.pdf (accessed April 13, 2015).

17. Leandro Prados de la Escosura, "Economic Freedom in the Long Run: Evidence from OECD Countries (1850-2007)," *CEPR Discussion Paper No. DP9918*, March 2014, http://ssrn.com /abstract=2444861 (accessed April 21, 2015).

18. Henry Hazlitt, *Economics in One Lesson* (New York: Three Rivers Press, 1979), p. 141.

19. Doug Altner, "It's Not the Unions—It's the Labor Laws," *American Thinker*, March 19, 2014, http://www.americanthinker.com/articles/2014/03/its_not_the_unions__its_the_labor _laws.html (accessed April 13, 2015).

20. Thomas Sowell, *Basic Economics* (New York: Basic Books, 2004), p. 172.

21. Krugman, *The Conscience of a Liberal*, p. 113.

22. Sowell, *Basic Economics*, p. 173.

23. James Pethokoukis, "Why We Can't Go Back to Sky-High, 1950s Tax Rates," *AEIdeas*, April 18, 2012, https://www.aei.org/publication/why-we-cant-go-back-to-sky-high-1950s-tax-rates/ (accessed April 21, 2015).

24. See, for instance, Arpit Gupta, "Revisiting the High Tax Rates of the 1950s," Manhattan Institute for Policy Research, April 2013, http://www.manhattan-institute.org/html/ib_19 .htm (accessed July 27, 2015).

25. U.S. Social Security Administration, "Table 5.A4 Number and Total Monthly Benefits, by Trust Fund and Type of Benefit, December 1940–2009, Selected Years," 2009, http://www .ssa.gov/policy/docs/statcomps/supplement/2010/5a.html#table5.a4 (accessed April 13, 2015) and U.S. Census Bureau, "U.S. Population by Year," Multpl.com, November 1, 2014, http:// www.multpl.com/united-states-population/table (accessed April 13, 2015).

26. Edmund Phelps, *Mass Flourishing* (Princeton, NJ: Princeton University Press, 2013), chapter 9.

27. John Micklethwait and Adrian Wooldridge, *The Right Nation* (New York: Penguin Books, 2005), p. 88.

28. Ronald Reagan, "First Inaugural Address," January 20, 1981, http://www.bartleby.com/124 /pres61.html (accessed April 21, 2015).

29. Hedrick Smith, *Who Stole the American Dream?* (New York: Random House, 2012), p. xxii.

30. See, for instance, Krugman, *The Conscience of a Liberal*; Reich, *Beyond Outrage*; Smith, *Who Stole the American Dream?*; Thomas Frank, *What's the Matter with Kansas?* (New York:

Metropolitan Books, 2004); Joseph E. Stiglitz, *The Price of Inequality* (New York: Norton, 2013); and Thomas Byrne Edsall, *The New Politics of Inequality* (New York: W. W. Norton & Company, 1984).

31. Frank, *What's the Matter with Kansas?*, p. 5.

32. Christopher Chantrill, "Spending in 20th Century," usgovernmentspending.com, April 13, 2015, http://www.usgovernmentspending.com/spending_chart_1900_2015USp_16s1li011l cn_F0f_Spending_In_20th_Century (accessed April 13, 2015).

33. Christopher Chantrill, "Total Recent Spending," usgovernmentspending.com, April 13, 2015, http://www.usgovernmentspending.com/spending_chart_1970_2015USp_16s1li111lcn _F0t_Total_Recent_Spending (accessed April 13, 2015).

34. Christopher Chantrill, "Recent Defense Spending," usgovernmentspending.com, April 13, 2015, http://www.usgovernmentspending.com/spending_chart_1970_2015USp_16s1li011lc n_30f_Recent_Defense_Spending (accessed April 13, 2015).

35. Christopher Chantrill, "Pensions and Health Care," usgovernmentspending.com, April 13, 2015, http://www.usgovernmentspending.com/spending_chart_1970_2015USp_16s1li011lc n_00t10t_Pensions_And_Health_Care (accessed April 13, 2015).

36. Christopher Chantrill, "Welfare Spending Trends," usgovernmentspending.com, April 13, 2015, http://www.usgovernmentspending.com/spending_chart_1970_2015USp_16s1li011lc n_40t_Welfare_Spending_Trends (accessed April 13, 2015); Ron Haskins, "Welfare Reform, Success or Failure? It Worked," *American Public Human Services Association*, March 16, 2006, http://www.brookings.edu/research/articles/2006/03/15welfare-haskins (accessed April 13, 2015).

37. Pierre Lemieux, "A Slow-Motion Collapse," *Regulation*, Winter 2014-2015, http://object .cato.org/sites/cato.org/files/serials/files/regulation/2014/12/regulation-v37n4-3.pdf (accessed April 13, 2015).

38. John W. Dawson and John J. Seater, "Federal Regulation and Aggregate Economic Growth," *Journal of Economic Growth*, June, 2013, http://www4.ncsu.edu/~jjseater/regulationand growth.pdf (accessed April 13, 2015).

39. Patrick McLaughlin, "The Code of Federal Regulations: The Ultimate Longread," *Mercatus Center*, April 1, 2015, http://mercatus.org/publication/code-federal-regulations-ultimate -longread-game-thrones-hunger-games (accessed May 27, 2015).

40. Lemieux, "A Slow-Motion Collapse."

41. John A. Allison, *The Financial Crisis and the Free Market Cure* (New York: McGraw-Hill, 2013), p. 133.

42. Steven Horwitz and Peter J. Boettke, *The House That Uncle Sam Built: The Untold Story of the Great Recession of 2008*, http://fee.org/resources/detail/the-house-that-uncle-sam-built (accessed April 21, 2015).

43. For our own account of the causes of the financial crisis see Yaron Brook and Don Watkins, *Free Market Revolution* (New York: Palgrave Macmillan, 2012), pp. 47–62. See also Allison, *The Financial Crisis and the Free Market Cure*, and David Beckworth (ed.), *Boom and Bust Banking: The Cause and Cures of the Great Recession* (Denver: Independent Institute, 2012).

44. Stiglitz, *The Price of Inequality*, p. 3.

45. Ibid., p. 3.

46. Ibid., p. 9.

47. Emmanuel Saez and Thomas Piketty, "Income Inequality in the United States, 1913-1998," *Quarterly Journal of Economics*, 118(1), 2003, 1–39 (2013 updates), http://eml.berkeley .edu/~saez/TabFig2013prel.xls (accessed April 21, 2015).

48. Donald J. Boudreaux and Mark J. Perry, "Donald Boudreaux and Mark Perry: The Myth of a Stagnant Middle Class," *Wall Street Journal*, January 23, 2013, http://online.wsj.com /articles/SB10001424127887323468604578249723138161566 (accessed April 12, 2015).

49. Mark J. Perry, "When It Comes to the Affordability of Common Household Goods, the Rich and the Poor Are Both Getting Richer," *AEIdeas*, October 3, 2013, https://www.aei.org /publication/when-it-comes-to-the-affordability-of-common-household-goods-the-rich -and-the-poor-are-both-getting-richer/ (accessed April 12, 2015).

50. Steven Horwitz, "Inequality, Mobility, and Being Poor in America," *Social Philosophy and Policy*, Spring 2015, http://ssrn.com/abstract=2559403 (accessed April 21, 2015).

51. United States Bureau of Labor, "Civilian Labor Force by Sex, 1970–2012," http://www.dol .gov/wb/stats/Civilian_labor_force_sex_70_12_txt.htm (accessed April 12, 2015)

52. Horwitz, "Inequality, Mobility, and Being Poor in America."

53. As inequality researcher Scott Winship explains, these surveys "do not capture enough people who are at the very top of the top, who drive the trends in concentration. A sample as large as 120,000 people . . . would be expected to have no more than twelve households from the top one percent of the top one percent [i.e., the top .01 percent of income earners], and year-to-year variations in that small sub-sample can make a big difference in trends." Scott Winship, "Whither the Bottom 90 Percent, Thomas Piketty?" Forbes.com, April 17, 2014, http://www.forbes.com/sites/scottwinship/2014/04/17/whither-the-bottom-90-percent -thomas-piketty/ (accessed April 12, 2015).

54. Winship, "Whither the Bottom 90 Percent, Thomas Piketty?"; Phil Gramm and Michael Solon, "How to Distort Income Inequality," *Wall Street Journal,* November 11, 2014, http:// online.wsj.com/articles/phil-gramm-and-michael-solon-how-to-distort-income-inequal ity-1415749856 (accessed April 12, 2015). IRS data is also sensitive to changes in the tax code. Harvard economics professor Martin Feldstein argues that much of Piketty's evidence for rising inequality in the U.S. is the result of tax code changes during the 1980s. Martin Feld-stein, "Piketty's Numbers Don't Add Up," *Wall Street Journal,* May 14, 2014, http://www.wsj .com/articles/SB10001424052702304081804579557664176917086 (accessed April 12, 2015).

55. Stephen J. Rose, "Was JFK Wrong? Does Rising Productivity No Longer Lead to Substan-tial Middle Class Income Gains?," *The Information Technology & Innovation Foundation,* December 2014, http://www2.itif.org/2014-rising-productivity-middle-class.pdf (accessed April 12, 2015).

56. Ibid.

57. Ibid.

58. Scott Winship, "Poor and Middle Class Incomes Have Increased Significantly," e21.org, November 13, 2013, http://www.economics21.org/commentary/poor-and-middle-class-in comes-have-increased-significantly (accessed April 12, 2015).

59. Timothy Noah, *The Great Divergence* (New York: Bloomsbury Press, 2013), chapter 4.

60. Donald J. Boudreaux and Liya Palagashvili, "The Myth of the Great Wages 'Decoupling,'" *Wall Street Journal,* March 6, 2014, http://online.wsj.com/news/articles/SB10001424052 7023040268045794113009312562562 (accessed April 12, 2015). Another estimate puts the change as 3.3 percent of total income in 1975 to 8.5 percent in 2005. See Terry J. Fitzgerald, "Has Middle America Stagnated?" Federal Reserve Bank of Minneapolis, *Region,* Septem-ber 1, 2007, https://www.minneapolisfed.org/publications/the-region/has-middle-america -stagnated (accessed April 12, 2015).

61. United States Department of Labor, "CPI Research Series Using Current Methods (CPI-U-RS)," *Bureau of Labor Statistics,* July 12, 2011, http://www.bls.gov/cpi/cpirsdc.htm (accessed April 13, 2015), Rob McClelland, "Differences between the Traditional CPI and the Chained CPI," *CBO Blog,* April 19, 2013, http://www.cbo.gov/publication/44088 (accessed April 13, 2015).

62. Alan Reynolds, "The Misuse of Top 1 Percent Income Shares as a Measure of Inequality," *Cato Institute,* October 4, 2012, http://www.cato.org/publications/working-paper/misuse-top -1-percent-income-shares-measure-inequality (accessed May 31, 2015). See also Alan Reyn-olds, "Why Piketty's Wealth Data Are Worthless," *Wall Street Journal,* July 9, 2014, http:// www.wsj.com/articles/alan-reynolds-why-pikettys-wealth-data-are-worthless-1404945590 (accessed June 1, 2015); and Phil Gramm and Michael Solon, "How to Distort Income In-equality," *Wall Street Journal,* November 11, 2014, http://www.wsj.com/articles/phil-gramm -and-michael-solon-how-to-distort-income-inequality-1415749856 (accessed June 1, 2015).

63. Richard V. Burkhauser, Jeff Larrimore, and Kosali I. Simon, "A 'Second Opinion' on the Economic Health of the American Middle Class," *NBER Working Paper No. 17164,* June 2011, http://www.nber.org/papers/w17164 (accessed April 13, 2015).

64. Jared Bernstein, "Piketty's Arguments Still Hold Up, After Taxes," *New York Times,* May 9, 2014, http://www.nytimes.com/2014/05/10/upshot/pikettys-arguments-still-hold-up-after -taxes.html (accessed April 13, 2015).

65. Scott Winship, "Middle Class Earnings Are Stagnant! (Because Retirees Have No Earnings)," Forbes.com, May 20, 2014, http://www.forbes.com/sites/scottwinship/2014/05/20/middle-class-earnings-are-stagnant-because-retirees-have-no-earnings/ (accessed April 13, 2015).

66. See for instance Rose, "Was JFK Wrong? Does Rising Productivity No Longer Lead to Substantial Middle Class Income Gains?"; Winship, "Poor and Middle Class Incomes Have Increased Significantly"; Bruce D. Meyer and James X. Sullivan, "The Material Well-Being of the Poor and the Middle Class Since 1980," *National Research Initiative,* October 23, 2011, http://www.aei.org/wp-content/uploads/2011/10/Material-Well-Being-Poor-Middle-Class.pdf (accessed April 13, 2015); Terry J. Fitzgerald, "Where Has All the Income Gone?," *Region,* September 1, 2008, https://www.minneapolisfed.org/publications/the-region/where-has-all-the-income-gone (accessed April 13, 2015).

67. James Kenneth Galbraith, "Muddling towards the Next Crisis: James Kenneth Galbraith in Conversation with 'The Straddler,'" *Straddler,* Winter 2013, http://www.thestraddler.com/201310/piece2.php (accessed April 13, 2015).

CHAPTER 3

1. Cory Emberson and Rick Lindstrom, *Pursuing Liberty: America through the Eyes of the Newly Free* (Livermore, CA: Founders Editions, 2012), p. 162.

2. Yoani Sánchez, "Freedom and Exchange in Communist Cuba," *Cato Institute,* June 16, 2010, http://object.cato.org/sites/cato.org/files/pubs/pdf/dbp5.pdf (accessed May 20, 2015).

3. Emberson and Lindstrom, *Pursuing Liberty: America through the Eyes of the Newly Free,* pp. 165, 167, 175.

4. Quoted in Peter Schwartz, "Cuba's Boat People, Socialism, and Double Standards," *The Intellectual Activist,* Volume 1, Number 14, May 15, 1980.

5. Sánchez, "Freedom and Exchange in Communist Cuba."

6. Quoted in Michael J. Totten, "The Last Communist City," *City Journal,* Spring 2014, http://www.city-journal.org/2014/24_2_havana.html (accessed May 20, 2015).

7. Ibid.

8. Sánchez, "Freedom and Exchange in Communist Cuba."

9. Frances Robles, "In Rickety Boats, Cuban Migrants Again Flee to U.S.," *New York Times,* October 9, 2014, http://www.nytimes.com/2014/10/10/us/sharp-rise-in-cuban-migration-stirs-worries-of-a-mass-exodus.html (accessed May 20, 2015).

10. Emberson and Lindstrom, *Pursuing Liberty: America through the Eyes of the Newly Free,* p. 178.

11. Ibid.

12. Ayn Rand, "Racism," reprinted in Ayn Rand, *The Virtue of Selfishness* (New York: Signet, 1964 Centennial edition), p. 149.

13. Ayn Rand, "Man's Rights," reprinted in Ayn Rand, *The Virtue of Selfishness* (New York: Signet, 1964 Centennial edition), pp. 108–109.

14. Ibid., pp. 109–110.

15. Ayn Rand, "The Only Path to Tomorrow," reprinted in Peter Schwartz (ed.), *The Ayn Rand Column* (Irvine, CA: Ayn Rand Institute Press, 1998), p. 114.

16. Diana Saverin, "The Chris McCandless Obsession Problem," *Outside,* December 18, 2013, http://www.outsideonline.com/outdoor-adventure/Death-of-an-Innocent.html (accessed April 21, 2015). Thanks to Wesley Kemp for bringing this example to our attention.

17. Interview in the PBS documentary *Triumph of the Nerds: The Rise of Accidental Empires* (1996).

18. Steve Jobs, "'You've Got to Find What You Love,' Jobs Says," *Stanford Report,* June 14, 2005, http://news.stanford.edu/news/2005/june15/jobs-061505.html (accessed May 20, 2015).

19. R. J. Eskow, "8 Signs the Rich Have Way Too Much Money," Salon.com, August 12, 2013, http://www.salon.com/2013/08/12/8_signs_the_rich_have_way_too_much_money_partner/ (accessed May 20, 2015).

20. Ayn Rand, "The Objectivist Ethics," reprinted in Ayn Rand, *The Virtue of Selfishness* (New York: Signet, 1964 Centennial edition), pp. 34–35.

21. Harry Binswanger, "The Dollar and the Gun," in Debi Ghate and Richard E. Ralston (ed.), *Why Businessmen Need Philosophy* (New York: New American Library, 2011), p. 270.

22. George Reisman, *Capitalism* (Ottawa, IL: Jameson, 1998), p. 331.

23. Leslie T. Chang, "The Voices of China's Workers," *TED,* September 2012, https://www.ted.com/talks/leslie_t_chang_the_voices_of_china_s_workers/transcript?language=en (accessed May 20, 2015).

24. Benjamin Powell, "In Defense of 'Sweatshops,'" *Library of Economics and Liberty,* June 2, 2008, http://www.econlib.org/library/Columns/y2008/Powellsweatshops.html (accessed May 20, 2015).

25. Ibid.

26. Ibid.

27. Richard Tedlow, *Giants of Enterprise* (New York: Collins, 2003), pp. 19–33.

28. Quoted in Jon Ward, "Paul Ryan Reads from 1850 Irish Government Poster to Make Case for Immigration Reform," *Huffington Post,* June 12, 2013, http://www.huffingtonpost.com/2013/06/12/paul-ryan-poster-irish-im_n_3428852.html (accessed April 8, 2015).

29. Franklin D. Roosevelt, "Address at Atlanta, Georgia," *Works of Franklin D. Roosevelt,* November 29, 1935, http://newdeal.feri.org/speeches/1935g.htm (accessed May 31, 2015).

30. Dean Alfange, "Respectfully Quoted: A Dictionary of Quotations," Bartleby.com, http://www.bartleby.com/73/71.html (accessed April 28, 2015).

31. For the record, we profoundly disagree with many of Carson's ideas, especially his religious views, but this does not detract from his achievements as a surgeon.

32. Ben Carson with Cecil Murphey, *Gifted Hands: The Ben Carson Story* (Grand Rapids, MI: Zondervan, 1990), p. 37.

33. Ibid., pp. 63–64.

34. Ibid., p. 103.

35. Ibid., p. 106.

36. Ibid., p. 117.

37. Mike Rowe in interview with Stephen Samaniego, "Cleaning Up 'Dirty Jobs,'" CNNMoney.com, May 18, 2011, http://money.cnn.com/2011/05/18/news/economy/mike_rowe_dirty_jobs/ (accessed April 28, 2015).

38. Emma Woolley, "How Much Do Plumbers Make?," *Career Bear,* April 17, 2012, http://careerbear.com/plumber/article/how-much-do-plumbers-make (accessed May 20, 2015).

39. Katherine S. Newman. Interview by Russ Roberts, "Newman on Low-Wage Workers," *EconTalk,* March 8, 2010, http://www.econtalk.org/archives/2010/03/newman_on_low-w.html (accessed May 20, 2015).

40. Katherine S. Newman, *No Shame in My Game: The Working Poor in the Inner City* (New York: Vintage, 2000), chapter 5.

41. Jason DeParle, *American Dream* (New York: Penguin, 2004), p. 79.

42. Miles Corwin, *And Still We Rise* (New York: Harper Perennial, 2001), pp. 36–37.

43. What explains the decline of opportunity-nurturing values is a difficult question. It isn't poverty per se: poverty was far worse in 1960 than today, both in absolute and relative terms, but as political scientist Charles Murray, among others, has shown, most poor Americans back then shared the same opportunity-promoting values and behaviors as their wealthier counterparts. Out-of-wedlock births were rare, crime was low, the work ethic was strong, individual responsibility was nurtured, and individual ambition was encouraged. Nor can we blame racial discrimination. Racism was far more virulent in 1960 than today, and poor white communities have seen the same negative trends as poor black communities. The actual causes are complex, but we place the blame ultimately on ideas and (to a lesser extent) government policies. See Don Watkins, *RooseveltCare: How Social Security Is Sabotaging the Land of Self-Reliance* (Irvine, CA: Ayn Rand Institute Press, 2014).

44. Michael Harrington, *The Other America: Poverty in the United States* (New York: Touchstone, 1997), p. 162.

45. Steve Large, "UC Davis Economics Professor: There Is No American Dream," *CBS Sacramento,* November 26, 2014, http://sacramento.cbslocal.com/2014/11/26/uc-davis-economics-professor-there-is-no-american-dream/ (accessed April 28, 2015).

46. Elias Isquith, "Paul Ryan's 'Blame the Victim' Disease: How He Epitomizes a Horrible New Consensus," Salon.com, July 26, 2014, http://www.salon.com/2014/07/26/paul_ryans _blame_the_victim_disease_how_he_epitomizes_a_horrible_new_consensus/ (accessed April 28, 2015).

47. Interview with Don Watkins, May 2015.

48. Newman, *No Shame in My Game: The Working Poor in the Inner City,* chapter 4.

49. Liam Murphy and Thomas Nagel, *The Myth of Ownership* (New York: Oxford University Press, 2002), p. 120.

50. Richard Wilkinson and Kate Pickett, *The Spirit Level* (New York: Bloomsbury Press, 2009), p. 157.

51. Quoted in Joe Gelonesi, "Is Having a Loving Family an Unfair Advantage?," ABC.com, May 1, 2015, http://www.abc.net.au/radionational/programs/philosopherszone/new-family-val ues/6437058 (accessed May 20, 2015).

52. Emberson and Lindstrom, *Pursuing Liberty: America through the Eyes of the Newly Free,* p. 178.

53. Joseph E. Stiglitz, "Equal Opportunity, Our National Myth," *New York Times Opinionator,* February 16, 2013, http://opinionator.blogs.nytimes.com/2013/02/16/equal-opportunity -our-national-myth/ (accessed April 28, 2015).

54. Paul Krugman, *The Conscience of a Liberal* (New York: W. W. Norton & Company, 2009), p. 249.

CHAPTER 4

1. "Life Expectancy at Birth," HumanProgress.org, http://humanprogress.org/static/1896 (accessed May 29, 2015).

2. "Infant Mortality Rate," HumanProgress.org, http://humanprogress.org/sharable/584 (accessed April 13, 2015).

3. "U.S. Wheat Yields," HumanProgress.org, http://humanprogress.org/static/us-wheat-yields (accessed April 13, 2015).

4. "U.S. Spending on the Basics as a Share of Disposable Personal Income," HumanProgress .org, http://humanprogress.org/static/us-spending-on-basics (accessed April 13, 2015).

5. Steve Wozniak with Gina Smith, *iWoz: Computer Geek to Cult Icon* (New York: Norton, 2006), pp. 12–13.

6. Ibid., p. 18.

7. Ibid., pp. 54–55.

8. Ibid., pp. 155–56.

9. "National Inventors Hall of Fame," Ohio History Central, http://www.ohiohistorycentral .org/w/National_Inventors_Hall_of_Fame?rec=1727 (accessed August 31, 2015).

10. Quoted in Sean Rossman, "Apple's 'The Woz' Talks Jobs, Entrepreneurship," *Tallahassee Democrat,* November 6, 2014, http://www.tallahassee.com/story/news/local/2014/11/05 /apples-woz-talks-jobs-entrepreneurship/18561425/ (accessed April 13, 2015).

11. Quoted in Alec Hogg, "Apple's 'Other' Steve—Wozniak on Jobs, Starting a Business, Changing the World, and Staying Hungry, Staying Foolish," BizNews.com, February 17, 2014, http://www.biznews.com/video/2014/02/17/apples-other-steve-wozniak-on-jobs-starting -a-business-changing-the-world/ (accessed April 13, 2015).

12. Walter Isaacson, *Steve Jobs* (New York: Simon & Schuster, 2011), p. 295.

13. Ibid., pp. 308, 318.

14. Ibid., p. 317.

15. Ibid., p. 337.

16. Ibid., pp. 318–19.

17. Ibid., p. 329.

18. William J. Bernstein, *The Birth of Plenty* (New York: McGraw-Hill, 2004), p. 125.

19. Isaacson, *Steve Jobs,* pp. 76–77.

20. Ibid., pp. 340–43.

21. Ayn Rand, *Atlas Shrugged* (New York: Penguin, 1999), p. 1065.

22. David Harriman (ed.), *Journals of Ayn Rand* (New York: Plume, 1999), p. 421.

23. Angus Deaton, *The Great Escape: Health, Wealth, and the Origins of Inequality* (Princeton, NJ: Princeton, 2013), pp. 45–46.

24. See, for instance, Katy Barnato, "'Enormous Increase' in Global Inequality: OECD," CNBC .com, October 1, 2014, http://www.cnbc.com/id/102048998 (accessed April 13, 2015).

25. Nathan Rosenberg and L. E. Birdzell, Jr., *How the West Grew Rich* (New York: Basic Books, 1986), p. 51.

26. Algernon Sidney, *Discourses Concerning Government*, 3.33. Sidney, whose influence on the Founding Fathers was surpassed only by Locke, would be put to death in 1683 for his defense of political liberty.

27. Deaton, *The Great Escape: Health, Wealth, and the Origins of Inequality*, p. 84.

28. Rosenberg and Birdzell, Jr., *How the West Grew Rich*, p. 22.

29. Deirdre N. McCloskey, *Bourgeois Dignity* (Chicago: University of Chicago Press, 2010), p. 397.

30. Thomas Jefferson, "First Inaugural Address," March 4, 1801, http://avalon.law.yale.edu /19th_century/jefinau1.asp (accessed May 4, 2015).

31. Quoted in Charles R. Morris, *The Tycoons* (New York: Owl, 2005), p. 39.

32. Alan Trachtenberg, *The Incorporation of America* (New York: Hill and Wang, 2007), p. 41.

33. "Centennial Exhibition Tours: Machinery Hall," http://libwww.library.phila.gov/CenCol /tours-machineryhall.htm (accessed April 23, 2015).

34. On the development of the corporate form, see Rosenberg and Birdzell, Jr., *How the West Grew Rich*, pp. 189–210. For an explanation of why corporations are the product of economic freedom, not "creatures of the state," see Robert Hessen, *In Defense of the Corporation* (Stanford, CA: Hoover Institution Press, 1979).

35. Rosenberg and Birdzell, Jr., *How the West Grew Rich*, p. 213.

36. Burton W. Folsom, Jr., *The Myth of the Robber Barons* (Herndon, VA: Young America's Foundation, 2003), p. 67.

37. Richard S. Tedlow, *Giants of Enterprise* (New York: HarperCollins, 2001), p. 164.

38. Quoted in Morris, *The Tycoons*, p. 56.

39. Jonathan Hughes, *The Vital Few* (New York: Oxford University Press, 1986), p. 560.

40. Alan B. Krueger and Jorn-Steffen Pischke, "A Comparative Analysis of East and West German Labor Markets: Before and after Unification," *NBER Working Paper No. 4154*, August 1992, http://www.nber.org/papers/w4154 (accessed May 4, 2015).

41. Ibid.

42. Norman Gelb, *The Berlin Wall* (New York: Simon & Schuster, 1988) pp. 51, 53.

43. "East Germany: They Have Given Up Hope," *Time*, December 6, 1963, http://www.time .com/time/printout/0,8816,898090,00.html (accessed April 21, 2015).

44. Julian L. Simon, *The Ultimate Resource 2* (Princeton, NJ: Princeton University Press, 1996), p. 498.

45. Ferdinand Protzman, "East Germany's Economy Far Sicker Than Expected," *New York Times*, September 20, 1990, http://www.nytimes.com/1990/09/20/business/east-germany-s -economy-far-sicker-than-expected.html (accessed April 21, 2015).

46. Thomas Piketty interview with Russell Roberts, "Thomas Piketty on Inequality and Capital in the Twenty-First Century," *EconTalk*, September 22, 2014, http://www.econtalk.org /archives/2014/09/thomas_piketty.html (accessed May 4, 2015).

47. See, for instance, John Cochrane, "Why and How We Care about Inequality," *The Grumpy Economist*, September 29, 2014, http://johnhcochrane.blogspot.com/2014/09/why-and-how -we-care-about-inequality.html (accessed May 28, 2015), and Ayn Rand, "Egalitarianism and Inflation," reprinted in Ayn Rand, *Philosophy: Who Needs It* (New York: Signet, 1984).

48. Kip Hagopian and Lee Ohanian, "The Mismeasure of Inequality," *Policy Review*, August 1, 2012, http://www.hoover.org/research/mismeasure-inequality (accessed May 4, 2015).

49. Andrew G. Berg and Jonathan D. Ostry, "Equality and Efficiency," *Finance & Development*, September 2011, http://www.imf.org/external/pubs/ft/fandd/2011/09/berg.htm (accessed May 4, 2015).

50. Georgia Levenson Keohane, "Inequality in America: Pox and Progress," *Next New Deal*, September 28, 2011, http://www.nextnewdeal.net/inequality-america-pox-and-progress (accessed May 4, 2015).

51. Scott Winship, "Inequality Does Not Reduce Prosperity," *e21 Report*, October 2014, http://www.manhattan-institute.org/pdf/e21_01.pdf (accessed May 4, 2015).

52. Paul Krugman, "Inequality and Economic Performance," *The Conscience of a Liberal* (blog), *New York Times*, December 2, 2014, http://krugman.blogs.nytimes.com/2014/12/02/inequality-and-economic-performance/ (accessed May 4, 2015).

53. Jared Bernstein, "The Impact of Inequality on Growth," *Center for American Progress*, December 2013, http://cdn.americanprogress.org/wp-content/uploads/2013/12/Bernstein Inequality.pdf (accessed May 4, 2015).

54. Kyle Smith, "Sorry, Liberals, Scandinavian Countries Aren't Utopias," *New York Post*, January 11, 2015, http://nypost.com/2015/01/11/sorry-liberals-scandinavian-countries-arent-utopias/ (accessed April 13, 2015).

55. Carl Svanberg. "What about Sweden?" Lecture, Objectivist Summer Conference, Chicago, July 6–8, 2013.

56. Ibid.

57. Ibid.

58. Erik Norrman and Charles E. McLure, Jr., "Tax Policy in Sweden," *National Bureau of Economic Research*, January 1997, http://www.nber.org/chapters/c6521.pdf (accessed May 28, 2015).

59. Svanberg. "What about Sweden?" See also Daniel J. Mitchell, "What Can the United States Learn from the Nordic Model?," *Policy Analysis*, November 5, 2007, http://object.cato.org/sites/cato.org/files/pubs/pdf/pa-603.pdf (accessed May 28, 2015).

60. Thomas Piketty, *Capital in the Twenty-First Century* (Cambridge, MA: Belknap, 2014), pp. 247–49.

61. Johnny Munkhammar, "The Swedish Model: It's the Free-Market Reforms, Stupid!" *Wall Street Journal*, January 26, 2011, http://www.wsj.com/articles/SB10001424052748704698004576104023432243468 (accessed April 13, 2015).

62. Piketty, *Capital in the Twenty-First Century*, p. 246.

CHAPTER 5

1. Joseph Stiglitz, "America Is No Longer a Land of Opportunity," *Financial Times*, June 25, 2012, http://www.ft.com/intl/cms/s/2/56c7e518-bc8f-11e1-a111-00144feabdc0.html (accessed April 28, 2015).

2. Barack Obama, "Remarks by the President on Economic Mobility," *The White House*, December 4, 2013, http://www.whitehouse.gov/the-press-office/2013/12/04/remarks-president-economic-mobility (accessed April 12, 2015).

3. Paul Krugman, *The Conscience of a Liberal* (New York: W. W. Norton & Company, 2009), pp. 247–48.

4. James Truslow Adams, *The Epic of America* (Garden City, NY: Garden City Books, 1933), pp. 184–88.

5. Scott Winship, "Mobility Impaired," *Brookings Institute*, November 9, 2011, http://www.brookings.edu/research/articles/2011/11/09-economic-mobility-winship (accessed May 26, 2015).

6. Richard Wilkinson and Kate Pickett, *The Spirit Level* (New York: Bloomsbury Press, 2009), pp. 157–59.

7. Thomas Sowell, "Economic Mobility," Townhall.com, March 6, 2013, http://townhall.com/columnists/thomassowell/2013/03/06/economic-mobility-n1525556/page/full (accessed May 26, 2015).

8. United States Department of Treasury, "Income Mobility in the U.S. from 1996 to 2005," http://www.treasury.gov/resource-center/tax-policy/Documents/incomemobilitystudy03-08revise.pdf. Cited in Steven Horwitz, "Inequality, Mobility, and Being Poor in America," *Social Science Research Network*, January 2, 2014, http://ssrn.com/abstract=2559403 (accessed May 28, 2015).

9. Timothy Noah, "The Mobility Myth," *New Republic*, February 8, 2012, http://www.newrepublic.com/article/politics/magazine/100516/inequality-mobility-economy-america-recession-divergence (accessed April 21, 2015).

10. Raj Chetty, Nathaniel Hendren, Patrick Kline, Emmanuel Saez, and Nicholas Turner, "Is the United States Still a Land of Opportunity? Recent Trends in Intergenerational Mobility," *NBER Working Paper No. 19844,* January 2014, http://obs.rc.fas.harvard.edu/chetty/mobil ity_trends.pdf (accessed April 13, 2015), and Raj Chetty, Nathaniel Hendren, Patrick Kline, Emmanuel Saez, and Nicholas Turner, *The Equality of Opportunity Project,* January 2014, http://www.equality-of-opportunity.org (accessed April 13, 2015).

11. Wilkinson and Pickett, *The Spirit Level,* p. 159.

12. Max Borders, *Superwealth* (Sioux Falls, SD: Throne, 2012), pp. 216–17.

13. Miles Corak, Matthew J. Lindquist, and Bhashkar Mazumder, "A Comparison of Upward and Downward Intergenerational Mobility in Canada, Sweden and the United States," *Labour Economics,* vol. 30, pp. 185–200, http://www.sciencedirect.com/science/article/pii /S0927537114000530 (accessed April 28, 2015).

14. For a more thorough review of the debate over mobility statistics, see Scott Winship, "Does America Have Less Economic Mobility? Part 1," e21.org, April 20, 2015, http://www .economics21.org/commentary/winship-economic-mobility-inequality-us-04-20-2015 (accessed May 26, 2015), Scott Winship, "Does America Have Less Economic Mobility? Part 2," e21.org, April 22, 2015, http://www.economics21.org/commentary/us-economic-mobility -great-gatsby-curve-miles-corak-04-21-2015 (accessed May 26, 2015), and Scott Winship, "Does America Have Less Economic Mobility? Part 3," e21.org, May 8, 2015, http://www.eco nomics21.org/commentary/america-economic-mobility-income-jantti-corak-05-07-2015 (accessed May 26, 2015).

15. Gary Wolfram, "Making College More Expensive: The Unintended Consequences of Federal Tuition Aid," *Policy Analysis* No. 531, January 2005, http://object.cato.org/sites/cato.org /files/pubs/pdf/pa531.pdf (accessed April 28, 2015).

16. "McDonald's CEO Don Thompson Is Still Lovin' It," *CBS News,* October 26, 2014, http:// www.cbsnews.com/news/mcdonalds-ceo-don-thompson-is-still-lovin-it/ (accessed April 28, 2015).

17. Paul Krugman, "The Living Wage," *The Unofficial Paul Krugman Archive,* September 1998, http://www.pkarchive.org/cranks/LivingWage.html (accessed April 28, 2015).

18. Paul Guppy, "Seattle's $15 Wage Law a Factor in Restaurant Closings," *Washington Policy Center,* March 11, 2015, http://www.washingtonpolicy.org/blog/post/seattles-15-wage-law -factor-restaurant-closings (accessed April 28, 2015).

19. Sean McElwee, "The Moral Case for a Higher Minimum Wage," Policy.Mic, August 7, 2013, http://mic.com/articles/58425/the-moral-case-for-a-higher-minimum-wage (accessed May 12, 2015).

20. David Neumark and William L. Wascher, *Minimum Wages* (Cambridge: MIT Press, 2008), p. 104.

21. Megan McArdle, "Everything We Don't Know about Minimum-Wage Hikes," *BloombergView,* December 29, 2014, http://www.bloombergview.com/articles/2014-12-29/every thing-we-dont-know-about-minimumwage-hikes (accessed May 12, 2015).

22. Ibid.

23. Krugman, "The Living Wage."

24. Alexander C. Kaufman, "Krugman Demolishes Classic Argument against Raising Minimum Wage," *Huffington Post,* September 9, 2014, http://www.huffingtonpost.com/2014/09/09 /krugman-minimum-wage_n_5790334.html (accessed May 12, 2015).

25. Jason DeParle, *American Dream* (New York: Penguin, 2004), p. 158.

26. "Untangling African Hairbraiders from Mississippi's Cosmetology Regime," *Institute for Justice,* http://ij.org/mississippi-hairbraiding-background (accessed May 12, 2015).

27. Pierre Lemieux, "A Slow-Motion Collapse," *Regulation,* Winter 2014-2015, http://object .cato.org/sites/cato.org/files/serials/files/regulation/2014/12/regulation-v37n4-3.pdf (accessed May 12, 2015).

28. Timothy Sandefur, "The Unknown Road Blocks to the American Dream," *The Blaze,* February 19, 2015, http://www.theblaze.com/contributions/the-unknown-road-blocks-to-the -american-dream/ (accessed May 12, 2015).

29. James Sherk, "Why Did This Union Oppose Higher Pay for Its Members?," *Daily Signal,* May 18, 2014, http://dailysignal.com/2014/05/18/union-oppose-higher-pay-members/ (accessed May 12, 2015).

30. Christina D. Romer, "The Business of the Minimum Wage," *New York Times*, March 2, 2013, http://www.nytimes.com/2013/03/03/business/the-minimum-wage-employment-and-in come-distribution.html (accessed May 12, 2015).

31. See, for instance, Edward Glaeser and Joseph Gyourko, "Zoning's Steep Price," *Regulation*, Fall 2002, http://object.cato.org/sites/cato.org/files/serials/files/regulation/2002/10/v 25n3-7.pdf (accessed May 12, 2015) and Sandy Ikeda, "Shut Out: How Land-Use Regulations Hurt the Poor," *The Freeman*, February 5, 2015, http://fee.org/freeman/detail/shut -out-how-land-use-regulations-hurt-the-poor (accessed May 12, 2015).

32. See, for instance, Thomas Sowell, *Applied Economics* (New York: Basic Books, 2004), pp. 97–120.

33. Nicolas Loris, "Free Markets Supply Affordable Energy and a Clean Environment," *The Heritage Foundation*, October 31, 2014, http://www.heritage.org/research/reports/2014/10/free -markets-supply-affordable-energy-and-a-clean-environment (accessed May 12, 2015).

34. Deborah Perry Piscione, *Secrets of Silicon Valley* (New York: Palgrave Macmillan, 2013), part I.

35. Ibid., chapter 4.

36. Ibid., Epilogue.

37. See Ayn Rand, "America's Persecuted Minority," reprinted in Ayn Rand, *Capitalism: The Unknown Ideal* (New York: Signet, 1967); Dominick T. Armentano, *Antitrust: The Case for Repeal* (Auburn, AL: Ludwig von Mises Institute, 2007); and Edwin S. Rockefeller, *The Antitrust Religion* (Washington, DC: The Cato Institute, 2007).

38. David Einstein, "Gates Steps Down as Microsoft CEO," *Forbes*, January 13, 2000, http:// www.forbes.com/2000/01/13/mu7.html (accessed May 12, 2015).

39. Sharon Pian Chan, "Long Antitrust Saga Ends for Microsoft," *Seattle Times*, May 11, 2011, http://www.seattletimes.com/business/microsoft/long-antitrust-saga-ends-for-microsoft/ (accessed May 12, 2015).

40. Michael Q. McShane, *Education and Opportunity* (Washington, DC: AEI Press, 2014), pp. 40–41.

41. James Tooley, *The Beautiful Tree: A Personal Journey into How the World's Poorest People Are Educating Themselves* (Washington, DC: Cato Institute, 2009). For more on the issue of education, see Andrew J. Coulson, *Market Education: The Unknown History* (New Brunswick, NJ: Transaction, 1999); Myron Lieberman, *Public Education: An Autopsy* (Cambridge, MA: Harvard University Press, 1995); and Leonard Peikoff, *Teaching Johnny to Think* (Irvine, CA: Ayn Rand Institute Press, 2014).

42. Glen Whitman and Raymond Raad, "Bending the Productivity Curve: Why America Leads the World in Medical Innovation," *Cato Institute*, November 18, 2009, http://www.cato.org /publications/policy-analysis/bending-productivity-curve-why-america-leads-world-medi cal-innovation (accessed May 12, 2015).

43. Michael F. Cannon and Michael D. Tanner, *Healthy Competition*, 2nd ed. (Washington, DC: Cato Institute, 2007), p. 52.

44. Lawrence R. Huntoon, "Medicare Myths and Facts," *Association of American Physicians and Surgeons*, December 15, 2011, http://www.aapsonline.org/index.php/article/medicare _myths_and_facts/ (accessed May 12, 2015).

45. Sandeep Jauhar, *Doctored: The Disillusionment of an American Physician* (New York: Farrar, Straus and Giroux, 2014), Introduction.

46. Ibid., chapter 5.

47. Devon Herrick, "FDA Slow to Approve Medical Devices," *National Center for Policy Analysis*, December 1, 2010, http://healthblog.ncpa.org/fda-slow-to-approve-medical-devices/ (accessed May 12, 2015).

48. Michael Tennant, "ObamaCare: Stifling Innovation," *National Center for Policy Analysis*, April 9, 2015, http://www.ncpa.org/media/obamacare-stifling-innovation (accessed May 26, 2015).

49. *Cato Handbook for Policymakers*, 7th Edition (Cato Institute, January 16, 2009), http://object .cato.org/sites/cato.org/files/serials/files/cato-handbook-policymakers/2009/9/hb111-16 .pdf (accessed May 26, 2015). See also Rituparna Basu, *The Broken State of American Health Insurance Prior to the Affordable Care Act: A Market Rife with Government Distortion*, 2013,

http://www.pacificresearch.org/fileadmin/templates/pri/images/Studies/PDFs/2013-2015/BasuF2.pdf (accessed May 26, 2015).

50. Lin Zinser and Paul Hsieh, "Moral Health Care vs. 'Universal Health Care,'" *Objective Standard,* vol. 2, no. 4 (Winter 2007–2008), http://www.theobjectivestandard.com/issues/2007-winter/moral-vs-universal-health-care.asp (accessed April 8, 2015).

51. Michael F. Cannon, "Google Co-founders Sergey Brin & Larry Page: Health Care Regulation Is Blocking Innovation," *Cato At Liberty,* July 10, 2014, http://www.cato.org/blog/google-co-founders-sergey-brin-larry-page-health-care-regulation-blocking-innovation (accessed May 26, 2015).

52. Michael D. Tanner and Charles Hughes, "War on Poverty Turns 50: Are We Winning Yet?," *Policy Analysis,* October 20, 2014, http://www.cato.org/publications/policy-analysis/war-poverty-turns-50-are-we-winning-yet (accessed May 26, 2015).

53. Ibid.

54. Robert Rector, "How Poor Are America's Poor? Examining the 'Plague' of Poverty in America," *Heritage Foundation,* August 27, 2007, http://www.heritage.org/research/reports/2007/08/how-poor-are-americas-poor-examining-the-plague-of-poverty-in-america (accessed May 26, 2015).

55. David Brooks, "The Nature of Poverty," *New York Times,* May 1, 2015, http://www.nytimes.com/2015/05/01/opinion/david-brooks-the-nature-of-poverty.html (accessed May 26, 2015).

56. Charles Murray, *Coming Apart* (New York: Crown Forum, 2012), pp. 226–27.

57. Lawrence M. Mead, *From Prophecy to Charity: How to Help the Poor* (Washington, DC: AEI Press, 2011), p. 34.

58. Ibid., pp. 30–31; Lawrence M. Mead, *The New Politics of Poverty* (New York: Basic Books, 1992), p. 50.

59. Jason L. Riley, *Please Stop Helping Us* (New York: Encounter, 2014), chapter 4.

60. Mead, *From Prophecy to Charity,* p. 40.

61. Katherine S. Newman, *No Shame in My Game: The Working Poor in the Inner City* (New York: Vintage, 2000), chapter 4.

62. Ibid.

63. Ken Auletta, *The Underclass* (New York: The Overlook Press, 1999), p. 85.

64. Ibid., p. 167.

65. Newman, *No Shame in My Game,* chapter 4, fn. 9.

66. Michael Tanner and Charles Hughes, "The Work Versus Welfare Trade-Off: 2013. An Analysis of the Total Level of Welfare Benefits by State," *Cato Institute,* 2013, http://object.cato.org/sites/cato.org/files/pubs/pdf/the_work_versus_welfare_trade-off_2013_wp.pdf (accessed May 26, 2015).

67. Paul Krugman, "Enemies of the Poor," *New York Times,* January 12, 2014, http://www.nytimes.com/2014/01/13/opinion/krugman-enemies-of-the-poor.html (accessed May 26, 2015).

68. Interview with Don Watkins, May 2015.

69. James Gwartney and Thomas S. McCaleb, "Have Antipoverty Programs Increased Poverty?," *Cato Journal* 5, no. 1, (Spring/Summer 1985), http://object.cato.org/sites/cato.org/files/serials/files/cato-journal/1985/5/cj5n1-1.pdf (accessed May 31, 2015).

70. See Don Watkins, *RooseveltCare: How Social Security Is Sabotaging the Land of Self-Reliance* (Irvine, CA: Ayn Rand Institute Press, 2014), and Marvin Olasky, *The Tragedy of American Compassion* (Washington, DC: Regnery, 1992).

CHAPTER 6

1. Jay Yarow and Kamelia Angelova, "CHART OF THE DAY: Apple's Incredible Run under Steve Jobs," *Business Insider,* August 25, 2011, http://www.businessinsider.com/chart-of-the-day-apples-market-cap-during-steve-jobs-tenure-2011-8 (accessed May 28, 2015).

2. JPL, "A Look at Berkshire Hathaway's Annual Market Returns from 1968–2007," AllFinancialMatters.com, April 2, 2008, https://web.archive.org/web/20080412003318/http://allfinancialmatters.com/2008/04/02/a-look-at-berkshire-hathaways-annual-market-returns

-from-1968-2007/ (accessed May 28, 2015); "Berkshire Hathaway Inc. (BRK-A)," *Yahoo! Finance,* May 28, 2015 http://finance.yahoo.com/q?s=BRK-A (accessed May 28, 2015).

3. Robert Nozick famously gives a similar analysis using the example of Wilt Chamberlain in *Anarchy, the State, and Utopia* (New York: Basic Books, 1974), pp. 160–64.

4. Andrew Bernstein, *The Capitalist Manifesto: The Historic, Economic and Philosophic Case for Laissez-Faire* (New York: University Press of America, 2005).

5. Burton W. Folsom, Jr., *The Myth of the Robber Barons* (Herndon, VA: Young America's Foundation, 2003), pp. 2–3.

6. To be fair to Fulton, he deserves enormous credit for launching the first commercial steamboat, in addition to many other achievements.

7. Ayn Rand, "The Money-Making Personality," reprinted in Debi Ghate and Richard E. Ralston (ed.), *Why Businessmen Need Philosophy* (New York: New American Library, 2011), p. 68.

8. David R. Henderson, "The Economics and History of Cronyism," *Mercatus Center,* July 27, 2012, http://mercatus.org/sites/default/files/Henderson_cronyism_1.1%20final.pdf (accessed May 28, 2015).

9. Matthew Mitchell, "The Pathology of Privilege: The Economic Consequences of Government Favoritism," *Mercatus Center,* July 9, 2012, http://mercatus.org/sites/default/files/The -Pathology-of-Privilege-Final_2.pdf (accessed May 28, 2015).

10. Timothy P. Carney, *The Big Ripoff* (New York: Wiley, 2006), pp. 59–61.

11. Chris Edwards, "Agricultural Subsidies," DownsizingGovernment.org, June 2009, http:// www.downsizinggovernment.org/agriculture/subsidies (accessed May 28, 2015).

12. Timothy P. Carney, *Obamanomics* (Washington, DC: Regnery, 2009), p. 122.

13. Hunter Lewis, *Crony Capitalism in America: 2008–2012* (Edinburg, VA: AC² Books, 2013), p. 104.

14. Timothy P. Carney, "Carney: How Hatch Forced Microsoft to Play K Street's Game," *Washington Examiner,* June 24, 2012, http://www.washingtonexaminer.com/carney-how-hatch -forced-microsoft-to-play-k-streets-game/article/2500453 (accessed May 28, 2015), Michael Kinsley, "Michael Kinsley: The Washington Lobbying Dance," *Los Angeles Times,* April 5, 2011, http://articles.latimes.com/print/2011/apr/05/opinion/la-oe-kinsley-column-micro soft-20110405 (May 28, 2015).

15. Carney, "Carney: How Hatch Forced Microsoft to Play K Street's Game."

16. Ibid.

17. Carney, "Carney: How Hatch Forced Microsoft to Play K Street's Game."

18. Kinsley, "Michael Kinsley: The Washington Lobbying Dance."

19. Ibid.

20. L. Gordon Crovitz, "Silicon Valley Makes Peace with Washington," *Wall Street Journal,* April 11, 2011, http://www.wsj.com/news/articles/SB100014240527487044151045762507637167 15484 (accessed May 28, 2015).

21. Thomas Piketty, *Capital in the Twenty-First Century* (Cambridge, MA: Belknap, 2014), p. 303.

22. "Yaron Brook and Dr. James Galbraith, Inequality: Should We Care?," *YouTube,* May 9, 2014, https://www.youtube.com/watch?v=_oee9iS5u-Y (accessed May 28, 2015).

23. Russ Roberts, "Luigi Zingales on the Costs and Benefits of the Financial Sector," *EconTalk,* Library of Economics and Liberty, February 2, 2015, http://www.econtalk.org /archives/2015/02/luigi_zingales_1.html (accessed May 28, 2015).

24. "Ranked Sectors," OpenSecrets.org, https://www.opensecrets.org/lobby/top.php?indexTy pe=c&showYear=2014 (accessed May 28, 2015).

25. Luigi Zingales, "Does Finance Benefit Society?," January, 2015, http://faculty.chicagobooth .edu/luigi.zingales/papers/research/Finance.pdf (accessed May 28, 2015).

26. Russell Roberts, "Gambling with Other People's Money: How Perverted Incentives Caused the Financial Crisis," *Mercatus Center,* April 28, 2010, http://mercatus.org/publication/gam bling-other-peoples-money (accessed May 28, 2015).

27. Jim Manzi, "Do CEOs Matter? Absolutely," *Atlantic,* June 5, 2009, http://www.theatlantic .com/business/archive/2009/06/do-ceos-matter-absolutely/18819/ (accessed May 28, 2015).

28. Steven N. Kaplan, "The Real Story behind Executive Pay: The Myth of Crony Capitalism," *Foreign Affairs*, April 3, 2013, https://www.foreignaffairs.com/articles/2013b04-03/real-story-behind-executive-pay (accessed May 28, 2015).

29. Piketty, *Capital in the Twenty-First Century*, pp. 302–303.

30. Albert R. Hunt, "Corporate Chiefs May Come to Rue Fat Paydays: Albert R. Hunt," *Bloomberg Business*, February 19, 2007, http://www.bloomberg.com/apps/news?pid=newsarchive&refer=columnist_hunt&sid=arth8j9wbrcc (accessed May 28, 2015).

31. Paul Krugman, *The Conscience of a Liberal* (New York: W. W. Norton & Company, 2009), p. 143.

32. Ibid., p. 144.

33. Piketty, *Capital in the Twenty-First Century*, p. 332.

34. Steven N. Kaplan and Joshua Rauh, "It's the Market: The Broad-Based Rise in the Return to Top Talent," *Journal of Economic Perspectives*, Summer 2013, http://pubs.aeaweb.org/doi/pdfplus/10.1257/jep.27.3.35 (accessed May 28, 2015).

35. Steven N. Kaplan, "Executive Compensation and Corporate Governance in the U.S.: Perceptions, Facts and Challenges," *Chicago Booth Research Paper No. 12-42; Fama-Miller Working Paper*, August 22, 2012, http://ssrn.com/abstract=2134208 (accessed May 28, 2015).

36. Ibid.

37. Carola Frydman and Dirk Jenter, "CEO Compensation," *NBER Working Paper Series No. 16585*, December 2010, http://www.nber.org/papers/w16585 (accessed May 28, 2015).

38. Piketty, *Capital in the Twenty-First Century*, p. 330.

39. Robert H. Frank and Philip J. Cook, *The Winner-Take-All Society* (New York: The Free Press, 1995), pp. 70–71.

40. Piketty, *Capital in the Twenty-First Century*, pp. 334–35.

41. Jim Manzi, "Piketty's Can Opener," *National Review*, July 7, 2014, http://www.nationalreview.com/corner/382084/pikettys-can-opener-jim-manzi (accessed May 28, 2015).

42. Jonathan R. Macey, "Market for Corporate Control," *The Concise Encyclopedia of Economics*, Library of Economics and Liberty, 2008, http://www.econlib.org/library/Enc/MarketforCorporateControl.html (accessed May 28, 2015).

43. David R. Francis, "Congress Pecks Away at CEO Pay," *Christian Science Monitor*, April 30, 2007, http://www.csmonitor.com/2007/0430/p15s01-cogn.html (accessed May 28, 2015).

44. Joe Nocera, "What if C.E.O. Pay Is Fair?," *New York Times*, October 13, 2007, http://www.nytimes.com/2007/10/13/business/13nocera.html (accessed May 28, 2015).

45. Quoted in Andrew Sullivan, "The Ebenezer Sermon," *Atlantic*, January 20, 2008, http://www.theatlantic.com/daily-dish/archive/2008/01/the-ebenezer-sermon/221010/ (accessed May 28, 2015).

46. Geoffrey James, "CEOs Are Just Glorified Sales Reps," CBS MoneyWatch, January 28, 2009, http://www.cbsnews.com/news/ceos-are-just-glorified-sales-reps/ (accessed May 28, 2015).

47. Thom Hartmann, *Threshold: The Crisis of Western Culture* (New York: Viking, 2009), p. 95.

48. Robert B. Reich, "CEOs Deserve Their Pay," *Wall Street Journal*, September 14, 2007, http://www.wsj.com/articles/SB118972669806427090 (accessed May 28, 2015).

49. Piketty, *Capital in the Twenty-First Century*, pp. 25–26.

50. Deirdre Nansen McCloskey, "Measured, Unmeasured, Mismeasured, and Unjustified Pessimism: A Review Essay of Thomas Piketty's *Capital in the Twentieth-First Century*," *Erasmus Journal of Philosophy and Economics*, November 2014, http://www.deirdremccloskey.org/docs/pdf/PikettyReviewEssay.pdf (accessed May 28, 2015).

51. Lawrence H. Summers, "The Inequality Puzzle," *Democracy: A Journal of Ideas*, Summer 2014, http://www.democracyjournal.org/33/the-inequality-puzzle.php?page=all (accessed May 28, 2015).

52. Ibid.

53. Ibid.

54. Daron Acemoglu and James A. Robinson, "The Rise and Fall of General Laws of Capitalism," August 2014, http://polisci2.ucsd.edu/pelg/AcemogluRobinsonGeneral%20Laws.pdf (accessed May 28, 2015).

55. For more on problems with Piketty's work, see Matthew Rognlie, "A Note on Piketty and Diminishing Returns to Capital," June 15, 2014, http://www.mit.edu/~mrognlie/piketty

_diminishing_returns.pdf (accessed May 28, 2015); Matthew Rognlie, "Deciphering the Fall and Rise in the Net Capital Share," *Brookings Papers on Economic Activity*, March 19, 2015, http://www.brookings.edu/about/projects/bpea/papers/2015/land-prices-evolution-capi tals-share (accessed May 28, 2015); Thomas H. Mayor, "Income Inequality: Piketty and the Neo-Marxist Revival," *Cato Journal*, Winter 2015, http://object.cato.org/sites/cato.org/files /serials/files/cato-journal/2015/2/cj-v35n1-4.pdf (accessed May 28, 2015); Daron Acemoglu and James A. Robinson, "The Rise and Decline of General Laws of Capitalism," *NBER Working Paper No. 20766*, December 2014, http://www.nber.org/papers/w20766 (accessed May 28, 2015); Phillip W. Magness and Robert P. Murphy, "Challenging the Empirical Contribution of Thomas Piketty's *Capital in the Twenty-First Century*," *Journal of Private Enterprise*, Spring 2015, http://papers.ssrn.com/sol3/papers.cfm?abstract_id=2543012 (accessed May 28, 2015).

56. "Yaron Brook and Dr. James Galbraith, Inequality: Should We Care?"
57. Steven E. Landsburg, "How the Death Tax Hurts the Poor," *Wall Street Journal*, October 29, 2011, http://www.wsj.com/articles/SB10001424052970203554104577001652652545814 (accessed May 28, 2015).
58. Carney, *The Big Ripoff*, p. 166.
59. Andrew Lundeen, "The Top 1 Percent Pays More in Taxes Than the Bottom 90 Percent," *The Tax Policy Blog*, January 7, 2014, http://taxfoundation.org/blog/top-1-percent-pays-more -taxes-bottom-90-percent (accessed May 28, 2015).
60. Jared Meyer, "The Rich Pay More Than Their Fair Share of Taxes," e21.org, January 9, 2015, http://economics21.org/commentary/rich-pay-fair-share-tax-foundation-income-2015-1 -09 (accessed May 28, 2015).
61. Stephen Moore, *Who's the Fairest of Them All?* (New York: Encounter Books, 2012), p. 70.
62. Kyle Pomerleau and Andrew Lundeen, "The U.S. Has the Highest Corporate Income Tax Rate in the OECD," *The Tax Policy Blog*, Tax Foundation, January 27, 2014, http://taxfoun dation.org/blog/us-has-highest-corporate-income-tax-rate-oecd (accessed May 28, 2015).
63. Lydia Saad, "U.S. '1%' Is More Republican, but Not More Conservative," *Gallup*, December 5, 2011, http://www.gallup.com/poll/151310/U.S.-Republican-Not-Conservative.aspx (accessed May 28, 2015).
64. "Political Action Committees," OpenSecrets.org, https://www.opensecrets.org/pacs/index .php?chart=P (accessed May 28, 2015).
65. "Super PACs," OpenSecrets.org, http://www.opensecrets.org/pacs/superpacs.php?cycle=2014 (accessed May 28, 2015).
66. "2014 Outside Spending, by Super PAC," OpenSecrets.org, http://www.opensecrets.org/out sidespending/summ.php?chrt=V&type=S (accessed May 28, 2015).

CHAPTER 7

1. Robert H. Frank, "Why Have Weddings and Houses Gotten So Ridiculously Expensive? Blame Inequality," Vox.com, January 16, 2015, http://www.vox.com/2015/1/16/7545509 /inequality-waste (accessed May 28, 2015).
2. Megan McArdle, "Not Everyone Can Work for Costco," *Bloomberg View*, October 1, 2014, http://www.bloombergview.com/articles/2014-10-01/not-everyone-can-work-for-costco (accessed May 28, 2015).
3. Hedrick Smith, *Who Stole the American Dream?* (New York: Random House, 2012), p. 20.
4. Quoted in Smith, *Who Stole the American Dream?*, pp. 179–80.
5. Smith, *Who Stole the American Dream?*, p. 190.
6. Senator Elizabeth Warren, "The Retirement Crisis," *U.S. Senate*, November 18, 2013, http:// www.warren.senate.gov/files/documents/Speech%20on%20the%20Retirement%20Crisis %20-%20Senator%20Warren.pdf (accessed May 28, 2015).
7. See Don Watkins, *RooseveltCare: How Social Security Is Sabotaging the Land of Self-Reliance* (Irvine, CA: Ayn Rand Institute Press, 2014).
8. Nicholas Eberstadt, "American Exceptionalism and the Entitlement State," *National Affairs*, Winter 2015, http://www.nationalaffairs.com/publications/detail/american-exceptionalism -and-the-entitlement-state (accessed May 28, 2015).

9. Cass R. Sunstein, *Democracy and the Problem of Free Speech* (New York: The Free Press, 1995), pp. 18–19.

10. Ibid., p. 19.

11. Paul Krugman, "Losing Our Country," *New York Times,* June 10, 2005, http://www.nytimes .com/2005/06/10/opinion/10krugman.html (accessed April 13, 2015).

12. Paul Krugman, *The Conscience of a Liberal* (New York: W. W. Norton & Company, 2009), p. 18.

13. Ibid., p. 18.

14. Ibid., p. 41.

15. Ibid., p. 48.

16. Ibid., p. 20.

17. Thomas Piketty, *Capital in the Twenty-First Century* (Cambridge, MA: Belknap, 2014), p. 1.

18. Ibid., p. 480.

19. See Leonard Peikoff, *Objectivism: The Philosophy of Ayn Rand* (New York: Dutton, 1991), pp. 276–91, and Don Watkins interviewing Gregory Salmieri, "The Debt Dialogues [Episode 27]: Gregory Salmieri on Justice," Voices for Reason, September 16, 2014, https://ari .aynrand.org/blog/2014/09/16/the-debt-dialogues-episode-27-gregory-salmieri-on-justice (accessed May 28, 2015).

20. Ayn Rand, "What Is Capitalism?" reprinted in Ayn Rand, *Capitalism: The Unknown Ideal* (New York: Signet, 1967), p. 9.

21. John Rawls, *A Theory of Justice* (Cambridge, MA: Harvard University Press, 1971), p. 62.

22. Ibid., p. 62.

23. G. A. Cohen, "Incentives, Inequality, and Community," The Tanner Lectures on Human Value, Stanford University May 21–23, 1991, http://tannerlectures.utah.edu/_documents/a -to-z/c/cohen92.pdf (accessed May 28, 2015).

24. G. A. Cohen, "Where the Action Is: On the Site of Distributive Justice," *Philosophy and Public Affairs,* Vol. 26, No. 1, Princeton University Press, Winter, 1997, http://philosophyfaculty .ucsd.edu/faculty/rarneson/Courses/COHENGAwhereaction.pdf (accessed May 28, 2015).

25. Cohen, "Incentives, Inequality, and Community."

26. Ibid.

27. Rawls, *A Theory of Justice,* p. 277.

28. Ibid., p. 62.

29. Ibid., pp. 101–102.

30. Ibid., pp. 103–104.

31. Barack Obama, "Remarks by the President in Conversation on Poverty at Georgetown University," *White House,* May 12, 2015, https://www.whitehouse.gov/the-press-office/2015 /05/12/remarks-president-conversation-poverty-georgetown-university (accessed May 28, 2015).

32. Piketty, *Capital in the Twenty-First Century,* pp. 630–31.

33. James Kwak, "Do Smart, Hard-Working People Deserve to Make More Money?," *The Baseline Scenario,* November 2, 2009, http://baselinescenario.com/2009/11/02/smart-hard -working-people/ (accessed May 28, 2015).

34. This distinction comes from Brynmor Browne, "A Solution to the Problem of Moral Luck," *Philosophical Quarterly,* Vol. 42, No. 168 (Jul., 1992), pp. 345–56. Cited in Diana Hsieh, *Responsibility & Luck: A Defense of Praise and Blame* (Self-published, 2013), chapter 3, part 3.

35. Hsieh, *Responsibility & Luck: A Defense of Praise and Blame,* chapter 1, part 5.

36. "The Superinvestors of Graham-and-Doddsville," *Wikipedia,* last modified March 12, 2015, http://en.wikipedia.org/wiki/The_Superinvestors_of_Graham-and-Doddsville (accessed May 28, 2015).

37. Larry S. Temkin, "Egalitarianism Defended," *Ethics,* Vol. 113, No. 4, July 2003, http://www .mit.edu/~shaslang/mprg/TemkinED.pdf (accessed May 28, 2015).

38. Jim Collins and Morten T. Hansen, *Great by Choice* (New York: Harper Business, 2011), p. 2.

39. Ibid., p. 154.

40. Ibid., p. 158.

41. Ibid., p. 160.

42. Ibid., p. 164.
43. Elizabeth Warren, "Elizabeth Warren on Debt Crisis, Fair Taxation," *YouTube*, September 18, 2011, https://www.youtube.com/watch?v=htX2usfqMEs (accessed May 28, 2015).
44. Barack Obama, "President Obama Campaign Rally in Roanoke," *C-SPAN*, July 13, 2012, http://www.c-span.org/video/?307056-2/president-obama-campaign-rally-roanoke (accessed May 28, 2015).
45. Ayn Rand, *The Fountainhead* (New York: Signet, 1993 Centennial edition), p. 679.
46. David Harriman (ed.), *Journals of Ayn Rand* (New York: Plume, 1999), p. 421.
47. Ayn Rand, "Collectivized 'Rights,'" reprinted in Ayn Rand, *The Virtue of Selfishness* (New York: Signet, 1964 Centennial edition), p. 120.
48. Peter Singer, *The Life You Can Save* (New York: Random House, 2010), pp. 17–18.
49. For Rand's analysis of altruism see Ayn Rand, "This Is John Galt Speaking," *For the New Intellectual* (New York: Signet, 1963 Centennial edition), especially pp. 136–48; Ayn Rand, "Faith and Force: The Destroyers of the Modern World," reprinted in Ayn Rand, *Philosophy: Who Needs It* (New York: Signet, 1984); and Peter Schwartz, *In Defense of Selfishness* (New York: Palgrave Macmillan, 2015).
50. Rawls, *A Theory of Justice*, p, 586.
51. Ayn Rand, "What Is Capitalism?" reprinted in Ayn Rand, *Capitalism: The Unknown Ideal* (New York: Signet, 1967 Centennial edition), p. 9.
52. Liam Murphy and Thomas Nagel, *The Myth of Ownership* (New York: Oxford, 2002), p. 66.
53. Ibid.
54. Ibid., pp. 66–67. It is worth pointing out that, contra the egalitarians, the inextricable connection between political equality and the right to property was well understood historically. Abolitionists, for instance, often stressed that the essence of the inequality between slave and master was that the slave worked, not for his own benefit, but for the benefit of his master.
55. Rawls, *A Theory of Justice*, p. 534.
56. Piketty, *Capital in the Twenty-First Century*, p. 244.
57. Ayn Rand, "The Age of Envy," reprinted in Ayn Rand, *Return of the Primitive: The Anti-Industrial Revolution* (New York: Meridian, 1999), p. 144.
58. Christopher Ake, "Justice as Equality," *Philosophy & Public Affairs*, Vol. 5, No. 1, Autumn 1975, http://www.jstor.org/discover/10.2307/2265021 (accessed May 29, 2015).
59. Larry S. Temkin, "Egalitarianism Defended," *Ethics*, Vol. 113, No. 4, July 2003, http://www.mit.edu/~shaslang/mprg/TemkinED.pdf (accessed May 28, 2015).
60. Quoted in Philip Short, *Pol Pot: Anatomy of a Nightmare* (New York: Henry Holt, 2006), chapter 9.
61. Quoted in ibid., chapter 9.
62. Ibid., chapter 10.
63. Ibid., chapter 9.
64. Ibid., Prologue.
65. Bono, "Transcript: Bono on the Oprah Winfrey Show (Part 1)," ATU2.com, September 20, 2002, http://www.atu2.com/news/transcript-bono-on-the-oprah-winfrey-show-part-1.html (accessed May 28, 2015).
66. Paul Krugman, "The Undeserving Rich," *New York Times*, January 19, 2014, http://www.nytimes.com/2014/01/20/opinion/krugman-the-undeserving-rich.html (accessed May 28, 2015), and Angie Drobnic Holan and Nai Issa, "In Context: Hillary Clinton and Don't Let Anybody Tell You That Corporations Create Jobs," PolitiFact.com, October 30, 2014, http://www.politifact.com/truth-o-meter/article/2014/oct/30/context-hillary-clinton-and-dont-let-anybody-tell-/ (accessed May 28, 2015).
67. Richard Wilkinson and Kate Pickett, *The Spirit Level* (New York: Bloomsbury Press, 2009), p. 262.
68. Thom Hartmann, *Threshold: The Crisis of Western Culture* (New York: Viking, 2009), p. 95.
69. Sean McElwee, "This Is Your Brain on Money: Why America's Rich Think Differently Than the Rest of Us," Salon.com, October 11, 2014, http://www.salon.com/2014/10/11/this_is_your_brain_on_money_why_americas_rich_think_differently_than_the_rest_of_us/ (accessed May 28, 2015).

70. Rob Kall, "'De-billionairize' the Planet," *OpEdNews,* May 5, 2011, http://www.opednews.com/populum/printer_friendly.php?content=a&id=131211 (accessed May 28, 2015).

71. Patrick Slevin, "Austerity Measurement: Fuck the Rich; Or, Polls Show Most Americans Agree with This Headline," *The Aquarian Weekly,* December 15, 2010, http://www.theaquarian.com/2010/12/15/austerity-measurement-fuck-the-rich-or-polls-show-most-americans-agree-with-this-headline/ (accessed May 28, 2015).

72. McElwee, "This Is Your Brain on Money: Why America's Rich Think Differently Than the Rest of Us."

73. Barbara Ehrenreich, "Rich People Are Being 'Demonized' for Flaunting Their Wealth. Poor Dears!," *Washington Post,* September 30, 2011, http://www.washingtonpost.com/opinions/rich-people-demonized-for-flaunting-their-wealth-are-under-attack/2011/09/28/gIQAcJn4AL_story.html (accessed May 28, 2015).

74. Matthew Yglesias, "The Case for a Maximum Wage," Vox.com, August 6, 2014, http://www.vox.com/2014/8/6/5964369/maximum-wage (accessed May 28, 2015).

75. Hamilton Nolan, "Let's Have a Maximum Income," *Gawker,* August 8, 2012, http://gawker.com/5932875/lets-have-a-maximum-income (accessed May 28, 2015).

76. Thom Hartmann, "The No Billionaires Campaign," *OpEdNews,* July 18, 2012, http://www.opednews.com/populum/printer_friendly.php?content=a&id=153218 (accessed May 28, 2015).

77. Piketty, *Capital in the Twenty-First Century,* pp. 505, 513, 517.

78. Ibid., p. 505.

79. Naomi Klein, *This Changes Everything: Capitalism vs. the Climate* (New York: Simon & Schuster, 2014).

80. Wilkinson and Pickett, *The Spirit Level,* pp. 225–26.

81. Ibid., p. 217.

82. Randal C. Archibold, "Inequality Becomes More Visible in Cuba as the Economy Shifts," *New York Times,* February 24, 2015, http://www.nytimes.com/2015/02/25/world/americas/as-cuba-shifts-toward-capitalism-inequality-grows-more-visible.html (accessed May 28, 2015).

83. Sean McElwee, "The Moral Case for a Higher Minimum Wage," Policy.Mic, August 7, 2013, http://mic.com/articles/58425/the-moral-case-for-a-higher-minimum-wage (accessed May 28, 2015).

84. Ayn Rand, "Philosophical Detection," reprinted in Ayn Rand, *Philosophy: Who Needs It* (New York: Signet, 1984), p. 18.

85. Ibid.

86. Joseph Epstein, *Envy* (New York: Oxford University Press, 2003), p. 52.

87. Alan Bullock, *Hitler and Stalin: Parallel Lives* (New York: Knopf, 1992), p. 359.

88. David E. Cooper, "Equality and Envy," *Journal of Philosophy of Education,* Volume 16, Issue 1, July 1982, http://onlinelibrary.wiley.com/doi/10.1111/j.1467-9752.1982.tb00594.x/abstract (accessed May 28, 2015).

89. Thomas Nagel, "Equal Treatment and Compensatory Discrimination," *Philosophy & Public Affairs,* Vol. 2, No. 4, Summer, 1973, http://www.jstor.org/stable/2265013 (accessed May 29, 2015).

90. James Truslow Adams, *The Epic of America* (Garden City, NY: Garden City Books, 1933), p. 317.

CONCLUSION

1. Thomas Piketty, *Capital in the Twenty-First Century* (Cambridge, MA: Belknap, 2014), p. 15.

2. Ayn Rand, *Atlas Shrugged* (New York: Plume, 1999), p. 1043.

3. Maria Popova, "The Secret of Life from Steve Jobs in 46 Seconds," *Brain Pickings,* December 2, 2012, http://www.brainpickings.org/2011/12/02/steve-jobs-1995-life-failure/ (accessed May 28, 2015).

4. Rand, *Atlas Shrugged,* p. 454.

5. Onkar Ghate, "The Basic Motivation of the Creators and the Masses in *The Fountainhead,*" in Robert Mayhew (ed.) *Essays on Ayn Rand's 'The Fountainhead'* (New York: Lexington, 2007), pp. 270–71.

INDEX